# The Spirit of Roman Law

# The Spirit of the Laws

Alan Watson, General Editor

# THE SPIRIT OF
# ROMAN LAW

*Alan Watson*

The University of Georgia Press
Athens & London

© 1995 by the University of Georgia Press
Athens, Georgia 30602
All rights reserved
Designed by Walton Harris
Set in Trump 10/14 by Tseng Information Systems, Inc.
Printed and bound by Thomson-Shore, Inc.

The paper in this book meets the guidelines for permanence
and durability of the Committee on Production Guidelines
for Book Longevity of the Council on Library Resources.

Printed in the United States of America
99  98  97  96  95    C    5   4   3   2   1

*Library of Congress Cataloging in Publication Data*

Watson, Alan.
  The spirit of Roman law / Alan Watson.
    p.   cm. — (The spirit of the laws)
  Includes bibliographical references and index.
  ISBN 0-8203-1669-5 (alk. paper)
    1. Roman law.   I. Title.   II. Series.
KJA147.W38   1995
340.5'4—dc20                               94-5969

*British Library Cataloging in Publication Data available*

*For David Daube*

# CONTENTS

# PREFACE

For Roman legal writers and subsequent scholars alike, Roman law was overwhelmingly private law [1] and in that respect has been the most admired and influential secular legal system. My aim in writing this book is to describe, and where possible account for, the features of the system. This is not a study of the rules and institutions, or even of the history, of Roman law. Rather, it is an attempt to understand the approaches and the values, express and implicit, of those who made the law. Such a book has been written twice before, by Rudolf von Jhering [2] and Fritz Schulz, [3] and admirer of their achievements as I am—indeed, von Jhering has long been an especial hero of mine—I am conscious that my understanding is different from theirs. I am equally conscious that had I tackled the subject three years ago, before I wrote *The State, Law and Religion: Pagan Rome* (Athens, Ga., 1992), the outcome would have been very different. Writing that book greatly changed my views on the dynamics of Roman law. Writing this book has further changed them. Richard Baumann has written to me: "Roman law is the perfect chameleon. Every time I look at it I see something different." The statement is not to be taken literally, of course, but it is insightful. The legal rules and institutions, even their history, are relatively clear and also remarkably simple. What seems to change color and to be difficult to perceive is the reason for Roman legal development. Much is veiled to our eyes because of Justinian's great *Corpus Juris Civilis*—a work, of course, unknown to the Romans. We see the *Corpus Juris,* not the concerns and hopes of those who shaped the earlier law. Moreover, in very large measure we see the *Corpus Juris* itself through its subsequent history in shaping Western law and in providing a structure for modern legal systems and instruction.

The book emerges inevitably from previous researches of mine. Passages, including some long ones, are taken almost verbatim from earlier work. It seemed superfluous when using these materials to illustrate a development or characteristic to change their wording, especially because I was often using them for a different end and because the audience I hope to reach with this book is largely different. Thus, in *Law Making in the Later Roman Republic* (Oxford, 1974) I sought to show that the jurists made little use of Greek philosophy. Here I use the same materials, but with the purpose of showing that this was just one aspect of a much wider legal isolationism. Elsewhere I discussed the two imperial rulings on gross inequality of exchange to account for the very different provisions on the subject in the modern French and German civil codes. Here I use much of that discussion to show the state's general lack of interest in regulating private bargains. My justification for the repetition is simply that the resulting thesis is very different. Indeed, my goal for this new series, the Spirit of the Laws, which this volume introduces, is that scholars with experience in particular systems set forth a synthesis of their experience. In the process their experience will change, but their past history will shape much of their synthesis.

Though it would be impossible to write a book on Roman law without mentioning the great codification of the Byzantine emperor Justinian I, the *Corpus Juris Civilis*, as it came to be called, really came too late to be part of "the spirit of Roman law." It appears here partly for what it reveals about earlier law and partly because of its own role as a successor to the tradition. The stress is on the period from the *Twelve Tables* around 451 B.C. to the end of the so-called classical period around A.D. 235. Because it is my hope also to reach an audience unversed in Roman law I have included, as a first chapter, a thumbnail sketch of its development. That chapter reproduces in very large measure my contribution to *Civilization of the Ancient Mediterranean: Greece and Rome*, vol. 2 (New York, 1988), edited by Michael Grant and Rachel Kitzzinger. I am grateful to Charles Scribner's Sons for permission to republish. Inevitably, much of the content of the chapter is repeated in subsequent chapters when I set the scene for dealing in detail with particular issues. Chapter 1 should be ignored by those with some acquaintance with the subject.

I should like to emphasize that in writing this book I had no intention of producing an anodyne, abstract account of Roman lawmaking. I wished to confront readers with the issues and problems that faced the Roman legal intelligentsia.

"The spirit of Roman law," as I conceive it, is remarkably cohesive and coherent—in itself a cause for suspicion among historians, as my friend Jerzy Linderski wrote to me in a different context. But the consequence is that examples used in one chapter would often fit as well, or almost as well, in other chapters and reinforce (I hope) their arguments. I would be grateful if readers could bear this in mind.

I wish to call special attention to the three appendices. For me they are important, and should be read as a contrast to the rest of the book.

# ACKNOWLEDGMENTS

A number of friends read drafts of this book: John Cairns, Patricia Crone, John Ford, Peter Hoffer, Frank Stewart, Jim Whitman. All gave constructive criticism that resulted in numerous changes in structure and substance. To all I am grateful.

The book has received the generous support of the Robbins Collection at the University of California at Berkeley, which is presently under the charge of Laurent Mayali. It is the result of decades of study of Roman law, and it is fitting that I dedicate it to my revered and beloved master, David Daube, who was long the director of the Robbins Hebraic and Roman Law Collection.

# ABBREVIATIONS

| | |
|---|---|
| *C.* | The *Code* of Justinian. |
| *Coll.* | *Collatio legum Romanarum et Mosiacarum.* |
| *C. Th.* | The *Code* of Theodosius II. |
| *D.* | The *Digest* of Justinian. |
| Daube, *Collected Studies* 1, 2 | David Daube, *Collected Studies in Roman Law*, vols. 1 and 2 (Frankfurt am Main, 1992). |
| Daube, *Roman Law* | David Daube, *Roman Law: Linguistic, Social and Philosophical Aspects* (Edinburgh, 1969). |
| *G.* | The *Institutes* of Gaius. |
| *h.t.* | The same title of *Code* or *Digest* as in the preceding text. |
| *J.* | The *Institutes* of Justinian. |
| Jolowicz and Nicholas, *Historical Introduction* | H. F. Jolowicz and B. Nicholas, *Historical Introduction to the Study of Roman Law*, 3d ed. (Cambridge, 1972). |
| Kaser, *Privatrecht* 1, 2 | M. Kaser, *Das römische Privatrecht*, vol. 1, 2d ed. (Munich, 1971); vol. 2, 2d ed. (Munich, 1975). |
| Kunkel, *Herkunft* | W. Kunkel, *Herkunft und soziale Stellung der römischen Juristen*, 2d ed. (Graz, 1967). |
| Lenel, *Edictum* | O. Lenel, *Das Edictum perpetuum*, 3d ed. (Leipzig, 1927). |
| *Pr.* | *Principio*, i.e., "in the beginning," the first part of a *Digest* or *Code* text. |

| | |
|---|---|
| *P.S.* | *Pauli Sententiae* (The Opinions of Paul). |
| *R.I.D.A.* | *Revue Internationale des Droits de l'Antiquité.* |
| Robinson, *Ancient Rome* | O. F. Robinson, *Ancient Rome: City Planning and Administration* (London, 1992). |
| Rotondi, *Leges publicae* | G. Rotondi, *Leges publicae populi romani* (Milan, 1912). |
| Schulz, *Legal Science* | F. Schulz, *Roman Legal Science* (Oxford, 1946). |
| Schulz, *Principles* | F. Schulz, *Principles of Roman Law* (Oxford, 1936). |
| Treggiari, *Marriage* | S. Treggiari, *Roman Marriage* (Oxford, 1991). |
| *T.v.R.* | *Tijdschrift voor Rechtsgeschiedenis.* |
| *Vat. Fr.* | *Fragmenta Vaticana.* |
| Watson, *Law Making* | A. Watson, *Law Making in the Later Roman Republic* (Oxford, 1974). |
| Watson, *Legal Origins* | A. Watson, *Legal Origins and Legal Change* (London, 1991). |
| Watson, *Obligations* | A. Watson, *The Law of Obligations in the Later Roman Republic* (Oxford, 1965). |
| Watson, *Roman Law and Comparative Law* | A. Watson, *Roman Law and Comparative Law* (Athens, Ga., 1991). |
| Watson, *Slave Law* | A. Watson, *Slave Law in the Americas* (Athens, Ga., 1989). |
| Watson, *State, Law and Religion* | A. Watson, *The State, Law and Religion: Pagan Rome* (Athens, Ga., 1992). |
| Watson, *Studies* | A. Watson, *Studies in Roman Private Law* (London, 1991). |

| | |
|---|---|
| Watson, *Succession* | A. Watson, *The Law of Succession in the Later Roman Republic* (Oxford, 1971). |
| Watson, *XII Tables* | A. Watson, *Rome of the XII Tables: Persons and Property* (Princeton, 1979). |
| *ZSS* | *Zeitschrift der Savigny-Stiftung (romanistische Abteilung).* |

*The Spirit of Roman Law*

# 1 Introduction to Roman Law

## THE SOURCES OF LAW

By tradition Rome was founded in 753 B.C. and was ruled by kings until Tarquin the Proud was expelled and the Republic was inaugurated in 509. The kings were supposedly the authors of some legislation. In the early Republic the population was divided into a small ruling elite, the patricians, and the others, the plebeians. The main elected public officers, the praetors (later called consuls) and the quaestors, had to be patricians. The same was true of the priests of the state religion, especially the members of the College of Pontiffs and College of Augurs. The tribunes of the plebs—the office was created in the early fifth century B.C.—were charged with protecting the lives and property of the plebeians.

The demand for codification of the law in the early Republic is said to have stemmed from the grievances of the plebeians, who could not know the law and felt exploited by the patrician magistrates. They demanded equality before the law and an articulation of the powers of the consuls. The patricians, in an attempt to block or delay reform, are said to have organized a delegation to Greece to study the law of Solon. If the tradition is accurate, the plebeians lost the battle. The *Twelve Tables* deal almost only with private law, with a very little criminal law, and with the law of disposal of the dead. The powers of the magistrates are not delineated, and the code does not deal with forms, whether for trials or for contracts or for freeing slaves. Without other knowledge, the *Twelve Tables* would not be protective of rights. And there is no real sign of Greek influence. In contrast to modern codifications, no attempt was made to set out the law systematically; rather, the code contained only clarifications of the law or innovations. Thus, dowry, which had long existed, is not dealt with, and the law of slavery appears only incidentally. There are seven known provisions on prescription (the acquisition of rights by lapse of time, presumably a new institution), but otherwise there is nothing about acquisition of property (as distinct from transfer, which also is not fully dealt with). The first group of ten officials, the *decemviri*, appointed to set down the law produced ten tables of law in 451 B.C. A second group was appointed to complete the work, and they produced a further two tables, but they turned tyrannous. To this second set is attributed the rule that a patrician could not marry a plebeian, which was overturned by the Canuleian law of 445 B.C.

Three bodies could legislate: the *comitia centuriata*, which was the main political assembly, the *comitia calata*, and the *concilium plebis* (council of the plebs). But in normal times legislation was used sparingly, and usually for private law the organ of legislation was the *concilium plebis*. Apart from the Canuleian law the most important private laws in the Republic were: the Aquilian law of about 287 B.C., which above all regulated damage to property; the Atilian law of about 210, which provided for the appointment by the praetor and a majority of the tribunes of the plebs of a tutor to a fatherless child who otherwise would have no guardian; the Cincian law of 204, which restricted large gifts; the Plaetorian law of 193 or 192, which gave remedies when a person under twenty-five was defrauded; and the Atinian law of about 150 B.C., which provided that the ownership of stolen property could not be acquired by long usage until the property had come back into the hands of the person from whom it was stolen.

The individually elected higher magistrates could not legislate, but they could issue edicts setting out how they would act within their spheres of competence during their terms of office. While their powers were limited, those in charge of law courts could refuse to grant an action where one was provided by civil law, they could allow a remedy where none was provided, and they could reinterpret the law. The most important magistrates in this regard were the subsequently created praetors, especially the urban praetors and perhaps also the peregrine praetors, although the boundaries between their jurisdictions are not clear. Among their other duties, the praetors had control of the major law courts. It became established that when a praetor was elected he would issue an Edict announcing his intentions in a number of clauses, which were mainly of two types: individual edicts setting out that the praetor would grant an action in particular circumstances, and model forms of action called *formulae*, sometimes even in the absence of a relevant edict. Each year saw the possibility of much reform because of three factors: praetors were elected for only one year at a time and could not be reelected; the Edicts were valid only during their terms of office; and the praetors did not need to obtain further support for their Edicts. In practice they took over much of their predecessor's Edict, but often with changes. The praetor's Edict was the most important vehicle of legal change in the Republic: the praetors, for instance, remodeled the whole of the law of succession and were largely responsible for the law of contract, especially the highly significant consensual contracts.

The curule aediles (those entitled to a curule chair as a symbol of rank of office) had their own court and jurisdiction over streets and marketplaces. They issued important edicts governing the sale of slaves and animals, the keeping of wild beasts near public places (often for games), and the suspension of things over or allowing them to fall on public places.

The interpretation of the *Twelve Tables* was entrusted to the patrician College of Pontiffs. It was thus important for those who were well connected and who wished to be pontiffs to know the law. The opinion of the college was authoritative, and each year one member was chosen to be the spokesman. The position was one of great significance. Plebeians could become pontiffs only after the Ogulnian law of 300 B.C., and in time the pontiffs lost their monopoly of legal interpretation. But people of social importance continued to seek to be pontiffs and to give legal advice, although individually and no longer authoritatively, and this practice was treated with respect. Until the early first century B.C. the leading jurists were of senatorial rank, but thereafter in the Republic they were knights (*equites*).

In time the jurists began to produce books of varying types. The first major step was the *Tripertita* by Sextus Aelius Paetus, who was consul in 198 B.C. This contained the provisions of the *Twelve Tables*, a commentary on them, and a description of the relevant forms of action. Quintus Mucius Scaevola, *pontifex maximus*, consul in 95 B.C., is said to have first divided the civil law into categories or classes (*genera*), and he produced the first commentary on the civil law, in eighteen books. This seems to have been old-fashioned and to have covered only topics that were dealt with by the *Twelve Tables* or could be pegged to a discussion of that code. Other jurists such as Servius Sulpicius Rufus, consul of 51 B.C., wrote commentaries on particular topics, including the Edict, and even compiled collections of their answers to legal problems, real and hypothetical.

Augustus, who was given perpetual tribunician power in 23 B.C., restored the use of legislation, but primarily through the *comitia tributa*, not the *concilium plebis*. He had a number of laws enacted concerned mainly with family law and the manumission of slaves. Subsequently, few statutes were passed except under Claudius (A.D. 41–54), who, in keeping with his reputation as a true lover of the Republic, legislated through the *concilium plebis*. By the end of the first century legislation had died out.

No change was made in the right of the magistrates to issue edicts, but they ceased to innovate and made only a few minor alterations. The emperor Hadrian (A.D. 117–39) gave the jurist Salvius Julianus the task of consolidating the Edict of the urban praetor. Julian made a substantial alteration in the organization and a minor one in substance, but thereafter no change could be made.

Augustus gave selected jurists the right to issue replies on his authority. The import of this change is unclear, but it would bring lawmaking by jurists more under his control. (A modification to this, again unclear, was introduced by Hadrian.) The jurists wrote more and more books and, largely as a result of their writings, the first 250 years of the empire are known as the classical period of Roman law. Great innovations had died with the Republic, and subsequent jurists dedicated their efforts to ever greater refinements. Bestowing authority on jurists to make law allows for flexibility and continuing suggestions for improvement, but it has a serious defect. In the absence of a system that ranks the jurists, there is no authoritative way of determining the outcome when a point of law is disputed. Many problems argued by the jurists in the early Empire were settled only by Justinian. Prominent in the disputes were the rival schools—probably true teaching establishments—of the Sabinians and the Proculians, who seem separated by no ideological divide.

One juristic work, the *Institutes* of Gaius (published around A.D. 161), deserves particular mention, partly because it is the only classical work to survive largely intact, partly because it served as the main model of Justinian's *Institutes* and hence became the structural basis for most modern civil codes. This elementary textbook for beginning students is organized in four books: book 1 covers sources of law and persons; book 2, property and testate succession; book 3, intestate succession and obligations; and book 4, the law of actions.

By about A.D. 235 the writing of juristic books had virtually come to an end. New sources of law came into being in the Empire. Decrees of the senate (*senatus consulta*) gradually came to have lawmaking force, and by the time of Hadrian they could be directly applied as law.

The emperor could issue edicts like any magistrate, and since his jurisdiction was universal they could be on any matter. The *constitutio Antoniniana* of A.D. 212, which gave Roman citizenship to all free inhabitants of the Empire, was an imperial edict. The emperor's decisions in lawsuits (*decreta*), though technically binding only in the particular case, were treated as authoritative in others, and collections of these decisions were made. Instructions (*mandata*) issued to governors and other officials were also authoritative for succeeding generations. Most significant of imperial constitutions (legislative enactments) for future development were the rescripts (*epistulae*), replies sent to private individuals who had asked for a ruling by the emperor on a point of law.

Between the death of Severus Alexander (A.D. 235) and the accession of Justinian I (527), a number of external factors had an impact on the legal tradition. Until at least the end of the reign of Diocletian (305), classical law was retained despite the intervening political and economic chaos. Constantine the Great was a convert to Christianity; it was he who moved the center of the Empire to Constantinople in the Greek East. Subsequent centuries saw the loss of the Latin West. But what the period has in common is the absence of innovative juristic works and in their place the centrality of imperial rescripts. There were some juristic books, of course, but they are abridgments of elementary commentaries on earlier works or collections of earlier texts. A problem for using imperial rescripts was the difficulty of finding the one that clearly applied to the given situation. An unofficial collection, the *Codex Gregorianus*, appeared in 291 and another, the *Codex Hermogenianus*, in 295; neither has survived. The *Codex Theodosianus*, compiled and published (438) on order of Theodosius II, has survived; it is an official collection, brought up to date, of all the general imperial constitutions since the reign of Constantine.

Theodosius II issued the famous Law of Citations in A.D. 426. This made authoritative all the writings of five of the classical jurists: Ulpian, Paul, Papinian, Modestinus, and Gaius. Jurists whom they cited also had weight. When the five expressed differing opinions, the will of the majority was to prevail. When they were equally divided the opinion supported by Papinian was to win. When they were equally divided and Papinian had expressed no opinion the judge could follow whom he wished. This does not mark a low point of Roman jurisprudence as is often suggested. Rather, it ranks the jurists of more than two centuries before and makes their opinions important when a point was still unsettled. Naturally, any imperial rescript would take precedence, and these would be drafted by jurists who had become imperial functionaries. Thus, a contemporary lawyer (or one in the recent past) writing in the name of the emperor would take precedence over the great jurists of the distant past.

Justinian I joined his uncle Justin (who had risen from the ranks) as coemperor of the Eastern (Byzantine) empire in 527, and on the latter's death in the same year he became sole emperor. He immediately began to restate the law. His first step in 528 was to set up a ten-man team including Tribonian (quaestor in 529) and Theophilus, a professor, to prepare a collection of imperial rescripts drawn from the three previous codes and later enactments. They were to bring the rescripts up to date and make desired alterations. This first *Code* was published in 529 and has not survived.

Justinian turned to juristic writings and as a preliminary he resolved some of the disputes of the classical writers by promulgating the *Fifty Decisions*, which have not independently survived. In December 530, he instructed Tribonian to choose a commission, and he in fact appointed sixteen men. They were to make extracts from the great jurists of the past and to arrange them in fifty books, divided into titles according to subject matter. The commissioners were to choose the best view on every point, eliminating all dissension along with whatever was superfluous or obsolete or already in the published *Code*. Contrary to a widely held view, they were not given the power to change the substance of the texts. The commissioners retained at the beginning of each extract the name of the jurist and the work from which it was taken; more than one-third of the *Digest*, as it is called, is taken from Ulpian, and a further sixth comes from Paul. Justinian claims that almost two thousand books were read and reduced to one-twentieth of their length. The *Digest* was published in 533. Thus were the writings of the great jurists reduced to a manageable whole. To keep them that way, and also to preserve the *Digest*'s authority, Justinian forbade all commentaries and allowed only direct translations into Greek.

While work on the *Digest* was under way, Justinian ordered the preparation of a new elementary textbook, the *Institutes*; this task was entrusted to Tribonian, Theophilus, and Dorotheus. The work was to be based on elementary works of classical jurists, especially Gaius's *Institutes*. The *Institutes* of Justinian are in four books: book 1 contains sources and persons; book 2 deals with property and testate succession; book 3 with intestate succession, contracts, and quasi contracts; and book 4 with delict and quasi delict, crimes, and actions. The *Institutes* came into effect on 30 December 533, the same day as the *Digest*.

All this while, from 529, fresh imperial constitutions were issued and instructions were given for a new *Code*. This was issued in 534 in twelve books subdivided into titles in which the rescripts are arranged chronologically. Like the *Digest* and *Institutes*, the second *Code* has survived.

Although the work of codification was complete, new rescripts continued to be issued, now known as the *New Constitutions* or *Novellae*. At a much later date, the *Digest, Institutes, Code,* and *Novellae* came to be called the *Corpus Juris Civilis*.

## ACTIONS

A remedy in Roman law exists only where there is an appropriate action. The two main types of legal procedure up to and including classical law were both in two stages. The older type, the *legis actio* procedure, contained a small number of forms that had to be used in front of the praetor or other elected magistrate. Each form could be used for a variety of claims. They were so rigid that after their demise Gaius (probably mistakenly) believed that a party who made a mistake in the wording lost his case. The second stage, in front of a judge or arbiter after the praetor had given his approval, was less stylized. The *legis actiones* were gradually replaced between the third century B.C. and the first century A.D. by the formulary procedure. The first stage here, before the praetor, led to his issuing a *formula*, a formal statement of the claim that if proved before the judge led to the condemnation in damages of the defendant. For an action ordinarily to be available the alleged facts had to fit within the scope of an existing *formula* set out in the Edict. Thus, for a long period an action under the *formula* that applied to sales would be successful only if there was an actual contract of sale; if the agreement did not concern a sale but something akin, or if the contract was void, the action would fail. The praetor filled in many gaps either by inserting a fiction (the action was to proceed as if something were the case when it was not) or by giving an ad hoc remedy, an action on the facts. Some of these last became standardized, particularly for damage to property. From the early Empire onward there gradually developed a more bureaucratic system of procedure, the *cognitio*, with official judges.

# THE LAW OF PERSONS

## Marriage and Divorce

In early Rome reciprocal promises of betrothal were made by the contract of *sponsio* on behalf of the bride and groom, but before the beginning of the second century B.C. the promises ceased to be actionable. Nonetheless betrothal had some legal standing: from the time of the betrothal relatives of the pair were in-laws, and a sexual involvement by the woman with another man was adultery. By the fourth century A.D., the fiancé gave the woman a gift to ensure the marriage, which he forfeited if he did not marry her; if she would not marry him she had to return a multiple of the gift.

There were two types of marriage. In the earlier, marriage *cum manu*, the wife came into the power, the *manus*, of her husband or of his father if he were still alive. In marriage *sine manu* the wife remained in the power, the *potestas*, of her own head of family if he were alive and otherwise remained independent. *Manus* was created in three ways. *Confarreatio* was a religious ceremony involving a cake of spelt (*far*, a kind of wheat), and it required the presence of the *pontifex maximus* (chief priest) and the *flamen dialis*, one of three major priests responsible for consecration and sacrifice. Hence its use must have been restricted to the top level of society. *Coemptio* was an imaginary, possibly once real, purchase of the bride by a modified form of *mancipatio*, which was the form of transfer reserved for certain important kinds of early property. A wife who was not married with either of these formalities came into the power of her husband by *usus* (use) after a year of cohabitation unless she stayed away for three nights. The *Twelve Tables* contained a provision whose point was the intentional avoidance of *usus* by absence of the wife. So the second type of marriage, *sine manu*, was also early. It was common by the beginning of the second century B.C., and, as a result of deliberate misinterpretation of another provision of the *Twelve Tables*, marriage *cum manu* became virtually obsolete early in the first century B.C. *Confarreatio* was restored early in the Empire but only with religious effect. No ceremony was needed for marriage *sine manu*, but celebrations including the leading of the bride to her husband's home were usual. Marriage required agreement, and this was commonly evidenced by a dowry, which, however, was not essential to a marriage.

Only marriage between Romans or with someone from a state that had been granted the right of intermarriage with Romans constituted full civil law marriage. Marriage between patrician and plebeian was forbidden by the *Twelve Tables* but was permitted again by the Canuleian law of 445 B.C. Marriage between persons of senatorial rank and freed persons was frowned on in the Republic but was first actually prohibited for senators and their descendants by Augustus. Later, Jews and Christians were forbidden to marry. Slaves could not contract any marriage. Close relationship was also a bar, but the prohibited degrees varied with time. Originally, second cousins could not marry, but by the first century B.C. first cousins could. Uncles and nieces, aunts and nephews could not intermarry until a *senatus consultum* permitted marriage with a brother's (though not sister's) daughter so that the emperor Claudius could marry Agrippina the Younger. Almost four centuries later the old law was restored, with the death penalty for such incest. By the time of Augustus the female had to be at least twelve years old, but whether she had reached puberty was irrelevant. The Proculians required that the male be fourteen, but the Sabinians demanded actual puberty, to be determined by physical examination.

The consent of the *paterfamilias* of the bride and of the groom was required, as was the consent of the parties, although in early law the wishes of the woman were legally irrelevant. Where the woman was independent, the consent of her tutor was needed when the marriage was to be *cum manu* from the outset (but not otherwise); it was also needed for any dowry.

Except when it was *cum manu*, marriage had little impact on the status of the parties. In early law the husband could punish his wife, but for serious offenses it was her family that judged her and, with the husband's consent, put her to death. The main consequence of a valid Roman marriage was that the children were born into the power (*patria potestas*) of the husband or his father.

Divorce was permitted to the husband in early Rome only on specific grounds: adultery, tampering with keys, poisoning a child (abortion?). The wife or her father then had no right to the return of the dowry. If the husband cast her off for any other reason he had to give her one-half of his property, the remainder being forfeited to the goddess Ceres. This continued until about 230 B.C., after which it came to be established that a husband (and a wife, too) could divorce for any reason. It then became sensible for the parties to make their own arrangements for the return of the dowry if the marriage failed. Otherwise, on divorce the dowry had to be returned, but the husband could retain fixed fractions if, for instance, there were children or the wife had committed adultery. No action or formalities were required for divorce unless the marriage was by *confarreatio,* in which case a reverse ceremony was needed. In the Christian empire Constantine enacted that upon divorce an offending wife would be deported and a husband could not remarry. If he did, the ex-wife could seize the second wife's dowry. Justinian enacted that if a wife divorced her husband, except for specified reasons, she would be confined in a nunnery for life and all her property would be forfeited. Nonetheless the divorce was valid.

## Patria Potestas

Children born in a civil law marriage were in the power (*potestas*) of their father (*pater*) or remoter male relative and so remained all their lives unless the *potestas* was ended by death or by emancipation. The *pater* had enormous power. He could put children to death for just cause (proven apparently by an investigation by the family council) or could sell them into slavery; his consent was necessary for marriage; and he could bring about their divorce. A father who abused his power might be punished, and eventually after the *Twelve Tables* were promulgated some powers, such as the right to sell into slavery, were restricted. Originally only the *pater* (or a woman who was independent) could own property; however, it was customary to allow descendants and slaves to have a private fund, the *peculium,* which they might use as if it were their own although technically it belonged to the *pater.* When dependents made contracts with third parties the benefits accrued to the *pater,* but he could not be sued in disputes over the contract. This was obviously inefficient for trade, and the praetor eventually allowed third parties to bring actions against the *pater* in certain cases: when the dependent had a *peculium* then the *pater* could be sued up to the limit of the *peculium* and also to the extent that he had benefited; when the *pater* had authorized the third party to contract with the dependent; or when the *pater* had set someone up in business or put him in charge of a ship. Augustus permitted a son, so long as he remained a soldier, to dispose of military earnings by will, and this exceptional case was gradually widened until a son was effectual owner of all his military earnings (*peculium castrense*). Constantine extended this to earnings from certain public offices, and he also gave children ownership of property left them by the mother, although the father retained the use of it during his lifetime.

*Patria potestas* was also acquired by adoption, of which there were two forms. *Adrogatio* was used when the adoptee was independent. After investigation by the pontiffs into its suitability the matter went before the *comitia curiata*, a legislative body whose decision was in fact a law. Since only males above puberty could appear before the *comitia*, only they could be so adopted. Adoption of this type was not to provide a loving home for an orphaned minor but was mainly political, to preserve a family from extinction; but it did, of course, involve the extinction of the adoptee's family line. Adoption of the other type, which was used when the adoptee was already in *patria potestas*, arose from a deliberate misinterpretation of a provision of the *Twelve Tables* that said if a son were sold three times—probably a reference to *nexum*, an old form of bondage of freemen—he would be free from his father's power. The father transferred him by a modified *mancipatio* to a friend who released him; this was repeated twice and then the friend either reemancipated him to the father (so that he would be outside *patria potestas*) or retained him. The friend then claimed to be the father, the father did not counterclaim, and the praetor adjudged the son to the adopter. In time it was accepted that only one sale was necessary for a similar transfer of daughters or remoter descendants. The same procedure could be used for emancipation, the deliberate freeing of children from paternal power. In later law, at least, this was common.

# Guardianship

Both males and females under puberty who were not in *patria potestas* had a *tutor*, a guardian, whose office was treated as a very serious duty. As early as the *Twelve Tables* a *tutor* might be appointed by will, but only by the *paterfamilias* and only to those who became independent on his death. Failing this, the tutelage went to the nearest male agnates, relatives linked through males, who had themselves reached puberty. The nearest agnates would inherit the property of the ward or pupil if he died, but it should be noted that the *tutores* had no control over the person of the pupil. The Atilian law of about 210 B.C. allowed the praetor at Rome and a majority of the tribunes of the plebs to appoint a *tutor* to a pupil who had none. A further statute extended this to the provinces, and there was additional provision for appointment of a special *tutor* when there was a lawsuit between the pupil and the existing *tutor*.

To act as *tutor* was a public duty and could not be refused except for specific reasons. Until the fifth century A.D., while the pupil was *infans*, literally "unable to speak," he could not legally act; the *tutor* alone had to act. When the child was older, the *tutor*'s consent was needed for all legal acts of the pupil that might result in loss to the pupil. The *Twelve Tables* gave an action for theft from a pupil's account against an agnatic *tutor* for double the amount he had embezzled, but it was available only at the termination of the tutelage; another action for fraud by a testamentary *tutor* (one designated by a father's will) could be brought during the tutelage. Later, probably in the third century B.C., arose the action on tutelage, the *actio tutelae*, which is perhaps the oldest of the good-faith actions—those actions in which the judge is instructed to condemn the defendant to pay a sum equal to "what he ought to give or do in accordance with good faith."

From the earliest times, women who were independent and above the age of puberty also had *tutores* who were appointed as they were for children. But the women themselves had the power of administration, and the *tutor*'s job was restricted to giving his consent to certain acts. The arbitrariness of this was recognized, and various devices were introduced to enable women to replace obstructive tutors.

Lunatics and their property were placed under the curatorship—another form of guardianship—of their nearest agnates by the *Twelve Tables*. A prodigal who wasted an inheritance that he had received on intestacy, and later any prodigal, could be placed under curatorship and prohibited from dealing with his property. The Plaetorian law of 193 or 192 B.C. provided a fine for anyone who defrauded someone under the age of twenty-five; it also gave the minor a defense if he was sued by someone who was defrauding him. The praetor in time gave the minor a remedy for any transaction in which he might suffer loss. Later in the second century A.D. it became customary for a minor to have a *curator*; if he had, the minor was not liable in any transaction for more than he gained unless the *curator* had consented.

## Slavery

For much of its history, Rome was a slave state in the sense that slaves were the main means of production. Yet little law emerged peculiar to slavery. The main ways of acquiring slaves were by capture in a lawful war from a people who did not have a treaty of friendship with Rome or by birth to a slave mother. Exceptional cases are illuminating. A child was born free whose slave mother was free at any time between conception and birth. By the *senatus consultum Claudianum*, if a master forbade a woman to cohabit with one of his slaves and she persisted, then she and any resulting children could be enslaved by a decree of a magistrate. Or the woman could make a bargain that she would remain free but any children would be slaves. Again by the *Twelve Tables*, a thief caught in the act would be enslaved. So would those who avoided the census to escape conscription. A person above majority who had himself sold as a slave in order to share fraudulently in the price (when he was claimed as free) also actually became a slave.

A slave could own nothing, and anything he acquired belonged to his owner even if he were allowed a *peculium*. If he committed a delict, then (like a son) he could be given by the master to the victim in lieu of paying damages, a form of limited liability called noxal surrender. During the Republic there were no legal limitations on the master's right to punish; gradually restrictions crept in, but they were always limited and relatively ineffective.

There were three ways of freeing a slave that conferred citizenship as well as liberty. The slave might be enrolled in the census, so long as it was taken, as if he were a citizen. Or someone, with the connivance of the master, might wrongly claim before the magistrate that the slave was free, the master would put up no defense, and the slave would be declared free. These were dodges, but the *Twelve Tables* allowed slaves to be freed by will. This was the only means by which they could be freed conditionally, and an heir was allowed to do nothing to inhibit a slave's eventual freedom. Augustus imposed perhaps the most common restrictions on this type of manumission. Slaves informally freed in the Republic remained slaves but were protected by the praetor; eventually their freedom was recognized, but they did not become citizens.

Freed persons, but not their children, were subject to certain disabilities at public law. In addition they had certain obligations to their former masters, including the payment of promised days of work and, in varying degrees, payment of property on death. They were also restricted in bringing suit against their patrons.

## THE LAW OF PROPERTY

Legal genius is largely a matter of drawing the most appropriate distinctions, and the Romans showed their skill nowhere more than with property. A first distinction was between the things governed by divine law and those under human law. Under divine law were *res sacrae,* things such as temples dedicated by order of the Roman people to the gods above, and *res religiosae,* things dedicated to the gods of the underworld, namely tombs. *Res sanctae* were in an intermediate class, to some extent under divine law. They were the gates and walls of cities; climbing on them entailed the death penalty. Things under divine law could not be owned. Under human law were public and private things. Public things were owned by the state and included roads, harbors, and navigable rivers. Riverbanks were private but their use was public. Some things were classed not as public but as common to all, such as air, the sea, and running water. There was dispute as to whether the seashore below the high water mark was public or common to all. Things were further classified as corporeal or incorporeal, a distinction whose sole importance was that incorporeal things could not be transferred by the legal method that required actual physical delivery (*traditio*).

The main division of things that could be privately owned was between *res mancipi* and *res nec mancipi*, a division also important for transfer of ownership. *Res mancipi,* a classification that was early fossilized, were things important in an early agricultural community—Italic land and the four oldest land servitudes: slaves, cattle, horses, mules, and asses. (The Proculians included the animals of draft and burden only when they were broken in.) These *res mancipi* could be transferred only by *mancipatio* or *in iure cessio*.

*Mancipatio* was a formal ceremony requiring the presence of the transferrer, the transferee, five male witnesses who were Roman citizens above puberty, and another who held a bronze scale. The transferee grasped the object of transfer, struck the scale with a bronze or copper ingot, and said, "I declare this slave [for instance] to be mine by the law of the citizens, and let him have been bought by me with this bronze and this bronze scale." The transferrer said nothing, his silence showing his acquiescence. Obviously the ceremony goes back to a time before coined money came into use, and it required the actual weighing of the bronze. The ceremony contained an inherent warranty—not, oddly, for the transfer of ownership but that if the transferee were lawfully evicted (that is, if the thing was taken from him by someone with a better title) the transferrer would pay him double the price stated in the *mancipatio*. The action lay only if the price were paid or security given, and it could not be directly excluded by agreement of the parties. A dodge to circumvent the rule developed, though, of stating a ridiculously low price in the *mancipatio*. A similar warranty existed when the acreage of land was wrongly stated in the *mancipatio*.

Transfer by *in iure cessio* could be used for all kinds of property, including incorporeals. It was a fictitious lawsuit in front of the magistrate in which the transferee claimed to be owner, the transferrer put up no defense, and the magistrate adjudged the thing to the transferee. Unlike ordinary lawsuits, this decision actually transferred ownership and its effect was not only between the parties.

*Mancipatio* and *in iure cessio* gave ownership only to Roman citizens, as did *usucapio*, a form of prescription that occurred when someone had undisturbed control of land for two years or of movables for one, provided his control began in good faith, that the thing was not stolen property, and that it was susceptible to private ownership. In postclassical law a very different system was used. Possession for ten years—twenty if the owner was not in the same province—extinguished the owner's title without giving the possessor ownership. Even before Justinian, however, this possession did give ownership.

*Res nec mancipi* could be transferred by *traditio*, actual physical delivery, a transaction that was available to foreigners. However, there was some lessening of the strict requirement of physical delivery. There was delivery *longa manu*, by the long hand, when goods stored in a warehouse were sold and the seller gave the buyer the key within sight of the warehouse; and delivery *brevi manu*, by the short hand, when the transferee was already in possession. *Traditio* did not transfer ownership of *res mancipi*, but if other requirements were fulfilled the recipient would gain ownership by usucapion after one year (or two for land). The Publician action, perhaps of the first century A.D., allowed the recipient to recover the property from anyone during the intervening year as if the year had run.

There were other, less important ways of acquiring ownership. By *occupatio* one took physical control and so ownership of something that did not have an owner. *Specificatio*, the making of a new thing out of materials belonging to another who did not consent (say wine out of grapes) gave ownership, but the owner of the materials would usually have an action for compensation or even for theft. *Accessio* occurred where property of one person became inseparably joined to more important property of another. *Thesauri inventio*, treasure trove, was property hidden so long that the owner could no longer be traced. At first, this went to the landowner, but under Hadrian it was established that the landowner and finder shared equally.

The Romans also distinguished between ownership and possession. Generally speaking, a person had possession when he had physical control of a thing, even through an intermediary, and intended to keep it. Possession was important not only as a requirement for usucapion but because it was itself protected by remedies called interdicts. When ownership was in question the person who had possession, or was put into possession because of the interdicts, would be the defendant in any lawsuit, and it was only the plaintiff who had to prove his case in order to win. Usually, but not always, interdicts protected the present possessor: thus, by the interdict called *utrubi*, possession was in effect awarded to the person who had had possession neither by force, nor by stealth, nor by grant at will for the longest period in the preceding year. When someone held control but not in his own name, particular rules came into force. Thus, a pledge creditor to whom the thing had been delivered did possess, a lessee did not, and a tenant for life did. A grantee at will did, but his claim to possess did not prevail against the grantor.

Possession was a matter of both fact and law. One gained possession when one took control with the requisite intention. And one retained possession so long as one did not relinquish the intention and provided the intention was not unrealistic and no one else had taken control.

Property might also be subject to burdens. Some of these operated only between neighboring land, whether by operation of law or by arrangement. Several restrictions of the former type were contained in the *Twelve Tables*; for instance, five feet of land around the boundaries could not be usucapted, overhanging trees could be lopped by the neighbor up to fifteen feet from the ground, and nuts or fruit that fell onto neighboring land could be collected. Again, the code gave an action if work had been done on a neighbor's land as a result of which rainwater might now cause damage. There was also a remedy by which one might demand security for damage threatened by a neighbor's defective property.

The most significant rights over neighboring property were servitudes, whose prime characteristic was that they were attached to the land and survived changes in ownership. A servitude had to fall within a recognized class, and the four earliest—the right of way, the right to drive beasts, a combined right of these two, and the right of aqueduct—were *res mancipi*. Other well-known servitudes were the right of light and the right to let the rainwater from one's roof fall on a neighbor's land. With the sole exception of *oneris ferendi*, servitudes could not impose a positive obligation on the owner of the servient land, but by *oneris ferendi* he could be compelled to keep in good condition a wall that acted as a support of adjoining property. Servitudes could only be exercised for the benefit of neighboring land and had to be used in such a way as to create as little disturbance as possible.

Property could also be burdened by real security. The oldest form is probably *fiducia*, the transfer of ownership of a *res mancipi* with a clause requiring good faith from the creditor. This was a good security for the creditor because, since he became owner, he had a strong right against anyone who got control of the property. It could also be good for the debtor: because the creditor had such strong protection, he did not need to insist on physical control, and the debtor in possession could continue to work his slaves, beasts, or land. In *pignus*, which could relate to all kinds of property, the debtor transferred possession but not ownership to the creditor. The creditor, if he lost possession, had a special Servian action to pursue the thing from the debtor or from anyone else. When the debtor paid and the thing was not returned, the debtor could bring the normal action, *vindicatio*, for ownership of the security, or a contractual action. *Hypotheca* was a variant on *pignus*—the texts use the terms interchangeably—in which not even physical control was delivered. The creditor's rights to sell the pledge in the event of nonpayment of the debt varied from time to time.

Finally there were burdens that are sometimes termed personal servitudes. Usufruct (*usus fructus*) was the right to enjoy the use and fruits of a thing for one's lifetime without impairing its substance. *Usus* was the much more limited right to enjoy the use but not the fruits; and *habitatio*, the right to live in a particular building, was a variety of *usus*.

## THE LAW OF SUCCESSION

By the time of the *Twelve Tables* succession could be by will as well as by intestacy. Heirs were classed as *necessarii, sui et necessarii,* and *extranei.* The first were slaves of the deceased, appointed by will, and with no power to refuse. This was important because by Roman law an heir was responsible for all debts even when they exceeded the inheritance. The second were those persons in the power of the deceased who became independent on his death; they, too, had no power to refuse. Both *necessarii* and *sui et necessarii* became heirs automatically at the moment of death. All other heirs were *extranei;* they had the right to refuse and became heirs only when they accepted the inheritance by a formal act or by acting as heir. In early times the heir was responsible for the *sacra,* the private religious duties of the deceased, but this came to be regarded as burdensome, and Publius Mucius Scaevola, the *pontifex maximus,* was himself responsible for inventing a dodge to avoid the *sacra.*

When there was no will, succession was regulated at first by the *Twelve Tables.* For the freeborn, *sui heredes* (those who became independent by the death) came first. If there were no *sui heredes,* the nearest agnate (a person related through males) would become heir; and failing the agnate, the succession would fall to the *gentiles,* members of the clan. The identification of the nearest agnate was made very narrowly, so that if he died or refused the inheritance it did not go to the next-nearest agnate but to the *gentiles.* If a freedman died intestate, his *sui heredes* succeeded and failing them his patron. In the first century B.C. the law of intestate succession was remodeled by the praetor's edict and basically gave rights first to children (including those given in adoption), next to blood relatives up to the sixth (and in one situation, the seventh) degree, and then to the husband or wife.

As early as the *Twelve Tables* wills could be made in three ways: *in procinctu,* when the army was drawn up in battle array and when no formalities were required; before the *comitia calata,* which met only twice a year for this purpose and where the will was a legislative act; and *per aes et libram,* which developed from the practice of using a modified form of *mancipatio.* The first two procedures died out early on, although Julius Caesar reinstituted a military will. In the *testamentum per aes et libram* a figurehead acted as if he were transferee, but the inheritance went to the named heir, and the named legatees and *tutores* accepted without reference to the figurehead. The praetor modified this in the late Republic: if a written will were produced, with the seals of those necessary for a *mancipatio*, then the praetor gave possession to the person named as heir. Other forms of will came into being in postclassical times.

Only a sane Roman above puberty could make a will, and until Hadrian's time a woman could do so only if she had undergone a change of family (that is, had married *cum manu*); even then the consent of her *tutor* was required. A will was effective only if the designated heir was competent and accepted. Only Roman citizens could be named as heirs, with the exception that the slaves of Romans could also, whether they were slaves of the testator (provided they were given their freedom) or of another. Unborn descendants could be appointed: indeed if they were born after the will was made and they were unprovided for, the will became void. The Voconian law (169 B.C.) provided that a person in the first class on the census, the wealthiest, could not appoint a woman heir. This provision lost its significance with the decline of the census and the introduction of trusts. To avoid the danger of dying without an effective will, the testator could appoint a substitute, or a line of substitutes, to succeed if the institute (the first named heir) did not. Where the institute was a *suus heres* of the testator and under puberty, the will could be so written that the substitute would take even if the institute took but died before puberty.

In addition to designating an heir a will could contain legacies and trusts (*fideicommissa*) and appoint *tutores*. Legacies, like institutions of heirs, had to be written in proper form, and they were of different kinds depending upon the words used. The two most important kinds were legacy *per vindicationem*, by which the legatee became owner as soon as the will was effective, and legacy *per damnationem*, in which the heir was ordered to give the legacy to the legatee. If he failed, the legatee had a personal action against him. Trusts at first had no legal force and were binding only on the conscience of the heir. They were used primarily where the beneficiary was legally barred from inheriting. Augustus enforced them in some cases and they came to be legally effective. In some situations codicils (later additions to a will) were recognized as having legal force.

## THE LAW OF CONTRACT

Roman law is most highly regarded for its contract law even though the Romans did not develop a theory of contract but only individual types of contract. For an agreement to be a contract it had to fall within the scope of a particular type, say sale or hire, and then it had the legal characteristics of that type. With the sole exception of *stipulatio*, the earliest of the contracts that could be used for any lawful business, the individual contracts were all defined by their function. Yet the Romans classified them by their form as verbal, literal, real, and consensual.

### Verbal Contracts

Verbal contracts are those that require set spoken words or a set pattern of words to be effective. The most important was *stipulatio*, where the promisee orally asked, "Do you promise. . . ?" and the promisor replied "I promise." The verb had to be the same in question and answer, the promise had to correspond to the question, and no delay could intervene between question and answer. Originally only one verb, *spondere* (which suggests a sacred origin), could be used, but from quite early times any verb could be used. The contract was one of so-called strict law. The parties were supposed to mean what they said and only what they said. Hence it was difficult to imply unspoken terms. More important, the promisor was still bound even if he had entered the contract as a result of fraud or extortion. This was remedied by praetors in the first century B.C. Around 80 B.C. the praetor Octavius gave an action for extortion (*metus*) for four times the value involved; he restored the injured party to the position he would have been in but for the extortion; and he gave a special defense of extortion (*exceptio metus*) if the wronged promisor was sued. The last is particularly interesting. An *exceptio* is a clause inserted into pleadings when the defendant accepts the accuracy of the plaintiff's claim but insists another appropriate factor has to be taken into account. The *exceptio* had to be specifically pleaded. In 66 B.C. Gaius Aquilius Gallus gave the *actio de dolo* (action for fraud) for simple damages, but only if there was no other remedy, and also an *exceptio doli.* He defined fraud so narrowly that there had to be negotiations between the parties; hence the action was a contractual remedy. Since an action was available for fraud in other contracts, the *actio de dolo* was invented for fraud in the strict-law, as contrasted with good-faith, contracts. Within a short time the scope of the action for fraud was widened.

Not all stipulations were valid. A stipulation was void if it was illegal, immoral, or impossible or subject to such a condition. Nor could one be made for performance to a third party. A stipulation to be performed after the death of one of the parties was void as impossible, but the advantages of such an agreement (for life assurance, for instance) led to the dodge that if the promise were framed "to give me when I am dying," then it was valid as becoming effective at the last moment of life.

But a stipulation could be used to cover all the terms of another type of contract, say sale (in which case the contract was one of *stipulatio*), or some terms of another contract, say warranties against eviction and latent defects in sale. One standard use was as personal security, whereby the guarantor promised to pay the same—or a lesser but not greater—debt as the principal debtor, and the creditor could exact from either. There were three main forms depending on the verb used in the stipulation: *sponsio, fidepromissio,* and *fideiussio.* The rules here are complicated, but the important point is that so many rules developed to protect the guarantor that the two earlier forms ceased to be effective, and *fideiussio* emerged early in the Empire, without the restrictions.

In early law performance did not discharge a contract. There had to be a similar act of extinction, in this case called *acceptilatio.* When this ceased to be necessary, perhaps as early as the late third cen-

tury B.C., *acceptilatio* remained, but as a method of discharging a
stipulation (when the parties so agreed) without performance.

There were two other verbal contracts. *Dotis dictio* was one method
of promising a dowry and had the peculiarity that nothing was said
by the promisee. It could only be promised by the bride, her *paterfamilias*, or a debtor of the bride. *Iusiurandum liberti* was an oath
given by a new freedman that he would perform the services to his
patron that he had promised before manumission. It is the only contract of historical times that involved an oath.

## Literal Contracts

There was only one literal, that is, written, contract, and a great deal
about it is obscure. It was also a contract of strict law, and it existed
by the early first century B.C. but is probably older. Rather than being
an original contract it was a way in which an existing contract was
changed into another. The creditor wrote fictitiously in his formal
account books that an existing debt had been repaid and then made
another entry fictitiously stating that a loan of the same amount had
been made to the same debtor or another. Thereby the old contract was
extinguished and a new one created. Only Romans could be creditors,
but there was a dispute between the Sabinians and the Proculians as
to how far foreigners could be debtors. The contract died out, perhaps
in the third century A.D., with the demise of account books.

Justinian in his *Institutes* but not in the *Digest* treats of a literal
contract. If someone writes, he says, that he has received money when
he has not and two years pass, then if he is sued he cannot put up the
defense that he never received the money. This is not really a contract but amounts to saying that if a person granted an IOU and let it
stand without challenge, then after a period of time he is barred from
denying he took the loan.

## Real Contracts

The real contracts, contracts *re*—literally "by the thing," meaning by
delivery—show that the categorization by form does not correspond

to historical development. The oldest real contract, very different from the others, is *mutuum*, loan for consumption. A strict-law contract dating from the third century B.C., it was unilateral since only the borrower was bound, and he had to return the exact equivalent of what was lent. No interest was enforceable by the action although interest could be arranged through a separate stipulation. The action in this instance and also for the literal contract was the *condictio*, described below. In the first century A.D. the *senatus consultum Macedonianum* provided that someone who lent to a son in power had no remedy, even after the son became *sui iuris* (in one's own right), free from *patria potestas*.

The very different *commodatum* was a loan for use in which the borrower did not become owner and would not suffer the loss if the thing were destroyed or damaged unless he had failed to show the degree of care that was regarded as appropriate. The contract was introduced by a praetorian edict in the first century B.C., but inexplicably there was also a civil law action for what was proper according to good faith.

As early as the *Twelve Tables* there was an action for double damages where a depositee failed to return the article deposited. Whether we should see a contract in this or an action akin to theft is a matter of dispute. But early in the first century B.C. the praetor issued an edict giving double damages against someone who failed to restore a thing deposited with him as a result of a house falling down, shipwreck, or fire; only simple damages were allowed against his heir who failed to restore or to a depositee in other circumstances. Oddly, there also developed a civil law action. Normally the depositee was liable only for fraud.

## Consensual Contracts

The consensual contracts—contracts that come into being simply by the agreement of the parties and that require no formalities—are one of the great Roman inventions. There are four of them: hire; mandate; partnership, which comes from the law of succession; and sale, with roots in *mancipatio* and *stipulatio*. They have little in common in their origins except that, as consensual contracts, an action was provided for them by the praetor's edict.

Sale (*emptio venditio*) required agreement, a price, and a thing to be sold. No formalities were required, but for important transactions evidence would be provided by writing or by giving earnest money (*arra*), a deposit, which could also serve as part payment. This *arra* had no specific legal function. Justinian changed the law here: if the parties agreed that the contract was to be put into writing, there was no contract until the writing was completed and formalized, and either party could withdraw without penalty provided no *arra* had been given. If *arra* had been given and the buyer then withdrew, he forfeited the *arra*; or if the seller withdrew he had to restore the *arra* and as much again.

Since agreement was needed, error that blocked agreement prevented the sale from coming into being. Such error was sufficient if for instance it was about the identity of the thing sold or was the so-called *error in substantia*. The last is rather obscure but seems to mean error as to the material the thing is completely made of, such as bronze for gold (but not gold alloy for gold), or error as to the sex of slaves. A lesser error left the sale valid, but an action was available if the error was the result of misrepresentations by the seller— for the difference in value if the misrepresentation were innocent, for all subsequent loss if the misrepresentation was deliberate.

According to the Proculians, who prevailed, the price had to be set in coined money. The Sabinians had wished to extend the contract for sale to cover the legally inadequate rules of barter. The price also had to be certain in the sense that it had to be knowable, and it had to be seriously intended: a disguised gift was not a sale. A rule perhaps introduced by Diocletian (A.D. 284–305), only to disappear until it was restored by Justinian, stated that the sale of land was void if the price set was less than half the true value. There also had to be a thing to be sold: if a slave was sold who was already dead the sale was void. There could be a sale of a future thing, for instance of a growing crop. If this sale were construed as *emptio rei speratae*, a "purchase of a hoped for thing," then the sale came into effect only if the thing came into being; if as *emptio spei*, "purchase of a hope," then the expectation was what was bought, and the sale was valid even if no thing came into being. Originally there could be no sale of anything incapable of human ownership, such as a temple, but eventually it was accepted that such a sale was valid in the sense that an action on it might be brought.

The buyer was obliged to pay the price on time and, if he were in delay, interest and the seller's expenses. The seller's obligations were more complex. He had to keep the thing safe until delivery, deliver possession, give guarantees against eviction and hidden defects, and be free from fraud. As we have seen, ownership was transferred only by delivery, but under sale risk passed to the buyer as soon as the contract was perfect. The seller still in possession therefore was liable if he did not show proper care, but the standard of care demanded is not certain and may have varied. Oddly, the seller did not have to make the buyer owner. It was enough originally that he delivered the thing in good faith. So it became customary for the buyer to take a stipulation that his enjoyment would not be legally disturbed, and by a series of steps that culminated in the second century A.D. this guarantee came to be implied in the sale. Likewise, at first there were no innate guarantees against hidden defects, but they were often taken by stipulation. The curule aediles, who had control over the streets and markets, issued an edict giving an action where beasts or slaves had been sold and the declaration of defects was false or had not been given. Eventually, the warranty against latent defects was implied in all sales.

Hire (*locatio conductio*) may almost be described as a residual category after sale, covering every type of bilateral agreement where there is a money price on one side. As does hire in many modern Western systems, it thus covers hire of a thing, of a piece of work to be done, and of services. In hire of a thing the lessor had to give the lessee the use of the thing for the agreed period. If the thing was not fit for the purpose of the lease the lessee was excused from paying rent, and if the lessor unnecessarily caused the thing not to be used, then the lessee could sue for all resulting loss. In hire of a piece of work to be done the person hired agreed to produce a certain result on a thing delivered by the hirer—for instance, training a slave of the hirer to be a doctor, or to deliver the hirer's wheat to Rome. The person hired was liable for any loss caused to the thing, even if he were not negligent, unless the injury was the result of external force or robbery with violence. Hire of services was less important than it is today since much work would be performed by slaves, and when the services of another's slave were hired this would usually be hire of a thing. The so-called liberal arts, such as the teaching of philosophy, giving of legal advice, and surveying, were regarded as too noble to be the object of a contract.

Partnership (societas) had a long history before the introduction of the consensual contract. As early as the Twelve Tables, sui heredes who did not divide up the inheritance were partners (in all their assets, necessarily) but not as the result of contract. Then the praetor gave a legis actio for others who wished to form such a partnership. Even when consensual partnership came into being, the standard case was partnership of all the assets of the partners—obviously not a mercantile arrangement but one for close relatives who worked a farm together. Lesser partnerships were also available, including partnership for the purpose of one transaction, something unknown in modern law but useful for a society that does not accept direct agency, that is, where an obligation entered into by the agent becomes the obligation of his principal. Each partner had to contribute something, whether work or assets, and each had the right to some share of profits. Unless the partners agreed otherwise they would share equally in any profit or loss. The partners were liable to each other only for fraud, it being regarded as a person's own fault if he chose a negligent partner. Unlike modern partnership, Roman partnership was almost entirely turned inward and controlled the relationship between the partners. A partner's contract on partnership affairs with a third party was a contract solely between him and the third party, who could neither sue nor be sued by the other partners.

Mandate (mandatum) was the gratuitous undertaking—that is, for no reward—to do something on behalf of a friend, and the contract came into existence sometime in the second century B.C. If the undertaking was to enter a contract with a third party, then any resulting contract was between the third party and the person acting as mandatary. Hence mandate was not direct agency. Until performance was started, either party could withdraw from the contract. The mandatary was entitled to be reimbursed for any loss and expenses, and he was normally liable only for fraud.

Only the foregoing are described as contracts in Gaius's and Justinian's *Institutes*, but the *Digest* has a title on what later came to be called the innominate (not specifically named) contracts. These fall into two types. The first occurs where there is a clearly defined situation and where specific legal rules have come to govern a transaction that does in fact have a name, such as *permutatio* (barter) or *aestimatum* (sale or return). The second, described by the jurist Paul in the second century A.D., occurs when there is a bilateral agreement for each to give or do something, and an action would lie to one who performed his side of the bargain. As early as the Republic, the praetor also protected pacts in the sense that he allowed them to act as a defense although not as the basis of an action. There were subsequent developments.

There were also situations akin to contract but not to delict that gave rise to actions "as if from contract." The most important of such actions were the *actio negotiorum gestorum*, action for work done, and the *condictio*. The former lay when someone acted, without authorization but reasonably, on behalf of another. The actor could recover any expenses up to the value of the property saved. It was also the action where an authorized person acted for another in court, and the action for or against the *procurator*, the general agent. The *condictio* was an action that lay whenever, as a result of a transfer, the defendant owned something that he ought to give to the plaintiff: for instance, if the plaintiff had by mistake paid to the defendant something he did not owe him, or if the plaintiff had for an agreed reason given something to the defendant and the reason was not forthcoming. An anomalous case was the *condictio* against a thief to recover stolen property because the plaintiff had remained the owner.

## THE LAW OF DELICT

Delicts were private wrongs, but much of what we consider criminal law was covered by them. Only four delicts—theft, robbery with violence, damage to property, and verbal or physical assault—were dealt with in the *Institutes* of Gaius and Justinian.

As early as the *Twelve Tables, furtum* (theft) was divided into manifest and nonmanifest. The former meant that the thief was caught in the act, and originally if he were a slave he was beaten and thrown from the Tarpeian Rock; a freeman was beaten and adjudged to the victim as a bond servant. Later, by the Edict the penalty for manifest theft was four times the value of the stolen property. For nonmanifest theft the penalty was always double the value of the stolen property. Until the second century A.D., by a clause of the *Twelve Tables,* a thief at night could always be killed.

The physical requirement for theft was not carrying away but wrongful touching. This caused practical problems when only part of a larger whole, say some wine from a cask, was removed since the action lay for a multiple of the value, not of the owner's interest. The problem was compounded in that if the thief intended to use the thing only temporarily, he was still liable for theft of the whole thing. The necessary wrongful intention had to be to make a gain, but gain was understood in a wide sense and there were some doubtful borderline cases.

The *Twelve Tables* instituted a ritual search for stolen property, and if any was found the theft was treated as manifest. The Edict introduced an action for a fourfold penalty where a search was refused. If stolen property were found on someone's property without a formal search he was liable for a threefold penalty whether he was the thief or not (*furtum conceptum*), but in his turn he had a right of action for the same amount against the person who placed it there. These actions, established by the *Twelve Tables,* were repeated in the Edict.

*Rapina,* robbery with violence, was instituted as a separate delict by the praetor Marcus Licinius Lucullus (76 B.C.), with an action for a fourfold penalty. *Damnum iniuria datum,* wrongful damage to property, was dealt with by the Aquilian law of 287 B.C., although in part that merely consolidated earlier legislation. It was in three chapters, of which the second is out of place. That dealt with the situation in which by stipulation a friend of the creditor acted as alternative payee, payment was made to him, and he released the debtor by *acceptilatio* but did not hand the money over to the creditor. Until the introduction of mandate there was no contract between him and the creditor, hence this delictal action.

Chapter 1 of the Aquilian law gave an action when a slave or herd animal was wrongfully killed, and it lay for the highest value the slave or animal had had in the past year. "Wrongfully" at first meant without rightful cause, but before the end of the Republic it generally meant that the killing was malicious or negligent. The damages were doubled if the defendant denied liability. In the early Empire the action was interpreted restrictively and lay only if the defendant had killed, not if he had merely furnished a cause of death. The latter was the case, for example, if a midwife handed a drug to a pregnant slave and the slave herself drank it. In such an instance the praetor routinely gave an action on the facts.

Chapter 3 of the law gave an action for other damage to inanimate and animate things alike caused by wrongful burning, snapping, or breaking, and it lay for the loss that became apparent within thirty days. The reference to thirty days came to be neglected, and this chapter, too, came to be restrictively interpreted.

*Iniuria*, personal injury, was the object of three clauses of the *Twelve Tables*, whose meanings are not entirely clear. For *membrum ruptum*, presumably a serious bodily injury, the victim could inflict the same injury unless a compromise was reached. For *os fractum*, a broken bone, the action was for 300 *asses* (copper coins) if the victim were a free man, 150 if a slave. Probably this was the minimum for this subcategory of *membrum ruptum*. For minor assaults the action was for 25 *asses*. Depreciation of the value of the money made the awards absurdly low, and in the third century B.C. a general edict of the praetor made the assessment flexible. This effectively destroyed the distinctions between the categories, and the action was eventually extended to verbal assaults. Other edicts followed, giving actions for specific situations: public insult; following a matron, young boy, or girl, or removing a chaperone contrary to good morals; assaulting another's slave contrary to good morals, primarily by beating him or having him tortured; and *iniuria* to someone in power whose paterfamilias was absent.

In addition to the four main delicts there were a number of others, of which *metus* and *dolus* have been mentioned. Others included an action for double damages for taking in another's runaway slave or deliberately causing him damage, physically or morally, and one for wrongfully cutting down another's trees.

When a slave or son committed a delict without the master's knowledge, the action normally gave the master the choice of paying the whole amount of the condemnation or delivering the wrongdoer to the victim in so-called noxal surrender. This amounts to an early form of limited liability, as does the similar provision in the *actio de pauperie* when an animal caused injury and could be said to be at fault. The aediles also gave an action where a wild animal was kept near a road and did damage.

Finally, there were four situations akin to delict where an action was given for an obligation arising as if from delict. These were: where a judge made the case his own (a circumstance not fully explained); against the owner of a dwelling when something was poured or thrown from his dwelling (even without his knowledge) and caused damage; or for allowing something to be placed on or suspended from eaves or a projecting roof when its fall could cause injury; and against a ship's captain, innkeeper, or stablekeeper for any theft or fraud committed in the ship or building by an employee.

# 2 The Spiritual History of the Law

A legal system presents different faces to various groups: to the elite who make the law, to the educated and sophisticated persons living under the law, to the poor who suffer under the law, and to the outsiders looking in. To all of these law shows only a profile.

The lawmaking elite live their concerns and their culture. They see law from an elevated height, and the perspective is distorted. Thus, the leading English subordinate lawmakers, high court judges, who are concerned above all with details, can still write that English academics portray the law as if it were more systematic than it is. Those who make law by judgments in individual cases stress the particularity of each decision rather than the overarching structure.[1] Outsiders looking in see what exists or survives in an accessible form rather than the whole body of law. An outsider looking at the law relating to slavery in the Dutch colonies of Curaçao and St. Maarten in the seventeenth and eighteenth centuries would see above all the regulations, *placaaten*, that deal primarily with policing and control. The fact that behind the *placaaten* is the whole system of Roman slave law, that was understood to govern but was not stated, is much harder to grasp.[2]

For Roman law we all have to be outsiders looking in; there are no surviving Romans living the system. But the face presented to the outsiders is essentially that painted by the lawmaking elite, and especially by the jurists. The legal sources that survive reflect accurately their concerns but give little feel for how the law impacted on the population as a whole or even on the upper echelons. Thus, for example, to remain with slave law for a moment, whereas many laws survive from English-speaking America regulating the number or proportion of white free males on each plantation, only one nonlegal text proves that similar rules also existed in the Roman world.[3] The jurists were not interested in policing matters. Likewise, there is virtually no information in the legal sources on the building regulations that must have existed in each city[4] or (apart from the important clauses in the aeditilian Edict on the sale of slaves and beasts) on the regulation of the street markets.[5]

But in no sense am I in this book attempting to enter the minds of the lawmaking elite, and especially of the jurists. That elite lived its culture, and those living a culture are to a great extent unconscious of it. Rather, my goal is to show the psyche, the unconscious as well as the conscious, of that elite. I will attempt not only to describe their approach to law, their reasoning, the parameters of their legal thinking, and their concerns but also to explain their interests and their view of law.

It is the particular perspective of the elite on legal matters, above all of the jurists, that best brings out the innate spirit of Roman law. Yet, fortunately, there are the writings of Cicero, an outsider to the tradition of the jurists, that indicate other dimensions. Cicero's views will be discussed in appendix A. I said that the face presented to us as outsiders looking in is that shown by the Roman lawmaking elite. So it is, but we see it through colored and distorting glasses. Modern readers, and this writer too, view it through the prism of their own exposure to other systems. Often what seems strange to us is so only because we have come to know something else, somewhere else.

Astonishingly, the abiding characteristics of Roman law were fashioned mainly by events that occurred in a few years beginning around 451 B.C., in this early point in Rome's history. In this chapter, to lay the groundwork, I propose to sketch these events and describe in outline their consequences for the spirit of Roman law.[6]

After the expulsion of the last king, Tarquin the Proud, in 510 B.C. and the establishment of the Republic in 509, government was primarily in the hands of two magistrates, later called consuls, who were elected annually. From early in the Republic serious tension existed between the small number of leading aristocratic families, the patricians, and the great majority of the population, the plebeians.

Presumably we should see in this tension the ambition of leading plebeians who wished to break into the patrician monopoly of high public office.[7] For the mass of the plebeians it could make no practical difference whether political and religious power was restricted to patricians or was also open to the wealthiest and most ambitious plebeian families.

The patrician monopoly of power, established by law, was all embracing. Thus, in the religious sphere, the main state priests, including the members of the leading College of Pontiffs and the College of Augurs, had to be patrician. Only after the Ogulnian law (*lex Ogulnia*) passed in 300 B.C., despite patrician opposition, could plebeians be pontiffs or augurs.[8] Control of the state religion was a powerful political weapon. In the administrative sphere, only patricians could be consuls—and consuls were the normal heads of state—until the Licinian-Sextian laws (*leges Liciniae Sextiae*) of 367 B.C.:[9] thereafter one had to be a plebeian, but this provision seems not to have been regularly implemented until 320. From 444 B.C. three military tribunes might hold the chief magistracy (in place of the two consuls) and plebeians could hold that office, but according to Livy no plebeian was elected until 400 B.C.[10] Dictators, who could be appointed in an emergency, had to be patrician. The only other regular magistrates of the early Republic were the quaestors, who were chosen by the consuls; plebeians became legally eligible in 421 B.C.[11] The office of praetor was created in 367 B.C., specifically to deal with legal issues. This office is particularly significant for us since the praetors controlled the major law courts and had a great impact on legal change. Livy relates that the first plebeian praetor was elected in 337.[12]

Yet, to keep the record straight, it should be stressed that to open offices to the plebeians was not a big step toward democracy. The powerful plebeians who sought election had more in common with the patricians than with the great mass of plebeians. With time, rich plebeians had more wealth than many patricians, and Rome was a society as money-conscious as today's United States.

The main political legislative body was the *comitia centuriata*, which could meet only when summoned by the consuls and could discuss only the business they put before it. The *comitia* could vote down legislation but not amend it. The *comitia* in early Rome was divided into five military classes determined by wealth, and voting was by the centuries or electoral units into which each class was divided. Above the first, wealthiest, class were centuries of cavalry (*equites*), and the cavalry and first class together constituted a majority of centuries.[13] Voting was in descending order, the *equites* first, the first class next, and voting stopped as soon as there was a majority for the positive or negative. According to Livy, voting seldom went as far as the second class and almost never to the lowest class.[14]

In the subsequent turmoil, the plebeians' political demands came to center on the need for law reform.[15] In 462 B.C. a tribune of the plebs, C. Terentilius Harsa, attacked the arrogance of patricians toward the plebeians and above all the powers of the consuls. There were, he claimed, no restraints on the consuls, and he proposed that five men be appointed to write down the law on the powers of the consuls, which in the future they should not exceed. Terentilius made no progress that year, but proferred the same proposal the following year with the support of all the tribunes. Their demands encountered unfavorable religious omens. The Sibylline books were examined by the relevant two patrician officials, who found in them warnings against the danger of external attack and against factious politics. The tribunes treated these warnings as fraudulent and continued to press for their law reforms. Their demands were considered to be against religion—not surprisingly, given the composition of the priesthood— as well as against political order. Around 454 B.C. the consuls declared that the passage of a law by the people and the tribunes would never happen. The tribunes, who were by now discouraged, proposed a compromise: if the senate would not accept a law passed by the plebeians, the patricians and plebeians should appoint a team of lawmakers drawn from both sides to make laws beneficial to both and equalizing the liberty of both. The senators were not against the idea of lawmaking but insisted that they and they alone could make the law. The dispirited plebs accepted this, and a team was sent to Athens, says Livy, to write down the famous laws of Solon and to record the laws and customs of other Greek states. (In actuality, any Greek influence may have come from Magna Graecia, in southern Italy.) When the delegation returned, it was decided to appoint ten officials, as the sole magistrates, to draft the laws. After controversy over whether plebeians could be appointed to the office, the plebeians conceded that only patricians would be *decemviri*. The sources stress that the plebeians wanted the powers of the consuls to be limited and set down, and that they sought equality before the law.

These *decemviri* produced a code of ten tables which, after amendment, were successfully presented to the *comitia centuriata*. The *decemviri* proved to be very popular and, when it was felt that the code was incomplete, a second group of *decemviri* were elected for the following year. They produced two supplementary tables, and the resulting *Twelve Tables* became the basis of Roman law. The second set of *decemviri*, especially Appius Claudius, showed themselves to be tyrannous, remained in office after their term expired, but were eventually deposed.

Statute requires interpretation. According to the jurist Pomponius, writing in the second century A.D., the task of interpretation, specifically of the *Twelve Tables*, was allotted to the patrician College of Pontiffs, which each year selected one member for interpreting private law.[16]

Such were the historical events that, above all, in my view, determined the spirit of Roman law. The major characteristics that shaped Roman law forever flowed from these circumstances.

The plebeians lost the war to participate in creating the law and to delineate and delimit the powers of the chief public officials. Interpretation of the *Twelve Tables* was entrusted to patrician pontiffs.

The *Twelve Tables* were the work of patricians and very much a code of law drafted for the lesser plebeians, or at least a code of law that could be shared equally with plebeians. Thus, any subject that the patricians regarded as inappropriate for the plebeians was rigorously excluded. Public offices were the preserve of patricians. Hence (despite the plebs' original goals) nothing in the code sets out the powers and duties of consuls and other officials, and there are no provisions on the composition or functions of the assemblies. Public law does not appear in the code. Thereby arose the fundamental distinction between public law and private law.

The rituals of the state religion and the priestly offices were the monopoly of patricians. Accordingly, religious law was excluded from the *Twelve Tables* as a subject for which the plebs were unfit. This is one part of the explanation of the intensely secular appearance of Roman law. The pontiffs, as priests and patricians, were very conscious of the much greater importance of keeping the right relations between the gods and humans, especially the state, than of preserving them between individuals; and they did not carry over to private law the extreme formalism of Roman religion. This is the second part of the explanation for the secular nature of Roman private law. Indeed, even in the very few cases where religious oaths had an impact in private law, the use of the oath, as we shall see, was entirely secular.

The *Twelve Tables* were prepared by patricians as the law they were willing to share with plebeians, in response to the latter's demand for equal rights of liberty. This explains the extremely egalitarian nature of the contents of the *Twelve Tables* and of subsequent Roman private law. The severity of punishment for wrongdoing, for example, did not (as it did elsewhere) depend on the status of the victim so long as he was free. But this egalitarianism, so much part of the spirit of Roman private law, is an illusion. The inequalities in Roman law will not appear much in this book because the book is concerned with private law. But differences in political rights were enshrined in the law—in the structure of the assemblies and in the legal capacity in early times to hold political or priestly office. Until the *lex iudiciaria* of 122 B.C., only senators could be chosen to be judges whether in civil or criminal cases. That statute admitted *equites equo publico*, knights provided with a horse at public expense, and seems to have excluded senators.[17]

Just as none of us make our history just as we like but carry our past with us, so the interpreters of the *Twelve Tables* carried over from their pontifical roles their sacred-law approaches to legal reasoning. Accordingly, legal judgments could not be reached expressly on the basis of what was reasonable, economically advantageous, useful, or just. As we shall see, a very particular form of inturned legal logic was employed in reaching an opinion, with few references to social reality. This also explains the remoteness from legal discussion of particular political, social, or economic circumstances or events.

The original role of interpretation given to the pontiffs and the choice of one of their number to give authoritative rulings are the basis of two other characteristic features of the system: the importance subsequently attached by gentlemen (i.e., the jurists) to the giving of legal opinions, and the acceptance by the state of the individual's important role in lawmaking. Because to become one of the (originally) four pontiffs was an important step in a political career and because giving authoritative rulings in law was a significant pontifical function, it was valuable for a gentleman to have legal knowledge and provide legal opinions. Because the pontiffs were patricians and were appointed only after they had a known political track record, the ruling elite could usually feel confident in allowing them to declare what the law was. When the College of Pontiffs lost its monopoly of interpretation, tradition ensured that men of the same class regarded the task as important. Until the early first century B.C., the senators dominated the ranks of the jurists; and up to 95 B.C. eighteen jurists had held the consulate.[18]

The same facts explain fundamental approaches to legal sources. The role of interpretation given to the pontiffs entailed, as we will see, little scope for custom and judicial precedent in lawmaking. That role and the high social status of the pontiffs, and subsequently of the jurists, ensured that there would be close cooperation between jurist and praetor and meant that once praetors began to create law by setting out in edicts how they perceived their legal functions, much of the detail could be left unstated, to be filled in by the jurists.

On the same basis, too, is to be explained the absence of concern with the realities of court practice. The jurists as such were not directly involved with litigation. Their prestige (and wealth) did not depend on the outcome of a trial, and they were not concerned with strategies for winning. Thus arose the extreme separation of substantive law from the technicalities needed to support it. Formalities, for instance, were required to create the contract of *stipulatio*, but they were of such a nature that they provided no evidence for a court that a contract had actually been made.

Fundamental to the spirit of Roman law was the striving for clarity of legal concepts, even when this involved distortion of reality or resulted in practical disadvantages. In part, this was the result of putting interpretation into the hands of theorists who (as such) were not involved in practice. In greater part it results from the close relationship between praetors and jurists. The praetor would give, let us say, an action for sale and a different action for hire. It then became vital to determine what precisely counted as sale and what as hire. This was all the more important in that if the transaction was clearly not hire, yet not quite sale, then neither an action on hire nor an action on sale would lie, and no other action might be available. The precise delimitation of legal institutions, and the distinctions between one and another was essential, and this was a job undertaken by the jurists. No contrast with the growth of English common law could be stronger than this struggle for clarity of concepts.

Moreover, the way the *Twelve Tables* were created and their interpretation given to patrician pontiffs ensured that law would always retain a tinge of the aristocratic and that the notion of authority would always be prominent. The idea that law was the preserve of everyone was foreign to the spirit of Roman law.

As I have mentioned, the interpretation of civil law, specifically of the *Twelve Tables*, was entrusted to the College of Pontiffs. Within secular law, this civil law was the center of attention for the pontiffs, and subsequently for the jurists. When law was developed by the praetors in their Edicts, that praetorian law was kept separate from civil law. Even in the Empire, books were written on the civil law or on the Edict. Yet, despite appearances, there was only one system of law in operation: that enforced in the courts of the praetors. The praetorian Edict was not a separate system of equity such as appeared in England with the court of the Chancellor.

One fundamental characteristic was not the result of the *Twelve Tables*, but all that I have said above would be meaningless if it had not been central to the Roman legal psyche, namely tradition. There are no breaks in Roman legal history, only gradual evolution. The law was recognizably the same product around 200 B.C., in the late Republic, in Augustus's principate, in the disastrous later third century, in Diocletian's revival, and even in Justinian's codification. It was recognizably the same in a small republic and in a world empire, in economic growth and economic chaos, under paganism and Christianity, in Latin Rome and in Byzantine Constantinople. This is as true for family law and for the law of slavery as it is for the law of contract and property.[19]

# 3 Public Law and Private Law: Public and Religious Dimensions

Gaius's *Institutes*, written around A.D. 161,[1] was apparently the most widely used legal textbook.[2] In the hindsight of Justinian and of later ages it was the textbook par excellence, though there is no evidence that it was highly regarded by the classical jurists.[3] After a brief introductory section on the sources of law, Gaius states at *G.*1.8: "All the law that we use relates to persons or to things or to actions." And that is what he proceeds to discuss. He deals under persons with slaves, free persons subject to power, marriage, citizenship, adoption, marital power (*manus*), and guardians and curators, all in book 1. Things are the subject of books 2 and 3, and subjects treated include classifications of things, acquisition of ownership, testate and intestate succession, contracts, and delict. Actions are the subject of book 4. These topics are also the focus of interest for other jurists.

But Gaius claimed that *all* the law in use pertained to persons, things, or actions. Where in this classification is the law that we might regard as public law, such as constitutional law, administrative law, criminal law, military law, and the law relating to public property? Where is the religious law that governs the offices of the state priests, requirements for the performance of rites, and decisions on sacred law? (As a celebrated text of Ulpian, *D.*1.1.1.2, tells us, sacred law was part of public law.) To answer these questions we must look at what Gaius says about the state or state property and how issues touching religion appear in the *Institutes*.

Apart from the lawmaking functions of assemblies, praetors, and emperors, which are set out very briefly in *G.*1.2,3,4,5 and 6, public officials and bodies do not appear in any guise. There is nothing about election, powers, duties, and authority of any public person or body. There is nothing about military law or administrative law. Gaius's

concern with public bodies and officials is solely with their making
of private law.

Public property rights appear in two contexts. First:

> G.2.10: But these things which are under human law are either
> public or private. 11. Public things are regarded as no one's prop-
> erty: for they are considered to belong to the whole community
> of the people. Private things are those that belong to individuals.

Public property is not further described: what it is, how it is constituted or acquired, particular privileges attaching to it, its alienability
or otherwise, responsibility for its upkeep, actions against violators of
it—these topics are entirely missing. The texts just quoted are simply
part of the prelude to Gaius's treatment of private property.

The other mention of state property rights in Gaius—and let me
emphasize that he has no further references to state rights or obligations—is startlingly unimportant:

> G.2.61: Again, if the Roman people sold a thing pledged to
> it and the owner has taken possession of it, recovery by use
> (usus receptio) is permitted; but in this case land is recovered
> in two years. And this is the reason for the common saying that
> possession is recovered by usucapion from a land transaction
> with the people (praediatura): for a person who purchases from
> the people is called a land dealer (praediator).

Gaius is discussing in general when it is or is not possible to acquire
by prescription one's own property in which one's ownership has been
transferred in pledge. This is one case. Why a pledge to the people is
mentioned is not obvious, especially because no other aspect of state
property rights is discussed. Nor are any other peculiarities, if there
were any, of mortgages to the state. But Gaius's text, relatively insignificant as it is and strange because it alone concerns property law
involving the state, gains unexpectedly in stature for our purposes
when we take account of Cicero's speech *Pro Balbo* 20.45:

> For if that famous augur, Quintus Scaevola, when he was con-
> sulted about the law of public mortgages (ius praediaturum),

most skilled jurist though he was, referred those consulting him to the brokers (*praediatores*) Furius and Cascellius; if, with regard to water rights on my estate at Tusculum I consulted Marcus Tugio rather than Gaius Aquilius, because continued practice and dedication to one subject are frequently superior to ability and skill, who would hesitate to prefer our military commanders to all the most skillful jurists with regard to treaties and the whole law of war and peace?

Cicero's point is precisely that celebrated jurists are not the people to turn to when one has an issue relating to *praediatura*. For legal issues involving the state and state rights, including the law of war and peace, jurists are not the experts. Quintus Scaevola, the augur, is Quintus Mucius Scaevola, who was consul in 117 B.C.[4] Gaius Aquilius is Gaius Aquilius Gallus, praetor with Cicero in 66 B.C. and a famous jurist now known best for his introduction of the edict on fraud and his invention of the Aquilian stipulation.[5] Furius, Tugius, and Cascellius are not known.[6] Juristic law is private law.

Religion is scarcely more prominent in Gaius. Indeed no god is even named, though the priests (*flamines*) of Jupiter, Mars, and Quirinus are mentioned at G.1.112 as having to be born from a marriage consecrated by the religious ceremony called *confarreatio*. *Confarreatio* in Gaius's time had no civil law effects but is mentioned because of its past history, which is best discussed in the latter part of this chapter. A secular consequence of becoming a vestal virgin is mentioned at G.1.145; and roles for oaths, with a secular purpose, appear at G.3.96 and at G.4.13f, 16, and 28: they, too, will be discussed later in the chapter. At this point it is sufficient to stress that religion occupies a very restricted place in Gaius's *Institutes*; it occurs in only two further contexts. At G.2.55 Gaius explains that a person who knew he had no right to it could acquire an inheritance by prescription because the old (i.e., Republican) lawyers wanted those entitled to an inheritance to accept it quickly so that the family religious rites would be performed. Thus, one particular rule of private law had come into being for a religious reason.

The other context is G.2.2–9. Just as G.2.10–11 deal with public property, so do G.2.2–9 deal with things subject to divine law, but this time we are told how such a status originates. Things become sacred (res sacrae), consecrated to the gods above, only by authority of the Roman people; things become consecrated to the gods below (res religiosae) when someone buries a body in his own land and when the burial is properly his concern.[7] Sanctified things (res sanctae), such as city walls and gates, are also subject to divine law in some sense.[8] But the consequences of something being under divine, not human, law are not listed or discussed.

So public and sacred law are not really matters for discussion for Gaius. Indeed, his main concern with property in this context is really geared to showing that not all things are, or can be, privately owned. The law relating to such public and sacred things is then ignored.

But bearing Gaius's lack of interest in mind, we can jump to the end of our time scale. The *Institutes* of the Byzantine emperor Justinian were modeled on those of Gaius, a fact striking in itself since we have moved from the pagan Latin West to the Christian Greek East.

But in the body of that work, written in the hotbed of Christian religious debate under the auspices of an emperor famous for his fascination with theology, there is no mention of God or Jesus. No ruling is supported by the authority of scripture or of a father of the church; the role of authority is reserved for pagan jurists. Right at the beginning of the work, at J.1.1.1, Justinian declares "Learning in the law is the knowledge of things divine and human, the science of the just and the unjust."[9] But what precisely this knowledge of things divine is that is learning in the law, we are never told. God crops up only in the very last fragment, J.4.18.12, and only with the wish that, "God willing" (deo propitio), students will go on to study criminal law more deeply in the *Digest*.[10] God is not involved here for the substance of the law.

In even its widest sense religion makes only brief appearances in only a few contexts. Among the ways of freeing a slave is manumission in church, and it is simply listed as one way along with the others.[11] In explaining that *tutores*, guardians, are so called as being *tuitores*, protectors, Justinian tells us incidentally that *aeditui*, church wardens, are so called as those who protect buildings (qui aedes tuentur).[12] There is no legal point here. J.2.1.7–10 contain a discussion of religious property that is a precise parallel to the treatment we have looked at in Gaius's *Institutes*. And there is a detail on the ownership of treasure found on sacred land.[13]

The remainder of public law fares no better. Justinian introduces his subject at *J*.1.1.4:

> Of this study there are two branches, public and private. Public
> law is that which regards the state of Rome, private law is that
> which concerns the well-being of individuals. It must be said of
> private law that it is tripartite: for it is gathered together from
> the law of nature, from the law of all peoples and from state law.

But then he goes on to deal with only one branch, private law.[14] On public law he says nothing beyond mentioning public property[15] and again the detail on the ownership of treasure found on state land.

Exactly the same concentration on private law is found in the *Digest*, though several titles in book 1 are devoted to the duties of officials such as consul or prefect of the city guard.

We started in this chapter with legal education and with Gaius's *Institutes* in the second century A.D., then moved on to the time of Justinian, but the same strict separation of public and private law and concentration on private law are evident from the time of the *Twelve Tables* onwards. That codification, as was mentioned in chapter 2, has no provisions on public law.[16]

At least as striking as the separation of public and private law is the absence of a public or religious dimension to private law. A few examples will make this plain.

For example, no ceremony or formalities or public registration were required for the creation of a marriage. The basic requirements were the intention of the parties and the consents needed from parents, but the intention and consents could be shown in any way.[17] Festivities and religious celebration of marriage were common, but they had no place among the legal requirements.

Not just marriage, but also divorce, required no public authorization. There was no equivalent of a divorce court, with a judge pronouncing the end of a marriage, nor was there anything akin to public registration of divorce. Of course, evidence would be necessary, both for the benefit of husband and wife and for outsiders. Certain words of divorcing were traditional, for instance *"tuas res tibi habeto"* (take your things for yourself) in the Republic, but they seem not to have been set out in the *Twelve Tables* or other legislation.[18] Augustus, it would seem (though the matter is controversial), tightened the formalities and required that the announcement be made in the presence of seven witnesses.[19] Such evidentiary requirements are no indication of a public dimension in divorce. Indeed, divorce was freely a matter of intention. Certainly, in early times divorce by a husband for other than one of a few stated causes would cause him to suffer severe penalties, and subsequently the amount of dowry to be returned could be affected by the fault of one spouse or the other, and after the Empire became Christian severe penalties were again imposed for divorce except for a particular reason.[20] But in no way do these rules indicate state control of divorce, and there was none even under Justinian when he promulgated the *Digest* and *Code.* More than twenty years later, in A.D. 556, he did in fact prohibit divorce except for certain causes, but significantly this rule was itself rescinded by his successor only ten years later.[21] The notion that divorce was a private matter died hard.

Even slave law lacks a public-law dimension. There is nothing akin to the American South's legal system of patrollers whereby free men were organized against runaway slaves,[22] there is no system to restrict trading by slaves or to keep them off the streets, there is no compulsion on owners to brand or maim errant slaves.[23] There is little state interest in restraining masters from ill-treating slaves. Indeed, there were no restraints at all in the Republic, and when they were subsequently introduced the imperial decrees give the impression that they would not be strictly enforced.[24] The law does not come between the owner and his slaves. Thus, Gaius records at *G.*1.13:

It is provided by the *lex Aelia Sentia* that whatever slaves are bound by their owners on account of punishment or who have been branded or who have been tortured on account of wrongdoing and convicted of that offense or who have been handed over to fight with the sword or with wild beasts, or sent to the games or imprisoned, and who afterwards have been freed by the same or another owner, are free men in the same condition of those foreigners who capitulated (*peregrini dediticii*).

The status of free men classed as *peregrini dediticii* was very base, and Gaius here tells us that it was conferred on those who had been punished savagely by their former owner or by the state, but in the latter case only if the offense was proved. The question of the right-ness of the punishment by the *owner* was no business of the state. The concern of Gaius's text is not limits on the owner's right to pun-ish, but the status of persons who, when slaves, had been savagely punished.

Nor did the state present a high profile with regard to owners free-ing slaves. Three methods in the Republic conferred not only freedom but citizenship. Manumission by enrollment on the census (*censu*) occurred when the slave with the consent of the owner enrolled him-self as free on the census. Manumission *vindicta* was where an owner had a friend summon him before the praetor for holding a free man as a slave: the master did not defend, and the magistrate adjudged the slave to be free. Neither of these was a creation of the state but rather a device developed by individual owners and then acquiesced in by the state. The third method was manumission by will which, whatever its origins, did not involve the state in any way in historical times.

Nor were there restrictions on the owners' right to free slaves. Augustus introduced some, but to very limited effect. By the *lex Aelia Sentia* of 2 B.C. an owner could free *by will* only a proportion of his slaves. The owner of between three and ten slaves could free only half; of between ten and thirty only one-third; of between thirty and one hundred only one-quarter; of between one hundred and five hundred one-fifth; and in any event no more than one hundred could be freed. The owner of one or two slaves was not affected by the law which, it must be stressed, only applied to manumission by will.[25] The *lex Fufia Caninia* of A.D. 4 enacted that the owner had to be at least twenty or the manumission was void, unless the manumission was *vindicta* and good cause had been shown for it before a council.[26] The paucity of public restrictions is in sharp contrast to the multiplicity of laws in, say, the slave states in English-speaking America.[27]

From the early Empire, a slave could be freed informally by a letter conferring freedom or by a declaration among friends. A rescript of Constantine of 316 declared that it was long settled that an owner could free his slave in church, but the manumission had to be before the people, in the presence of priests, and there had to be a writing signed by the owner.[28] Five years later, another rescript declared that such manumission also conferred citizenship.[29]

What makes the absence of a public dimension to manumission truly significant is that freeing a slave had great social and economic consequences. Above all, it gave the ex-slave Roman citizenship, and Roman citizenship was a very prized possession.

This absence of a public dimension is marked throughout Roman private law and is one of its most characteristic features. A final example may be drawn from the law of contract. The earliest and in many ways the central Roman contract was the *stipulatio*.[30] This was a formal, unilateral, verbal contract in which one party asked the other if he would promise or give something, and the second party declared that he would, necessarily using the same verb.[31] Thus, though the contract was formal, its requirements were remarkably simple. They let the parties know that they had reached the point of agreement and were entering into a binding undertaking. But one usual element in legal formalities is missing. Since the contract requires no writing or witnesses, the formalities do not serve to provide evidence for a court that the contract was made.[32]

At this point I wish to introduce a theme that will recur throughout this book, one that surfaces so often in one form or another that three chapters will concentrate on its various manifestations, namely, legal isolationism. To an extraordinary extent Roman private law was kept apart from other aspects of society. As noted before in this chapter, there are very few texts in the traditional legal sources that mention activities in the market, except for those dealing with the aedilitian edicts concerned with the sale of slaves and beasts. Here we should look at these texts, of which there are, in fact, only two clear examples.

> D.1.12.1.11 (Ulpian, *On the office of urban prefect*, sole book): Supervision of the whole meat trade so that meat is provided at a fair price is in the charge of the prefecture, and so supervision of the pig market is within its charge. Indeed, providing cattle and other herd animals is also within its charge.

This text of Ulpian tells us that markets were under official supervision—in fact, at Rome, under the supervision of the city prefect. But it provides no detail, except that the prefect had to see to it that there was an adequate supply of meat. Significantly, the text is from a book of Ulpian's specifically on the duties of the city prefect. The "setting in life" of the text is not private law.

> D.42.4.7.13 (Ulpian, *On the Edict*, from book 59: The older jurists replied that a person, though he conduct business in the same market, would appear to be in hiding, if he lurks around pillars or stalls.

The subject of discussion was the praetor's edict that creditors might be put into possession of the property of a debtor who went into hiding. A person, it appears, might be regarded as being in hiding even if he did not leave the city, or even—in the extreme instance in the text—if he did not leave the market where he conducted business. So in this second text, the fact that the happenings occurred in the market is only incidental.

That these two are the only texts expressly referring to the market reveals more than the simple sharp separation of private law from public law. Some subjects are ignored as being unworthy of the attention of upper-class jurists. This is brought out even more if, as Olivia Robinson plausibly suggests,[33] some texts relating to false weights and measures concern market situations although the market is not mentioned and the legal point in them usually concerns something different.[34] One text gives the flavor:

D.47.2.52.22 (Ulpian, *On the Edict*, book 37): Someone lent you
heavier weights when you were buying by weight. Mela writes
that he will be liable to the seller for theft: you too, if you knew.
For you do not receive goods with the owner's consent when he
was mistaken about the weight.

The precise point of the text is much disputed,[35] but whatever it is,
it relates to the scope of the action for theft and has nothing specifically to do with markets. It may also be noted that theft, *furtum*, was
regarded primarily as a concern of the private law of delict and not of
public criminal law.

The absence of information on market regulation from the legal
sources is no accident: it reflects the concerns of the jurists. The same
is true for other aspects of administrative law where we have to rely
for our information on primarily nonjuristic texts: building regulations, demolition, road building, drains and similar sanitary conve-
niences, bars and eating places, *tesserae* (publicly issued cards) to the
games or food, and the control of animals.[36]

Just as Roman private law lacked a public dimension, so it lacked
a religious dimension. This is all the more striking in that until the
later second century B.C., the Romans regarded themselves, and were
regarded by others, as the most religious people in the world.[37] And
for the Romans, deities were everywhere and in everything.[38]

There is no religious dimension to the *Twelve Tables*. No provision
of the code deals with state cults, preservation of private cults, duties
of priests, or religious elements in private law. The one apparent exception, a clause relating to the vestal virgins, startlingly points the
message, because it concerns a secular issue: that vestals at private
law were to be free from guardianship.[39]

Indeed, religious ceremonial played almost no role at any time in
private law, whether as a requirement or as having some kind of impact. It appears in only two contexts.

*Confarreatio* was one of the three ways in which *manus*, marital
power over a wife, could be created. It was a wedding ceremony in
which the central part was a sacrifice to Jupiter Farreus of bread made

of spelt (*far*), fruits of the earth, and salt cake; it required the assistance of the *flamen dialis* and the *pontifex maximus* and the presence of ten witnesses.[40] Since the two priests were not only leaders in the priestly hierarchy but had to be patricians, we can be sure that *confarreatio* was restricted to the aristocracy.[41] It has even been suggested that the ceremony was restricted to the marriage of priests, but for this there is no evidence.[42] *Confarreatio* died out early and was later restored by Augustus and Tiberius, but only with religious effect: it did not otherwise affect the wife's status.[43]

*Adrogatio*, which probably existed as early as the *Twelve Tables* (though there is no direct proof), was the adoption of a male above puberty who was independent of paternal power. There were two stages. First came an investigation by the pontiffs (*pontifices*) into the advisability of the adoption; if they approved the matter went before the *comitia calata* summoned by the *pontifex maximus*. The adopter and the adoptee were each asked if they agreed to the adoption, then the members of the *comitia calata* were asked if they wished and ordered the adoption.[44] This part of the procedure was a legislative act.

It is important that it is precisely *confarreatio* and *adrogatio* where priestly involvement has private-law effects. *Confarreatio* and *adrogatio* are primarily institutions of sacred law rather than of private law. The emphasis is on sacred consequences. Thus, Dionysius of Halicarnassus, speaking specifically of *confarreatio*, which he believes was introduced by Romulus, says: "The law was to this effect that a woman joined to her husband by a holy marriage should share in all his possessions and sacred rites."[45] Of course, a woman *in manu* had no property; far less did she share in her husband's. But she did participate in the cult of her husband's family. Moreover, when *confarreatio* was reestablished in the early Empire, as has just been said, it had only religious effects. The priests (*flamines*) of Jupiter, Mars, and Quirinus had to have been married by *confarreatio* and be the sons of parents so married.[46] In *adrogatio*, the adoption meant that the adoptee would be the adopter's heir if he died intestate, and would thereby be responsible for the performance of the *sacra* of the adopter, his private family cult duties. Again, the adoption of a person not in paternal power involved the extinction of a Roman family, and with it its private cult; hence, in the *comitia* there was the solemnity of *detestatio sacrorum*, renunciation of the family's sacred rites.[47] So what we have with *confarreatio* and *adrogatio* are not private-law acts with priestly involvement but sacred acts with private-law consequences.

Even in secular systems use will be made of oaths. Roman law was no exception, but the use made of oaths is instructive for legal secularity.[48] They appear in only four contexts, three of them relating to procedure. Their purpose is always purely secular, never religious; they are tested, if at all, by secular means; and the penalty is always secular, never sacred. They are examples of what I have called "second best and the law." An authority needing to take a legal action may be in a dilemma: something has to be done, but he can do nothing that is fully satisfactory. Sometimes, in order to cope, the law may make a concession and permit a dodge to be used. That is the role of the oath in Roman private law.

The oath in substantive law is the *iusiurandum liberti*, the oath of a freedman. We do not know when it originated, but the probability is that it is republican. The dilemma was as follows.[49] Often an owner who wished to manumit a slave wanted to bind him to perform as a free man a number of days' work per year for him. But he could not create such a legal obligation before manumission, since there could be no contract between owner and slave. Yet if he freed the slave and then sought the *stipulatio*, the freedman might simply refuse to give it. Hence this device. The owner would have the slave swear an oath, and this (though it created no secular legal obligation) put the slave under a religious obligation to renew his promise after manumission. This second oath taken after manumission was the *iusiurandum liberti*, and it gave rise to a private-law obligation and action.[50]

Of the three procedural uses of an oath, that in the *legis actio sacramento*, the action of the law by an oath, dates back beyond the *Twelve Tables*, and the action was general in that it could be used when no other had been laid down by law. The action could be brought both *in rem* and *in personam*. In the former, in front of the magistrate, the first party claimed: "I affirm that this slave is mine by the law of the citizens according to his proper title. As I have declared, look, I have laid my staff on him." At that point he laid his staff on the slave. The second party said and did the same, and the praetor said, "Both let go the slave." The first party resumed: "I ask, will you say on what title you made your claim?" The other: "I exercised my right by laying on my staff." Again, the first party: "Since you have claimed wrongfully, I challenge you by an oath [*sacramentum*] of 500 [or 50] *asses*." The opponent rejoined: "And I you."

The claim of the action is purely secular; in the example just given from G.4.13–17, it is about ownership of a slave. The dilemma is that no appropriate action has been defined by law to establish the claim. So at the preliminary stage of the proceeding, before the praetor, one party challenges the other to swear an oath to the validity of the claim, and the matter is then sent to the judge whose task it is to discover the veracity of the oath. The oath's truth is determined by establishing who in fact is the owner of the slave, and this is done by purely secular means. The supernatural makes no appearance to discover the owner. The penalty for falsely swearing is again secular: forfeiture of a sum of money. The oath is used simply to bring a secular issue before a private-law court.

The second use of the oath in procedure was the *iusiurandum in litem*, the swearing of an oath in a lawsuit. A marked feature of Roman private-law actions was that the award against a defendant who lost his case was always fixed in money. The judge could not impose specific performance. But sometimes what the plaintiff reasonably wanted was performance of the obligation. Then, for a number of actions the instructions to the judge might contain the so-called *clausula arbitraria*, to order actual restitution to the judge's satisfaction, failing which condemnation in money terms was ordered. It is in the determination of the actual amount for financial restitution that the oath and the dodge are involved. What the plaintiff reasonably wanted was specific performance, which could not be directly ordered by the judge. How could it in fact be achieved? The answer was for the judge to put an oath to the plaintiff for the valuation of his claim; the plaintiff then swore the oath to an excessive valuation, and this valuation was accepted by the judge. The defendant then had the choice of making specific performance or paying the excessive valuation. The purpose of the oath was again purely secular and to bring about indirectly what could not be directly achieved. In keeping with its function, *iusiurandum in litem* was allowed only where the defendant was known to be fraudulent, malicious, or contumacious.[51] The texts make it plain that the plaintiff was expected to set too high a valuation; still, the judge could restrain him if the valuation was too blatantly excessive.[52]

The third and final use of an oath in procedure was intended to shorten the hearing. In some actions, before the plaintiff asked for his *formula* (form of proceedings), he might proffer an oath to the defendant on the essentials of the case. If the defendant swore his oath in the words put to him, the plaintiff automatically lost his case. If the defendant refused to swear, the defendant lost the case. The defendant might offer the oath back to the plaintiff, and then similar alternatives applied.[53]

The explanation of this exclusion of religion from private law must go back to the *Twelve Tables*. The patricians, who had conceded that a code should be made, won the right to draft it.[54] The plebeians had demanded that the law should apply equally to all. What they got was a code that was egalitarian in appearance because the patricians, legislating *de haut en bas*, inserted into it only rules and institutions that they were willing to share with the plebeians.[55] Priestly offices and functions were patrician offices and functions; how they were regulated ought not to concern the plebeians. Hence, religion was excluded from the code, and in a field as traditional as law the exclusion continued.

Nothing that has been said, though, excludes the possibility or probability that Roman religious values are enshrined in rules of private law without religion being expressly mentioned.[56] After all, it seems that the word for secular law, *ius*, originally meant "a religious formula that has the force of law."[57] This would account for the formation *iusiurandum* for "oath." It might also explain the phrase *iustae nuptiae*, a term for a valid Roman marriage that put children born in it into the power of the father; the words would then originally have meant a marriage created in the proper religious manner, or without a religious flaw. If this suggestion has any validity, then the lack of references to religion is all the more striking. Nowhere in the sources is there a suggestion that human law comes from the gods. There is even the famous line of Servius, *"ad religionem fas, ad homines iura pertinent,"* *fas* (sacred law) belongs to religion, *iura* belong to men.[58] And for the period for which we have evidence, *iustae nuptiae* have no apparent connection with religion.

# 4 Juristic Law and the Sources of Law

Students usually come to Roman law with no knowledge of other secular systems; otherwise they would be more struck by a most unlikely but characteristic feature: the extreme prominence of jurists who, as such, have no connection with government. One may come to accept that the role of governments in making private law is often more limited than one would expect,[1] but why should a state follow for its law the opinions of private individuals? And why should prominent individuals find it appropriate to fill their time without financial reward by giving legal opinions and writing legal treatises? One can readily see that persons might achieve prestige by judging disputes, or even by pleading causes before an audience; but writing law books is less obviously prestigious. Again, one can see that a state that appointed judges to adjudicate disputes might give some weight to their decisions as precedent and hence authoritative in similar cases, but for a state to give weight to opinions expressed outside of some official context is startling.

The prominence of jurists is unlikely and unusual only when the system of law is secular. It is not in the least surprising in a system based on religion, such as Jewish or Islamic law, that expounding the law will bring great prestige and attract scholars. Law as religion is law as truth, and to be recognized as uncovering the truth is always to obtain prestige.

Yet the prominent role of the jurists in Roman law is undeniable. Even under Justinian, the *Digest*, that part of his compilation that contains juristic opinions, is twice as long as his *Code*, which contains the rulings of the emperors. This is all the more significant in that the two works were not planned together, and the first aim was to collect and publish surviving and still relevant imperial rescripts.[2]

Thus, the compilers of the *Code* would have included rescripts that had not innovated but simply restated existing, even juristic, law. Moreover, the compilers of the *Digest* were instructed not to repeat law that existed elsewhere, namely, that is to say, in the *Code*.[3] Thus, the *Digest* is shorter than it would have been but for the prior publication of the *Code*, yet it is still twice as large as the *Code*.

Again, in collections of pre-Justinianian legal materials, surviving juristic writings are much bulkier than surviving laws.[4] And there are no surviving judicial decisions.

In the second chapter I gave an explanation—and it has come up again since—for the state allowing private individuals to make law, for prominent citizens wishing to become experts in private law, without practicing in the courts, and for the prestige attaching to this activity. I found the reason in the monopoly of interpreting the *Twelve Tables* given for political reasons to the patrician College of Pontiffs, which was composed of men with a political track record, and in the College's selection each year of one of its members to be the authoritative interpreter. Tradition dies hard and even when this monopoly of interpretation was ended, skill in giving legal opinions was a mark of great distinction, and juristic views were accepted by the state for the development of the law. It is not surprising that until about the end of the second century B.C. the great jurists were senators, being replaced in the last century of the Republic by men of the equestrian order.

But making juristic opinion authoritative (especially that of the pontiffs in early times) had of necessity important consequences for other usual sources of law, and that is the subject of this chapter.

In the first place custom as a source of law is virtually eliminated. If what the pontiff declares to be the law *is* the law precisely because he declares it so, then even if he bases his decision on what people do, the validity and authority of a practice will result from his ruling and not from custom. Thus, it can be no surprise that in none of the juristic listings of the sources of law does custom make an appearance.[5]

But there are a few legal rules whose authority is said to rest on customary practice, and in the circumstances this ascription to custom must be scrutinized. Three of these rules seem to go back to very early times; two date from the later Republic.

A rule that must be very old and is attributed to custom is the prohibition on marriage between closely related persons.[6] Apart from other reasons, the rule is too basic in the culture to be attributed to the decision or authority of any one person. Custom is the obvious source. The second early rule ascribed to custom is that a person under puberty could not be bound without the authority of his or her tutor.[7] Guardianship, *tutela*, of persons under puberty existed before the *Twelve Tables*,[8] and it was the subject of express provisions in that code.[9] The interposition of the tutor's authority was the central feature and presumably is as old as the institution. Thus, it will have existed before the pontiffs were given the monopoly of interpreting private law, so it could not properly be attributed to interpretation. The final early rule attributed to custom (which is, however, later than the *Twelve Tables*[10]) was to the effect that if a testator appointed as his heir a *suus heres* who was below the age of puberty, he could appoint a substitute heir to take the inheritance if the *suus* survived the testator but died before attaining puberty.[11] For this attribution to custom of *substitutio pupillaris*, as it is called, I have no explanation.

A later rule attributed to custom was the prohibition of gifts between husband and wife.[12] This had to be so ascribed precisely because the *lex Cincia* of 204 B.C., which forbade gifts in general above a certain (unknown) amount, made some express exceptions including for gifts between spouses.[13] The rule, therefore, was contrary to statute, and juristic opinion could not be allowed to prevail against statute. The final rule attributed to custom is that a banker—only a banker—could be sued on a debt owed by a partner.[14] There is no evidence to explain this, but I would suggest that bankers might commonly pay on their partners' debts to maintain the confidence of clients, and the practice became regularized to such an extent that an action was eventually allowed.[15]

A few other legal texts do indeed talk of custom, and one attributed to the jurist Julian in *D*.1.3.32.1 goes so far as to state that custom may abrogate statute. The accuracy of that text for classical law need not detain us at the moment. What matters is that the paucity of legal texts and their lack of specificity have led many scholars to dispute whether the classical jurists regarded custom as a source of law at all.[16] Of *D*.1.3.32 it has been said, "There is unanimity that the passage as it stands is not the work of Julian."[17] Custom was important in early times before the *Twelve Tables* and was recognized in the codification of Justinian, but in between it scarcely existed, thanks to the role of the jurists.

In exactly the same way, the role given to the College of Pontiffs would put an end to any significant contribution to legal development from judges. In other systems judicial decisions may contribute to legal development in various notable ways: a judgment may be treated as binding precedent, or two or three similar judgments may be seen as marking a tradition from which judges will not readily depart, or the judgments of a court may be regarded as the best evidence of what the custom is. But in Rome, judges would follow the interpretation of jurists, who themselves were the best, authoritative, source of evidence of the law.[18]

Still, in any society judicial decisions must have some importance, even if only as statements of what the law seems to be.[19] It then becomes significant that so little mention is made of them at Rome. There is nothing at all in the legal sources, whether juristic, statutory, or rulings of the emperors, and in the literary sources we have only the slightest indications that orators might refer to previous decisions in their speeches.[20]

Of course, in the Empire, the emperors had great judicial powers, and their decisions were treated as authentic statements of the law.[21] But this is a different matter and is simply one aspect of the proposition that what the emperor declares has the force of law. The Romans never formulated a theory of what was needed to make an imperial pronouncement a declaration of law.

But the impact of the jurists on the sources of law is best brought out by the other major source, the praetor's Edict. In the absence of much legislation on private law after the *Twelve Tables*, legal interpretation alone would have been insufficient to produce a satisfactory, supple, and relatively complete system. But it became the practice for the praetor, the magistrate in charge of the courts who was elected for a year only, to put up a conspicuous notice saying how he was going to enforce the law. All of the higher elected officials could issue edicts informing the public how they saw their duties and how they would perform their functions. Technically, the praetor could not change the law, but since he controlled the granting or refusal of an action, in effect he had control over legal development. He might issue individual edicts setting out the circumstances in which he would grant an action, and, for each type of action, he issued a model form for the procedure, the *formula*.[22] It is instructive to give here two of the early *formulae:* that for the buyer in a contract of sale and that of the lessor in a contract of hire of a thing.

> Whereas Aulus Agerius bought from Numerius Negidius, the man on account of whom the action is brought, and this is the subject matter of the action, whatever Numerius Negidius ought to give to or do for Aulus Agerius on that account in accordance with good faith, in that, judge, condemn Numerius Negidius to Aulus Agerius; if it does not appear, absolve him.

> Whereas Aulus Agerius leased to Numerius Negidius the farm on account of which the action is brought, and this is the subject of the action, whatever Numerius Negidius ought to give to or do for Aulus Agerius on that account in accordance with good faith, in that, judge, condemn Numerius Negidius to Aulus Agerius; if it does not appear, absolve him.[23]

Thus, for the first of these actions there had to be a contract of sale and not some transaction that did not amount to a sale; for the second there had to be a contract of hire. So fundamental was this that it was long held that if an agreement fell within the scope of a type of contract, and in the event the particular contract was void, the action was unavailable. In effect, without a valid contract of sale there could be no contractual action of sale. For example, some things were regarded as "outside of commerce" (*extra commercium*), such as things sacred to the gods above or below and public property, and they could not be the object of sale. Thus, until the early Empire the actions on sale would be refused even to an unwitting buyer,[24] and even then the trend was toward declaring that the sale was valid even though what was sold could not be owned.[25]

This approach has important consequences. But first we should take note of the astounding amount of information that is not included in a *formula*. For example, it does not relate what is necessary for the existence of a contract of sale—whether, for instance, any formalities are needed, whether the price has to be in coined money, whether future goods can be sold. It tells nothing about the duties of the seller, whether he has to transfer ownership (in fact, he is under no such obligation) or whether he warrants good title or absence of hidden defects. Nothing is revealed about the passing of risk in the sold goods before delivery. In fact, the *formula* is postulated on the basis that the nature of the contract of sale is already somehow known. Although, of course, there can be no such thing as a legal contract of sale before there is a means or action to enforce a contract, and the *formula* is the action and so its creation brought the contract into existence, the substantive rules of the contract are treated as if they were logically prior to the creation of the action. There was, it should be stated, no Roman Sale of Goods Act or any official initiative other than the praetor's *formula* to mark the creation of the contract of sale. The praetor created the contract of sale when he inserted *formulae* for it in his Edict, but he did not say what made a contract of sale or what its rules were.

The extreme lack of information in the *formulae* makes sense only if the substantive law could be treated as already known and the only people to whom it could be known and who had the authority to declare the law were persons such as the jurists. This means in turn that there must have been active cooperation from the jurists both in drafting *formulae* and edicts and in suggesting modifications to them. In large measure the credit for building up the Edict must be given to the "academic" and very upper-class jurists. The same must be true for *actiones utiles* and *actiones in factum*. These are ad hoc remedies granted when no action was available under the Edict but a remedy was considered desirable. When a jurist says the praetor will grant an *actio utilis,* he means that the praetor will follow the advice of jurists and give the ad hoc remedy that they have devised. Praetors and jurists, it should be remembered, come from the same very small social class.

Thus, allowing private citizens—first pontiffs, then jurists—to make authoritative pronouncements on the interpretation of law had important repercussions for other sources of law.

# 5 Legal Isolationism: I

Separation from private law of public and sacred law may, I suggest, be explained by the historical sketch set out in chapter 2. The paucity of religious elements with private-law effect may be explained in the same way.

But that does not account for the absence of reference to religious rites even where they did not produce legal consequences. After all, we do know that religious ceremonies were standard accompaniment for weddings.[1] The attainment of puberty by males had important legal consequences, and it was also celebrated with sacred rites.[2] From Cato the Censor one might conclude that oaths were a frequent accompaniment to some kinds of contract.[3] Something more is involved in this absence of mention of religious rites in the legal sources.[4]

In fact, isolation from the rest of life is a strong characteristic of Roman private law. Whole legal institutions, such as usufruct, which must have had particular social and economic implications, are set out with no hint on the face of the texts of their social realities.[5] Were the rules created with particular, normal, circumstances in mind? Were usufructs established during the owner's lifetime or on death? In the standard case, was it the widow who received a usufruct of her husband's property when their children were appointed heirs? Was the usufruct usually of an entire inheritance (if created on death), over part of someone's property, of a single house, of a conglomerate such as a flock of sheep, or of a single item such as a slave? Did the general legal rules come into existence with no input from their setting in life? No answers to these questions are forthcoming. Nor are we better informed when it comes to anomalous details. Thus, when there was a usufruct in any female animal, her offspring belonged at once to the usufructuary (as was the case with wool, milk, dung), yet exceptionally, a child born to a slave woman went—after there had been a prolonged juristic dispute on the matter—not to the usufructuary but to the bare owner. Modern explanations are instructive. J. M. Kelly (as reported by David Daube) suggests that commonly a man would die leaving a son as his heir, with a usufruct to the widow.[6] A slave woman who was part of the estate would give birth. Regularly, in Kelly's view, the son would be the biological father of the slave's child. Certainly, the widow would have no direct biological connection with it. Notice, the argument goes, was taken of this common pattern of events, and it was held that the owner of the slave woman became owner of her offspring. I find Kelly's hypothesis attractive, but the point that is important for us now is that there is no textual evidence for it. A second approach, that Daube inclines to call the academic, is that in effect *fructus* meant for the jurists a regularly recurring return from another thing as a result of husbandry;[7] a slave child, the suggestion would be, does not fit this definition. Though it is perfectly appropriate for modern scholars to reach a definition of *fructus* from an examination of the instances denominated as such, still we have no textual evidence that the jurists based their decision about a slave child on that account. A third explanation, by P. Birks, is "founded in the socio-moral assumptions evident in the [Roman] agriculturalists": it was unacceptable, he says, that slaves were used like animals for planned breeding.[8] Apart from the difficulty that the Romans, including the jurists, certainly regarded the offspring of slave mothers as a fruitful source of slaves,[9] there is no evidence in our sources for Birks's notion that the jurists anywhere drew a line at the callous exploitation of human sexuality.[10] The fourth explanation is my own, expressly based on Gaius's own reason given in *D.22.1.28.1*: "for it seemed absurd to include human beings among fruits since nature procured the fruits of all things for the sake of human beings."[11] Whether I am right in giving credence to Gaius's idealistic, philosophical explanation is here beside the point. What matters is that (as I observed) there is an emptiness in the application of the philosophical principle. Moreover, the natural result of the decision is the separation of mother and child, with a diminished survival rate for the latter.[12]

The point I wish to make is, of course, that even on a disputed point of law Roman jurists argue as if they lived in a vacuum, remote from economic, social, religious, and political considerations. This instance is, of course, not alone. One further example may suffice at this stage. There was a dispute among the Sabinian and Proculian jurists, the former holding that there could be a contract of sale when the price named was something other than money, the latter denying that this could constitute a contract of sale and claiming that the arrangement was barter.[13] The sole argument produced by the Sabinians was a text from Homer, and the main argument for rebuttal by the Proculians was a second Homeric text, invoked to show that the Sabinians had misunderstood the first. The Sabinians' understanding of their Homeric text was simply that an exchange for money was regarded as the same as an exchange for something else. But what was at issue was a serious economic matter. In Roman law, contractual actions of a particular type, say sale, were only available if that kind of contract was involved. The Roman contract of sale was in general very satisfactory, hence so were the available contractual remedies. The defendant who lost his case would be adjudged to pay the plaintiff a sum of money equal to what he ought to give or do in accordance with good faith. In contrast, at the relevant time, the first or second century A.D., there was not really a contract of barter, and a wronged party to such an arrangement who had performed his part of the bargain would be restricted to using the general action known as the *condictio*, specifically on the ground of *"causa data causa non secuta"* (a consideration given but no consideration followed). All that this remedy would grant him would be a sum of money equivalent in value to what he had given. The Sabinians' argument—and, presumably, their concealed purpose—would allow the satisfactory remedies for sale also to be available where one thing was promised for another and neither prestation was to be in coined money. But so far as we are told, the Sabinians made no use of this economic argument or of any other social argument but only of the text of Homer, who is scarcely an authority for Roman law. The only explanation is that arguments from economic and social realities were not acceptable. This explanation is supported by the second ground of rebuttal of the Proculians, namely, that otherwise one could not decide which party was buyer and which seller. This is a formalistic argument which could have no appeal to result-oriented lawyers. Indeed, there could have been a simple but very un-Roman rejoinder: an agreement to exchange goods for goods was a contract of sale in which each party was both buyer and seller.

The above examples are chosen from situations where the jurists were in disagreement. But equally there could be widespread agreement on a case and still little sign of concern for the social appropriateness of the result. One example will suffice here:

> D.45.3.9.1. (Ulpian, *On Sabinus*, book 48): If, when a slave had two owners, and he took a stipulation for this or that one of his owners, it has been asked whether the stipulation is good. Cassius wrote that the stipulation was ineffective; and Julian approves the opinion of Cassius; and that is the law in force.

A slave was owned in common by Titius and Maevius. He took a promise by stipulation for payment or performance "to Titius or Maevius." Cassius, Julian, and Ulpian were all agreed on the law: the stipulation was ineffective. The slave certainly could not sue. But neither could Maevius nor Titius because it could not be established which of them was the creditor since for voluntary performance the choice of payee was the promissor's. So what is a valid stipulation is rendered ineffective at law with no apparent regard for the loss to Titius and Maevius of a valuable asset. And any possible fraud is on the part of the promissor.

Again, even when we know the date or the author of legislation it is not easy for us to give to it a precise economic, social, or political message. Thus (apart from the *Twelve Tables*), the most important Roman statute was the *lex Aquilia*. The opening text of D.9.2, which is the title that deals with the law, tells us:

> The Aquilian law derogated from all laws that dealt with wrongful loss before it, whether the *Twelve Tables* or any other. Now

it is not necessary to refer to them. 1. This Aquilian law is a plebiscite, since Aquilius, tribune of the plebs, asked for it from the plebs.

That is all the information we are given about its promulgation. As with other Roman statutes, if we want to know more we have to look outside of the ordinary Roman legal sources, in this instance at Theophilus, *Paraphrasis* 4.3.15, who tells us that it was passed at the time of dissension of plebs and patricians. This will give us the probable date of 286 B.C.[14]

It is, of course, characteristic of the jurists not to be interested in recounting the historical background. But those of us who are now interested in such things are at a loss. Can we in any way connect events of 286 B.C., such as the trouble between patricians and plebeians, with particular provisions of the *lex Aquilia*, which was a plebiscite, and the main statute on damage to property?[15] The short answer must be negative.[16]

Another important republican statute is the *lex Falcidia* of 40 B.C. Gaius succinctly tells of its contents at *G.*2.227: "And so the *lex Falcidia* was passed, which provided that one could not leave more than three-quarters of one's estate in legacies. Thus, it is necessary that the heir have one quarter of the inheritance. And that is the law we now observe." As was the case with the *lex Aquilia*, we have a whole title of the *Digest* devoted to it. But this time we have not the slightest indication in the legal sources of the historical and social context of the law. Yet it must have had political significance because it is mentioned in various nonlegal works. From these we know its date and that it was a plebiscite introduced by the tribune Falcidius.[17] It is tempting to link it with an edict issued during the civil war, which was greeted with fury by the people[18] and which placed a tax on ownership of slaves and property acquired by legacy. If a connection between the two provisions is justified, then the purpose of the *lex Falcidia* would have been to encourage testate succession so that the tax on legacies could be collected.[19] A testamentary heir could refuse the inheritance, and then the inheritance would devolve an intestacy and legacies would not come into effect. The *lex Falcidia*, by

ensuring that the testamentary heir would get a reasonable proportion of the estate, would render it more likely that he would accept
the inheritance. But on the purpose of the law the legal sources are
silent.

Further, with very few exceptions, juristic texts cannot be related
to the doings of determinate individuals.[20] Even when the *Digest* texts
are concerned with historical events, they often reveal little. There
was, for instance, the rare event of a birth of triplets, which comes up
in *D*.1.5.15 (Tryphoninus, *Disputations*, book 10):

> By last will Arescusa was ordered to be free if she gave birth to
> three children. At the first birth she bore one, at the second three
> offspring. The question is raised whether any, and if so which, of
> the children were free? This condition attached to freedom now
> is to operate for the woman. But one should not doubt that the
> last child is born free. For nature does not permit two infants
> to emerge from the mother's womb at the same time by the
> same push, in such a way that by the uncertain order of birth
> it does not appear which is born in slavery or in freedom. The
> fulfillment of the condition at the beginning of the birth brings
> it about that the last born emerges from a free woman.

The jurist is interested only in the legal problem. But why would the
testator free a slave woman under such a condition? Obviously, he
wanted a financial benefit from slave breeding. In return for providing him with three little slaves, the mature slave woman Arescusa
would receive her liberty. Presumably the testator was well disposed
toward this slave, but the very condition in the will is indicative of
the callousness that slave-owning breeds. And there is no trace of
humanitarianism in the argument of the jurist. Strict legal logic is
alone treated as relevant.

We are given so little information about surrounding circumstances
that have no bearing on the legal decision that in the overwhelming
majority of instances we cannot tell whether the jurist was responding to a real or hypothetical problem. Sometimes the fact that unnecessary details are given alerts us that the jurist had a real case in
mind. Thus, in *D*.41.1.44, when Pomponius mentions that the neigh-

bor's dogs, which recovered "my" pigs from wolves, were "strong and powerful," we may believe he had a real happening in mind.[21]

Perversely, this very abstraction of facts from their background and the isolation of a legal situation from social realities may best be revealed by a text whose mention of immaterial details shows that an actual factual situation is under discussion. Thus:

> D.16.3.27 (Paul, *Replies*, book 7): When Lucius Titius had a daughter, Seia, in his power, he gave her in marriage to Pamphilus, who was a slave belonging to another. He also gave to Pamphilus a dowry which he set out in a written document under the title of a deposit. No denunciation was made by his owner, the father then died, and a little later so did Pamphilus. I ask by what action can Seia sue for the money when she herself was heir to her father? Paul replied, since dowry could not be constituted, the money was to be reclaimed by the action on the *peculium* on account of deposit.

There are two unnecessary details. First, there was no need to present Seia as being in the power of her father: for her right to any action, it was alone relevant that she was her father's heir. Second, there was no need to mention that there had been no denunciation. The denunciation in question would have been from Pamphilus's owner forbidding her as a free woman from cohabiting with Pamphilus. If proper denunciation were made and she had not desisted, she would have been subject to enslavement and the present issue could not have arisen. Part of the legal background is that a slave could not marry, hence Seia and Pamphilus could not become husband and wife, and without a marriage there could be no dowry.

On its face the text says nothing about social circumstances, and no reason is given for Paul's legal decision. That is what is really significant. Still, much can be deduced. To begin with, Lucius Titius cannot have been among the poorest members of society; otherwise he would not have wished to give his daughter a dowry. (A dowry was not a requirement of marriage but was common among those who had property. It is significant in this regard that so few texts talk of a married woman *indotata*, "without a dowry." Because the dowry was not legally necessary, Daube stresses, mention of it was surplus to requirements.[22]) Again, the father must have regarded the liaison of his daughter with a slave as not only tolerable but respectable, or he would not have given the dowry into Pamphilus's hands. If he had wished to maintain good personal relations with his daughter and provide her with financial support, other means lay at hand that did not involve committing money to Pamphilus. Third, Lucius Titius and Pamphilus are showing considerable legal sophistication. Their wish is to constitute a dowry but this is not possible, so a scheme is devised by which the intention is cloaked in a different guise. One reason for the choice of deposit as the cover is that this will stop Pamphilus's owner from producing any claim to the property. The type of transaction envisaged is probably not ordinary deposit but *depositum irregulare,* in which the recipient could make use of the deposit for the benefit of the depositor. It looks as if Pamphilus runs a business—conjecturally he is a banker—and Lucius Titius is making an investment in the business. The slave Pamphilus should also be seen as rather well off in fact if not in law. Finally, the jurist Paul is not offended by the sexual relationship between this slave and a propertied woman or he would have declared the transaction void as *fraus legis:* instead he accepts the appearance of a deposit. None of this suggested background appears to be a concern of the jurist.

This form of legal isolationism is compounded by two other, related issues. The first is that even when jurists were asked their opinion, they usually did not investigate the facts but gave their ruling on what the law, on the basis of the facts, stated to them. Indeed, they had no machinery to investigate the facts. Cicero tells us:

Indeed I have often heard my father and my father-in-law say that our people who wanted to win high honor for knowledge would embrace all subjects that were then known in the land. They remembered Sextus Aelius. We have actually seen Manilius walking across the forum, and what is remarkable is that in so doing he was putting his store of advice to the use of all citizens. People resorted to them both walking and sitting in their seat at home, not only to consult them about the civil law, but also about marrying a daughter, buying a farm, cultivating a field, in short about every duty or business.[23]

In these circumstances, there can have been no question of the jurist's trying to establish the facts. What he was interested in, what he believed his prestige depended upon, was not winning a case for his client but expounding the law. This derives from the early pontifical monopoly on interpreting the civil law. When the pontiffs annually selected one of their number to interpret the law, he was not charged with determining facts, applying the law to them, and then giving the equivalent of a court decision. Rather, he was charged with declaring what the law was on the basis of facts submitted to him.[24] Even in sacred matters, the pontiffs usually did not examine the facts.[25] This approach was so ingrained that much later, in the Empire, the emperor would give written replies on the law to questions put to him in writing, with no inquiry into the accuracy of the facts submitted to him. The emperor's response would not enable the petitioner to win his or her lawsuit—the alleged facts would still have to be established—but it would give a conclusive answer to a point of law.

The second relevant issue is precisely that, as I have said, jurists' prestige came from their presentation of points of law, not from winning lawsuits in court. They might present cases as advocates,[26] but that was not how they made their reputation as jurists. The significance of this is that their interests were not those of practicing lawyers. They were not influenced in their legal decision by the morality of the parties to a case, they reduced the relevant facts to an abstract minimum, and they were not much concerned with procedural dodges and devices. All this is very much part of the characteristic feature of Roman law that, if we take the sources as we find them, substantive law and procedure were kept very separate. All this, too, derives from the monopoly given to the pontiffs. They were not to fight lawsuits as attorneys, and what was significant for them was skill in interpreting the law.

The jurists' position is well summarized by Cicero:

*Topica* 11.50: A little while ago I gave an example of argument from corollaries and many corollaries would have to be added if we decided that under the edict possession should be given according to the written will made by one who did not have testamentary capacity. But this topic has more worth in conjectural issues that come up in trials, when the question is what is the position, or what happened, or what will happen, or what can happen at all. 12.51. That is the bare outline of the topic. The topic does suggest, however, that one should ask what happened before an event, what happened at the same time, and what happened afterwards. My friend Gallus used to say "This has nothing to do with law, but with Cicero," if anyone brought an issue to him that involved a question of fact. But you will not allow me to pass over any part of the textbook I began, lest you appear to be too selfish if you think that only matters of interest to you should be included. This topic in great measure is of interest to orators, but not to jurists, and not even to philosophers.

What I want to stress at this stage from these examples is that in large measure the jurists were not interested in private law as social engineering.

# 6 State Law: Statute and Edict

From the promulgation of the *Twelve Tables* around
451 B.C. to 23 B.C., when Augustus was given perpetual tribunician
power, there were passed, so far as our information goes, about twenty
statutes of general import dealing with what we would regard as private law. In contrast there were close to one thousand laws dealing
with foreign relations or temporary matters. Again, though we have
textual information showing that six of the statutes on private law
were *plebiscita—lex Canuleia* (445), *lex Aquilia* (287), *lex Cincia*
(204), *lex Furia* (before 169), *lex Voconia* (169), and the *lex Falcidia*
(40)—we have no evidence that in normal times, when the state was
not governed by a dictator, the main assembly, the *comitia centuriata*,
concerned itself with private-law matters. It seems, indeed, that it did
not.[1] As tribune Augustus at first brought his private-law legislation
before the *concilium plebis: lex Iulia de maritandis ordinibus*, the
Julian law on the marriage of the orders, and the *lex Iulia de adulteriis
coercendis*, the Julian law on restraining adulteries, both of 18 B.C.[2]
Later, he had private-law legislation passed by the consuls, such as
the *lex Fufia Caninia* on manumissions (2 B.C.)[3] and the *lex Papia
Poppaea* of A.D. 9.[4] Tiberius continued the practice of having laws
introduced by consuls, but the antiquarian Claudius restored the use
of *plebiscita*.[5] Thereafter, legislation as a source of law disappeared.

That in the Republic in normal times the *concilium plebis* but not
the *comitia centuriata* legislated on private law must have significance, though it is not easy to know what that is. Perhaps, because the
*Twelve Tables* set out the law that the patricians were willing to share
with the plebeians, the subject matter of that code was thought to be
the special preserve of the *concilium plebis*. Or perhaps the earliest
law after the code, the *lex Canuleia* of 445 B.C., set the pattern. That

statute was of political necessity a plebiscite since it repealed the provision of the tyrannous *decemviri* that prohibited intermarriage between patrician and plebeian.

More significant than which body passed the legislation is its paucity.[6] With his usual acumen, David Daube says, almost in passing: "Legislation was less suitable for the continuous day-to-day adjustments called for in private law. For one thing, it involved a cumbersome machinery, as a rule set in motion only for political purposes. In private law, it was something of a last resort."[7] Normally, law reform was left to the praetors in their Edicts. And some of the small number of laws were either not appropriate for the Edict, or the Edict could not have been used. A first example is the *lex Aquilia,* the most important of all the Roman statutes. The *Twelve Tables* had regulated physical assault in three provisions, though their scope is a matter of dispute.[8] For maiming a limb (*membrum ruptum*), they provided for a retaliation in kind if the parties could not agree on composition; for a broken bone (*os fractum*), there was a penalty of 300 *asses* if the victim was a freeman or 150 *asses* if the victim was a slave; for simple harm (*iniuria*), there was a penalty of 25 *asses.* The main purpose of chapter 3 of the *lex Aquilia,* which is to be dated around 287 B.C., was to replace the first two of these provisions where the victim was a slave (though herd animals were also covered) with flexible damages related to the owner's financial loss. Inflation produced a need for this legislation for valuable property where the previous penalty was a fixed sum. At this early date, the Edict was not used for substantive reform. Even before, chapter 1 of the *lex Aquilia* had provided a remedy for the wrongful killing of another's slave or herd animal.

But subsequently these three provisions of the *Twelve Tables* were further modified by state intervention—all three to give flexible damages when the victim was a free person and the one pertaining to *iniuria* reworked to give the same effect when the victim was a slave. This time the changes were introduced not by a plebiscite but by the so-called *edictum generale* of the praetor's Edict. The *edictum generale* seems to date from the last quarter of the third century B.C. and to be the oldest known edictal clause.[9] But how are we to account for the turnaround in law reform technique? I would suggest that once it became acceptable to introduce legal changes by an edictal clause—at this early date changes only of procedure or assessment of damages, not of substantive law—reform was usually left to the praetors except where the Edict was not a suitable vehicle.

The *lex Poetilia*, which ended the status of bond debtors (*nexi*), took effect before such a change could be introduced by Edict, since it was promulgated in the early fourth century B.C.[10] There was, moreover, public outcry for the reform on account of the sexual and other abuse of the unfortunately handsome debtor C. Publilius by his creditor L. Papirius. No edict could have been issued with a scope equivalent to the *lex Atilia* (probably around 210 B.C.), which allowed at Rome the praetor and a majority of the tribunes of the plebs to appoint a *tutor* to someone who did not have one. This statute went beyond the jurisdiction of the praetor, as did the *lex Titia* (of around 91 B.C.), which extended similar powers to magistrates in the provinces. Again no praetor could have declared, as did the *lex Minicia* (before 90 B.C.), that children born to parents who did not have the right of civil law marriage took the lowest status.

Another explanation should be given for a group of four laws being promulgated as statute. The *lex Furia* (perhaps around 200 B.C.), the *lex Appuleia* (which was earlier), the *lex Cicereia* (of uncertain date), and the *lex Cornelia* (of around 81 B.C.) all gave protection to those who had or would become personal guarantors of debtors. Their passage must be related to the intense and continuing interest in the debt question.

As was observed in chapter 5, because of "legal isolationism" we can seldom spot the social or political background to a Roman legal innovation. I would suggest that if we knew more, we would see in other cases that particular factors were responsible for the use of statute rather than the Edict. This might be especially true for another concentration of four statutes that regulated testate succession.[11] It can scarcely be coincidental that, in contrast with testate succession, the numerous changes in intestate succession were all brought about by the Edict.[12]

Cicero informs us that most people thought that knowledge of the law was to be drawn from the praetor's Edict and that in former times it was thought to be drawn from the *Twelve Tables*.[13] This corresponds to reality. No mention is made by Cicero of statutes subsequent to the *Twelve Tables*, but the Edict of the praetor had become basic to legal knowledge and development.

As I have said, all the higher elected officials had the right to issue edicts, which were in fact public declarations of their orders and intentions within their sphere of competence. The edicts that affected legal development came from those magistrates who had jurisdictional competence: the praetors, especially the urban and peregrine praetor; provincial governors, whom we will not consider here (just as the Roman jurists, with the exception of Gaius, ignored them);[14] and the curule aediles. The urban praetor, above all, had control of the main private-law courts.

One who had charge of a court could state how he would perform his duties, and this gave him enormous freedom to change the law in fact. He could set out the form of an action for a situation that had never given rise to a remedy before: this was the case, for example, with the contracts of sale, hire, and mandate. He could set out a clause stating new circumstances in which he would give a remedy together with a model action, as was the case with *commodatum*, loan for use.[15] He could issue an edict showing that he would give an action according to different legal prescriptions from those laid down by statute, as he did in the case of deposit, which had been regulated by the *Twelve Tables*.[16] In this way, too, by several edicts he changed the whole law of intestate succession. He could also refuse to grant an action where the civil law gave one. In addition, of course, he would issue a model form of action to enforce a civil law right when he was not considering changing the scope of an existing right. In fact, the praetor's Edict in its developed form contained all the remedies that the magistrate considered within his jurisdiction, whether he only set out a model form of action or also issued an edictal clause.

With these powers, and with the very active cooperation of the jurists, the praetorian Edict was the great factor in legal change.[17] Each Edict was effective only so long as the proposing magistrate remained in office, which was for a year only. But it was very much the case that a praetor would retain the bulk of his predecessor's Edict, making only such changes as he saw fit. Thus, the Edict made for stability in the law while allowing changes to be made easily. Though our evidence is sparse it clearly suggests that most edictal clauses underwent changes during their lifetime.[18]

The gradual development of the urban praetor's Edict can be plotted. As early as the end of the third century B.C. the praetor could issue edicts, but the development of the Edict proper had scarcely begun. What edicts there were touching private law were restricted to making alterations in the measure of damages (and probably in procedure). Changes in substantive private law were not yet made by the Edict. As late as 140 B.C. major changes in the substantive law, which later would have been introduced by edictal clauses in the Edict, still could not be so made. Instead, they were instituted by the introduction of new actions without an edictal clause but with model forms of action inserted in the Edict which were later (at least) regarded as civil law *formulae*, though they were the work of a praetor. But even before this the praetor was substantially changing the law by introducing into the Edict a praetorian action *in factum*, though no edict was issued. By the second-to-last decade of the second century B.C., edicts were being promulgated that profoundly modified the *ius civile*, but it is quite probable that the force of these was limited to restricting the rights of a plaintiff in a civil law action. Apparently only around 100 B.C. was the Edict so developed that individual edicts giving totally new actions on substantive law could be issued. The main period of the Edict was the following decades, but the development was not complete by the end of the Republic. Interdicts—concerned with the peacekeeping duty of the praetor—could be issued before 160 B.C.; decretal, ad hoc, remedies before 70 B.C.; and both civil law and edictal actions could be refused by the praetor by this latter date. Very few new edicts were issued by praetors in the Empire, no doubt because of the changed political circumstances. Though the evidence is sparse and late,[19] it seems that the emperor Hadrian (died A.D. 138) appointed the outstanding jurist Julian to revise or finalize the Edict: Julian's finished work was confirmed by a *senatus consultum* at Hadrian's request.[20] Julian introduced one new substantive rule, and since it is termed the "new clause of Julian" we may assume there were no others. He may have made some changes in the arrangement, as has been suggested,[21] but certainly he made no attempt to arrange the edictal clauses systematically (see chapter 12). Thereafter, no praetor could make changes, but the Edict continued to be used to develop new law, thanks to the major commentaries *ad Edictum* of outstanding jurists like Pomponius, Paul, and Ulpian. They approached the interpretation and conceptualization of the Edict in the same way as they had approached the *Twelve Tables* and subsequent commentaries on the civil law, such as those of Quintus Mucius and Sabinus. In addition, the emperor could issue edicts.

The Edict of the urban praetor was *the* Edict at Rome. The Edict of the peregrine praetor—whose jurisdiction is disputed and may have been limited to suits between peregrines or have extended to cases where one party was a citizen[22]—was shorter and contained only clauses that could not apply to citizens.[23] In other cases the Edict of the urban praetor would prevail. Apart from the ambiguous *D.*4.3.9.4a (Ulpian, *On the Edict*, book 11) there is no sign that any jurist wrote a commentary on the Edict of the peregrine praetor, and this is surely a cause for surprise. The reason is that the jurists were little concerned with what happened outside Rome. We have, thus, another important example of their lack of interest in social and economic matters.

Even shorter than the Edict of the peregrine praetor was the Edict of the curule aediles, who had control over the streets and markets. This contained only three clauses. Since they must have allowed other actions in their court, in other matters they would have followed the general law, namely, that in the urban praetor's Edict. Hence, their own clauses were restricted to remedies not (originally, at least) paralleled in the praetorian Edict.[24]

It is appropriate to note at this stage that the common notion that the praetors exercised an equity jurisdiction must be treated with great caution. In the first place, there was basically only one system of courts at Rome, that of the praetors: there was not one system of civil law courts and another of edictal courts.[25] Again, though the Edict was the main vehicle of law reform, it was in this regard much the same as legislation in some other systems. *D.*1.1.7.1 (Papinian, *Definitions*, book 2) should not mislead: "Praetorian law is that which in the public interest the praetors have introduced to help or supplement or correct the civil law." Of course it was, but the innovations were no more specifically equitable than is most legislation. What is striking is that though we know the names of many praetors, and though we know specific innovations in the Edict of a few of them,[26] we have no information to suggest that any praetor achieved a reputation as a law reformer (see chapter 10). Equitable remedies of the praetors are to be seen not so much in the Edict as in their granting of ad hoc remedies, *actiones in factum,* and *actiones utiles* for situations not covered by the forms of action set out in the Edict. In this, as I have claimed, the praetors would be largely guided by the jurists.[27]

Another equitable remedy was the fiction, a clause in the form of action that permitted the action to be brought in a situation where otherwise there could be no action. Perhaps the oldest is *"si civis Romanus esset"* (if he were a Roman citizen), which allowed a foreigner to sue in an action that was restricted to citizens. Apart from any equity, what is striking about a Roman fiction is again the preservation of clarity in institutions and actions. There is no falsehood in a Roman fiction. The *fictio* makes it plain on its face that (in this instance) the plaintiff is not a Roman citizen but the judge is to proceed as if he were. The contrast with English law is marked: the fiction there states untruths as truths and obfuscates the law.

*Senatus consulta,* decrees of the senate, were always legally significant, but throughout the Republic the senate had no direct lawmaking powers.[28] Technically, a *senatus consultum* was only advice or direction to the magistrate who had asked for the decree, and its binding force came from his authority. A change occurred in the early Empire, and the *senatus consultum Silanianum* of A.D. 10 was given legal effect by a clause inserted into the praetor's Edict.[29] Likewise the *senatus consultum Velleianum* of A.D. 46, which forbade women guaranteeing the debts of others, was given effect by a clause of the Edict which gave an *exceptio,* a defense, to a woman sued on such a guarantee.[30] Subsequently, *senatus consulta* became legally binding without the intervention of the praetor. The earliest sure example is the *senatus consultum Tertullianum* of Hadrian's reign,[31] but there may have been earlier examples. I do not feel that the history of *senatus consulta* is revealing of "the spirit of Roman law."

The emperors, too, as will be seen later, came to have lawmaking powers (see chapter 12).

# 7 Juristic Law: Reasoning and Conceptualization

Though the pontiffs, as we have seen, kept religion out of law and did not make legal forms so rigid as those of religion, still they did, probably subconsciously, introduce pontifical modes of reasoning into their interpretation of private law. As priests, the pontiffs' main function was to keep humans in proper contact with the gods, and this was very much a matter of sacred law. May a vow of an uncertain sum of money be made to a god? What authority is needed for the proper dedication of a temple? May one chapel be made sacred to two deities? To reach the right answer to those questions some arguments cannot be used. One cannot permit the answer to an issue of sacred law (law as truth) to turn upon an argument of equity or justice, usefulness or economic efficiency, or advantage to the state. Obviously such considerations are perfectly appropriate for settling issues of private law, but since they were not used by the pontiffs for sacred law they were not introduced by them for secular law. And so it continued. Roman legal reasoning is self-contained and based on a notion of "lawness" and is suffused with an internal legal logic.[1] The point is best made with examples.

(1)  *G.*3.179: Our statement that there is novation (*novatio*) if a condition is added ought to be understood in this way that there is novation only if the condition is realized: for otherwise, if it fails, the prior obligation endures. But we should consider whether he who sues on it cannot be defeated by the defense of fraud or of pact, because it seems to have been agreed between the parties that an action should lie only if the condition of the second stipulation was realized. But Servius Sulpicius held

that novation was made at once even during the pendency of the stipulation and, if the condition failed, an action could be brought on neither ground, and so all claim would be lost. Consistently he further advised that if someone stipulated from a slave for what Lucius Titius owed him, novation occurred and the claim was lost, since one cannot sue a slave. But in both cases we use a different rule; and novation takes place in those cases no more than where in stipulating for what you owe me from a peregine who is outside the communion of *sponsio* I use the word *spondes.*

Novation, which made use of a *stipulatio,* was the termination of an obligation, most commonly of a *stipulatio,* by replacing it with the same debt and by adding some new element, such as a new debtor or a new condition.[2] For Gaius, around the middle of the second century A.D., there is novation only when the condition is fulfilled. This is contrary to the intention of the parties. For instance, if I owe you a debt unconditionally, and we make a novation that I will pay you "if my ship arrives from Alexandria," our intention is that I am released from the debt if my ship is lost. The stipulation was a formal contract whose validity and scope depended not on the intention of the parties but on the words used. Presumably the rule about conditional novation current in Gaius's time was that a conditional stipulation came into being only when the condition was fulfilled, hence if the condition failed there was no second stipulation and the first survived because there was no novation. This very formalistic approach was not necessary, as we see from the fact that the republican Servius accepted that novation occurred at the moment the second stipulation was made. One can reasonably hold that a conditional stipulation is valid when made, but its effectiveness depends upon fulfillment of the condition. Moreover, the rule current in Gaius's time was also pointless if it were held (as he indicates may have been the case) that if the creditor sued on the first stipulation he would be rebutted by the defense of fraud or of pact.

But in his turn Servius Sulpicius himself was needlessly formalistic when he held that when the second stipulation was taken from a slave the first was extinguished. He could have claimed that when the second stipulation was void from the start there was no novation.

(2)  D.12.1.2.2. (Paul, *On the Edict*, book 28): The giving of a loan for consumption (*mutuum*) is so called because what is mine (*meum*) becomes yours (*tuum*). Therefore, if it does not become yours, the obligation does not arise.

What is under discussion is the scope of the action known as the *condictio*, specifically with regard to *mutuum*, a loan for consumption. The loan was of fungibles, things consumed by use, such as money or grain, and the obligation of the borrower was to restore the equivalent, not the actual object lent. The *condictio* was rather a general action that was given in a number of specific situations, including *mutuum*, and the usual requirements were that the plaintiff was not the owner of the object of the action, that there had been a giving to the defendant, and that for some reason the defendant was under an obligation to give the thing to the plaintiff.

For the specific ground in the text, *mutuum*, the scope of the action is defined by the supposed etymology of the word. *Mutuum* derives from *meum* and *tuum* because what was mine became yours. The text is rather enigmatic because we cannot tell whether the supposed etymology was originally used to define the scope of the *condictio* here or whether the scope was fixed, and the etymology was then brought in to justify the scope. What matters, though, is the formalistic nature of the sole argument for the scope of the action, an argument that in no sense has any social bearing.

Indeed, the scope of the action is contrary to the equity of the situation. Someone who was very likely acting in good faith but was not the owner handed something over to another for consumption on the understanding that he would receive the exact equivalent at some future time. He is denied a remedy because he did not make the recipient owner. But the recipient had the benefit of the transaction. And the lender might have been possessor in good faith and even in course of becoming owner by usucapion. Moreover, he might be liable to the owner for the value of the thing.

(3)  *D.9.2.2pr.* (Gaius, *On the Provincial Edict,* book 7): In the
first chapter of the *lex Aquilia* it is provided: "Whoever will
have wrongly killed another's male slave or female slave or four-
footed farm animal (*pecus*), let him be condemned to pay so
much money, as was the highest value of the property in the
preceding year." 1. And next it is provided that the action was for
double against one who denied his liability. 2. As it thus appears,
four-footed animals which were counted as *pecudes,* such as
sheep, goats, oxen, horses, mules and asses, were equated with
our slaves. But the question is asked whether pigs are contained
within the term *pecudes.* And Labeo rightly holds that they are.
But a dog is not among the *pecudes.* Much more are wild beasts
such as bears, lions, and panthers not included. But elephants
and camels are, so to say, "mixed," (for they perform the work
of draft animals, but they are by nature wild), and accordingly
should be within the scope of the first chapter.

*J.4.3.1:* The provision specifies not exactly four-footed animals,
but it is restricted to those classed as *pecudes,* to this purpose
that we understand that it does not provide for wild beasts or
dogs, but only for those which properly are said to graze, such as
horses, mules, asses, oxen, sheep, and goats. The same has been
decided for pigs: for even pigs are included in the term, *pecudes,*
because they, too, graze in herds. Thus, even Homer says in the
*Odyssey,* as Aelius Marcianus reports in his *Institutes:* "You
will find him sitting with his pigs grazing by the Raven's Crag
near the spring of Arethusa."

I have several reasons for this example, not least that the issue is not
wholly explicable. The question is why are pigs a problem? *Pecus* is a
standard term for any four-footed farm animals, and pigs certainly are
such.[3] Indeed, texts even in the Republic specifically use *pecudes* for
pigs.[4] Why, indeed, should one want to exclude pigs from the scope
of the first chapter of the *lex Aquilia,* which gave a greater measure
of damages than was permitted under the other appropriate chapter,
chapter 3? Pigs were an important part of the farm economy, and pork
was the most usual meat.[5]

The *lex Aquilia* was the first Roman statute specifically to refer to both male and female, probably in response to an argument on a previous statute that where the masculine term was used, females were not within the scope of the law. Thus began the use in late republican statutes of setting out a list to cover all possible contingencies.[6] Against this background we must see the attempt to define precisely what was included within the term *pecudes*. The choice of that term is treated as being very significant. *Pecudes* assuredly did not include dogs. But the argument was made that pigs were also excluded because they were not grazing animals. Presumably, the argument was based on some (false) etymology linking *pecudes* with the verb *pasci*, "to graze." At any rate, the argument was rebutted, so that pigs counted as grazing animals, by a text of Homer that used the Greek verb νέμομαι, "to graze," of pigs. This was the approach of Aelius Marcianus and was approved by Justinian.

There may have been other approaches. It should be noted in any event that the issue of whether pigs were *pecudes* was a live one in the time of Labeo (who died between A.D. 10 and 21) and still in the time of Aelius Marcianus, who was active in the early third century.[7] Moreover, it was regarded as sufficiently important for Justinian to spend considerable space on it in his *Institutes*.

In the present context the most significant point must be that the argument that the term *pecudes* was restricted to grazing animals was taken seriously for the interpretation of a statute, with no regard for the economic consequences. That was not the usual scope of the word, but once the argument was produced the appropriate course was to counter it by the assertion that pigs were, indeed, grazing animals, as Homer himself had said.

(4)   D.21.2.31 (Ulpian, *On Sabinus*, book 42): If someone, in response to one taking a *stipulatio* from him, promises that "the slave is healthy, is not a thief, and is not a corpse robber," etcetera, the *stipulatio* in the view of some is valueless, because if the slave is in that condition, then what is promised is an impossibility, if he is not in that condition the *stipulatio* is taken in vain. But I think it is more accurate that this stipulation "he

is not a thief, he is not a corpse robber, he is healthy" is useful; for its point is the interest of buyers in such being or not being the case. But if it were added "reparation will be made if" the *stipulatio* would have more validity. On any other view, the *stipulatio* set out by the aediles would be useless, which no sane person would accept.

For a long time the Roman contract of sale contained no inherent warranty of quality, especially with regard to psychological issues. A buyer who wished protection, as many did, against hidden defects would have to take an express promise by the formal verbal contract of *stipulatio*. The point here is that for some jurists, a *stipulatio* in the form "I promise that the slave is not a thief and is not a corpse robber" was ineffectual. If the slave did not have these defects, the guarantee would produce no effect and was thus unnecessary. If the slave did have these defects, the promise was of an impossibility, and a *stipulatio* for an impossibility was void.[8] Again we have reasoning remote from the real world. But this time, we have the unusual feature that the author of the text, Ulpian, brings in the real world: the point is, he says, the interest of buyers. But what he says next is most revealing. First, he says the stipulation would have more validity if the guarantor had said "reparation will be made if." So he is making some concession to the force of the formalistic argument. Next he brings in the edict of the aediles that a seller in the marketplace must declare a slave's faults and promise he had no others. Ulpian's point is that the second provision in the edict involves a stipulation in the form that some jurists regard as valueless, and so he declares that that juristic opinion cannot be right. We are back to a very formalistic argument. Lastly, Ulpian overdoes his response: no sane person, he says, would accept that the stipulation proposed by the aediles would be useless. He clearly does not find it easy to rebut the logic of the jurists he is disagreeing with.

(5)   D.45.1.38pr (Ulpian, *On Sabinus*, book 49): This *stipulatio*, "Do you promise we will be allowed to have" is to this effect that one be permitted to have, nor will anything be done by

anyone to prevent that person to have. The stipulation therefore seems to have promised the act of another, but no one is bound by promising the act of another, and that is the law we use. But he binds himself to do nothing to prevent the other's holding. He is further bound that neither his heirs nor any of his other successors brings it about that the other is prevented from having.

The text is again from Ulpian, and we see the extent of his embarrassment in the text just discussed. Here we are concerned with the analogous problem that in a contract of sale the buyer did not receive an inherent guarantee of quiet enjoyment, and if he wanted such, as most would in important transactions, he would have to take an express promise by *stipulatio*. But by a stipulation one could not promise the act of another; hence for Ulpian the stipulation "I promise you will have quiet enjoyment" was ineffectual against an attack on the buyer's title by anyone other than the seller or a successor of his. The stipulation should have run something like, "I promise to pay you $X$ if you are not permitted quiet enjoyment."[9] Ulpian's view is as far from considering justice, equity, or economic considerations as anything proposed by those with whom he disagreed in *D*.21.2.31. Ulpian's position is the more striking in that it would give much comfort to slave dealers, who had a reputation for crooked dealing in the ancient world.

(6) *J*.2.14pr: It is permitted to institute as heirs both free men and slaves, both the testator's own slaves or another person's. At one time the opinion of many was that one's own slave could be instituted properly only with a grant of liberty. But by our constitution, nowadays they can be instituted without a grant of liberty. We introduced this not as a novelty but because it was more equitable, and had been approved by Atilicinus as Paul reports in his works on Massurius Sabinus and on Plautius.

Thus, many classical jurists, including obviously Paul, held that if a testator instituted his own slave his heir but did not make him an express grant of freedom, the slave would be neither free nor heir.

Not only (as Justinian says) does this offend against equity, it is also clearly contrary to the intention of the testator.

Two further features from pontifical sacred responses also affected private law. First, frequently, the pontiffs gave no reason for their opinion.[10] One example from private law will suffice for this.

> D.16.3.1.5 (Ulpian, *On the Edict,* book 30): The things that are accessory to what is deposited are not deposited; for instance if a clothed man is deposited his clothing is not deposited; nor if a horse is deposited with a halter, for only the horse is deposited.

In this instance not only is no reason given for the decision but I can find none. Certainly the context of the opinion is not the formulation of the action, specifically how detailed the pleadings must be. What the decision comes to is a ruling that when something is deposited and accessories go with it, the accessories are not regarded as being part of what was deposited; they are thus outside the scope of the action on deposit. This means that in response to the action the depositee could simply hand over a naked slave or a horse without a halter. No doubt, the depositor could sue by some other action such as the *vindicatio,* the claim of ownership, but this seems excessively inconvenient for a relatively trivial amount.

The other feature from sacred jurisprudence that affected private law was cautelary jurisprudence, when the pontiffs (or other priests, such as the *fetiales*) were asked if a proposed course of action were permitted.[11] The jurists, in turn, were active in cautelary jurisprudence, giving *responsa* on the effects of proposed conduct.[12]

A further, but not obviously pontifical, characteristic of juristic argumentation is its reliance upon the authority of other jurists. The characteristic was so marked that Cicero could poke gentle fun at it. He playfully wrote to his friend, the jurist Trebatius, who was campaigning with Caesar, "I very much fear you will freeze during the winter. Therefore I think (and the same was the decision of Mucius and Manilius) that you should make use of a blazing fire, especially since you have no abundance of cloaks."[13] Cicero's humor lies in citing other jurists as authority, and there would be no point to this unless it were a common practice.

A further outstanding feature of Roman law was also the result of juristic involvement, namely, its very high degree of conceptualization. We saw in chapter 4 that the brevity of edicts and edictal *formulae,* such as those on sale and hire, were the result of the interaction of jurists with praetors. But a different issue, that of conceptualization, arises when we consider these *formulae* side by side. They indicate what is in fact the case: that sale and hire are different contracts, and that different actions are provided for the various contracts. If AA sued NN on the *formula* for sale and it developed that the contract was one of hire of a thing, then AA lost his case. And he could not subsequently sue on hire because of the basic principle of Roman law that once the decisive stage (the *litis contestatio*) of the action occurred, the plaintiff could not initiate a new action on the same facts. As a result it was extremely important in Roman law to decide precisely the outer limits of a legal institution or act, to determine what counted as sale and what as hire of a thing. There was, accordingly, enormous effort expended to determine exactly the legal elements of something such as the contract of sale. The nature of Roman actions was such that they demanded that the substantive law be highly developed in its own right.

The nature of the issue and some of its impact are well illustrated by a text from Gaius's *Institutes* 3.146:

> Likewise if I deliver gladiators to you on the terms that twenty denarii are given to me for each one that emerges uninjured, on account of his exertions, but a thousand denarii for each one that is killed or injured, the question arises whether this is a contract of sale or of hire. The prevailing opinion is that a contract of hire was made of those who emerged uninjured, but of sale of those who were killed or injured. This emerges from the outcome, it being understood that there was a conditional sale or hire of each one. For it is not now doubted that things can be bought or sold or hired conditionally.

Only one of these actions, either sale or hire of a thing, was the correct one. Consequently, in this as in other situations it was essential to determine precisely what would count as a contract of sale and what as a contract of hire. It was thus important that the *substance* of law be developed as fully as possible.

The working out of conceptualization may be demonstrated by the further example of possession. The recognition of possession as an institution separate from ownership, worthy of protection in its own right, seems to be a Roman invention. It had two main functions by the late Republic, both very important. First, possession (begun in good faith) was an essential requirement for the acquisition of ownership by prescription (*usucapio*). For prescription, land had to be possessed for two years, other things for one. Second, the fact of possession determined who would be the defendant in any dispute over ownership. The plaintiff had to prove his title to the property; the defendant did not. Hence the allocation of possession that might be made in a preceding magisterial pronouncement could determine the outcome of a battle over ownership.

There seems to have been no legislation on the basic elements of possession before Justinian, but much credit must be given to praetors who protected it by particular remedies called interdicts. Basically, an interdict was a pronouncement forbidding someone to do something. But we must be careful in estimating the role of the praetors. They also gave interdicts in situations where possession was not relevant; that is, interdicts were not specific to the protection of possession. Again, possessory interdicts do not always contain words denoting possession, such as *possessio*. Praetors never defined possession, never laid down general requirements for it, never gave a list of the circumstances in which someone possessed. They said nothing about the physical control or the intention needed before possession could begin or would continue. Moreover, interdicts sometimes protected existing possession, and sometimes their purpose was to permit someone who had lost possession to recover it.

An examination of the praetorian interdicts as they can be reconstructed does not lead to the conclusion that the praetors had a clear notion of what possession was. Rather, in very particular circumstances the praetors felt that some protection was required, and they granted it (probably after consultation with jurists). There is no theoretical foundation that links the interdicts together as protecting some definable type of control. Quotation of the two most important interdicts, *utrubi* for movables, *uti possidetis* for immovables, is revealing. The former read: "At whichever of you two, this man, who is the object of the dispute, was for the greater part of the year not with violence, not surreptitiously, not on sufferance from the other, I forbid violence to be used to remove him."[14] The latter: "As one of you possesses the building which is the object of the dispute, not with violence, not surreptitiously, not on sufferance, from the other, so that you do not cease possession I forbid violence to be used."[15] The first does not use words like possession, and there is nothing in it that indicates that a legal conception of possession existed or that, if it did, possession in the legal sense was the key to obtaining the interdict. Even more to the point, neither these interdicts nor others cast light on the troubling issue of when one person acquires possession or continues to possess through the physical control of another. Does the depositor continue to possess through the depositee, or the pledge-debtor through the creditor? Does an infant acquire possession through his *tutor* or even through his slave? and so on.

In these circumstances it was the jurists (acting in that capacity) who subsequently created the separate concept of possession based on the individual remedies granted by the praetors for discrete situations of fact. They gave the notion substance and sought to create rules of general application. In the process the jurists exhibited the traits discussed in chapter 6. They gave the rules a life of their own, based on their cultural notions, at times without considering practical consequences. This appears most clearly when we look at texts that indicate historical development.

> D.41.2.1.3 (Paul, *On the Edict*, book 54): A lunatic and a pupil acting without the authority of his *tutor* cannot begin to possess because they do not have the intention to hold, however much they are in physical contact with the thing, just as though one put something in the hand of a person asleep. But a pupil with the authority of his *tutor* does begin to possess. However, Ofilius and Nerva the son say that a pupil even without the authority of the *tutor* begins to possess: for possession is a matter of fact, not

of law. This opinion may be accepted if they are of an age to be capable of understanding.

Ofilius was a jurist of the late Republic, Nerva the son of the early Empire, and Paul was active in the early third century A.D. Paul, as is well known, believed that to begin to possess, one had to have sufficient physical control and the appropriate intention.[16] Hence for Paul, a pupil—that is, a male under fourteen or a girl under twelve—could not begin to possess because they could not form the appropriate intention. Paul, however, would allow a pupil of an age capable of understanding to begin to possess. But for the earlier Ofilius and Nerva, a pupil could begin to possess even without the *tutor*'s authority. The position of Ofilius and Nerva is certainly the more benign. Possession as a legal concept, as something distinct from mere physical control or ownership, could never lead to harmful consequences. It could only be beneficial.

But with the development of a theoretical content of the concept of possession by the jurists, situations occurred when theory prevailed over just results.

> D.41.2.3.5 (Paul, *On the Edict*, book 54): By contrast, several people cannot possess the same thing as a whole: for it is contrary to nature that when I hold something you can also be regarded as holding it. Sabinus, however, writes that a person who gives something in *precarium* both possesses it himself and so does the person who receives in *precarium*. Trebatius takes the same view on the basis that one person can possess justly, another unjustly, but there cannot be two unjust or two just possessors. Labeo takes him to task on the ground that in the matter of possession it does not much matter whether one possesses justly or unjustly. This is the more correct view. For it is no more possible for two persons to have the same possession, than that you should seem to stand on the same spot where I stand, or sit in the spot where I sit.

Trebatius was a jurist of the late Republic; Sabinus and Labeo came slightly later. *Precarium* was a grant of land for use and enjoyment with no time set for its termination but which could always be revoked at will by the grantor. The opinion of Paul and Labeo that two people could not possess the same thing seems appropriate in theory, but in practice it is less satisfactory than the opinion of Trebatius and Sabinus. For Paul, the person who would possess was the recipient of the *precarium*, and the grantor would have no possession. Hence, if a third person wrongfully took the land from the grantee, the grantee could successfully bring the interdict *uti possidetis* against him, but the grantor could not. For Trebatius and Sabinus, either the grantor or the grantee could successfully bring the interdict against the third party. It is easy to imagine circumstances in which in practice the interests of a grantor of a *precarium* were best served by allowing him also to have possession vis-à-vis an intruder.[17]

The development of possession is an example—as is also the development of contracts to be discussed in chapter 11—of the phenomenon I should like to call "no visible hand." Every student of economics is familiar with Adam Smith's doctrine of the "invisible hand." When demand is greater than supply the price will rise, which will induce producers to produce more so the supply rises. When the supply comes to exceed demand, the price falls, producers will produce less, and eventually and ideally, an equilibrium will result among supply, demand, and price. For law, I have long argued, there is no invisible hand that promotes an equilibrium between law and the society it serves. The difference, for me, is that to become law, society's demand must pass through a formal means of lawmaking, whether this is a supreme legislature or subordinate lawmakers such as jurists, law professors, or judges. Law, accordingly, is often out of step with society. But in addition to the absence of the invisible hand there is often no visible hand. Law develops in stages. New law often does not drive old law out, but builds on it without the lawmakers taking a fresh look at the issues. The result may be something approaching chaos. In this instance, the praetor gave interdictal protection in particular situations, with no regard for a consistent theory. Working with this material, the jurists and in particular Paul try to give some coherence to the notion of possession in order to determine the circumstances in which an interdict will be given. But the origins of the interdicts meant that there could be no coherence despite juristic attempts to impose one. The attempts of scholars of such eminence as Friedrich Karl von Savigny[18] and Rudolf von Jhering[19] to find a principle are quite misguided. For Savigny, the *animus* (intention) involved was to be owner; hence a person who had de facto control of a thing and intended to exercise that control for himself was the possessor. For Jhering, who stressed the element of physical control, a person possessed if he had the control that an owner normally had, together with an intelligent awareness (*animus*) of the factual situation. The objections to both theories and their successors are well known.[20] But mention of Savigny and Jhering raises an important issue for us. The success of Roman law after Justinian has caused later scholars to misunderstand the difficulties that the Romans had in creating it and to attribute to it qualities that it never possessed. To this issue we will return.

At times the drive toward conceptualization leads to exaggeration, as in the famous statement of Ulpian, "Ownership has nothing in common with possession."[21] It was, of course, important to keep the concepts of ownership and possession distinct, but to say that they had nothing in common much overstates the case. For things that had no owner but were capable of being owned, ownership was acquired by a taking (*occupatio*) that gave the taker possession. And possession for the period required for prescription was a necessary element for acquiring ownership by usucapion.

One consequence of this drive to conceptualization, which also became a force toward further conceptualization, was the granting by the praetor, as already mentioned, of ad hoc remedies, termed either *actiones utiles* or *actiones in factum*. When a situation occurred that merited a legal remedy but none was provided for in the Edict, the praetor could grant an analogous action or an action on the facts. If we consider the agreement to supply gladiators that was discussed earlier in this chapter, we can see the value of the approach. According to Gaius, the agreement will be the contract of sale or of hire, depending on the outcome. But what if there is no outcome, because the supplier simply fails to provide gladiators? Then there will be no way to decide whether the contract was sale or hire. And then there could be no action on sale or on hire. But it was open to the praetor from the first century B.C. onward to grant an ad hoc remedy when this seemed reasonable. Though there is no direct evidence for how this practice came about, we can proffer a plausible scenario. The jurists were active in discussing the boundaries of a legal construct. Was an agreement to allow a neighbor to pasture his flock for a season on your land for a fixed sum of money sale of the grass eaten or hire of the land? What contract, if any, was involved when the prestation on one side was transfer of a farm, on the other side to pay a fixed sum of money plus an obligation to rent another farm for two years? But the more that boundaries were fixed the more often would arise meritorious situations that fell just outside the scope of a construct and its remedies. Three approaches were possible, if in any way justice was to be taken into account. First, the boundaries of the construct could be redrawn, and no doubt this was sometimes done. Second, there could be some fudging and a remedy would be given under the construct. This was, for a long time, not the Roman way. Third, it could be admitted that the situation was outside the scope of a construct and so the relevant action was not available, but the praetor would grant an action based on the facts. This third approach was accepted, and we can assume that it was the work of the jurists who wished to preserve the clarity of their concepts. But once the notion was accepted that such actions would be granted, it enabled the jurists to be even more theoretical and to go further with conceptualization. Thus, the *lex Aquilia* gave actions for damage to property, but only to owners. Once it was accepted that the praetor would grant ad hoc remedies to certain nonowners, such as possessors in good faith and pledge creditors, the jurists had a green light to clarify further notions such as ownership and possession in good faith.

To this conceptualization of the jurists we must note a qualification. As David Daube brilliantly demonstrated,[22] many of the technical legal terms so well known to modern students of Roman law were unknown to the Romans, or were rare or late. Among the unknown from property law, for example, were *thesauri inventio, inaedificatio, satio, commixtio,* and *specificatio.* Instead of the abstract noun such as *thesauri inventio,* "treasure trove," the Romans used the active verb *thesaurum invenire,* "to find treasure." Daube emphasizes: "To say that the classics preferred the verb for stylistic reasons is not enough. Style may be a contributory factor, but the phenomenon calls for a deeper explanation: it has to do with the slowness of systematizing, institutionalizing, mastery of the discipline."[23]

# 8 Jurists and Reality

In previous chapters I have stressed the jurists' central role in shaping the law, their distance from the courts, their artificial (for private law) mode of reasoning, and their conceptualization, even at the expense of sensible development. Nonetheless, they were not always and entirely remote from reality. Indeed, it is another characteristic of Roman law that jurists sometimes struggled—and struggle is the appropriate term—to come up with a sane solution, although their difficulties are easily overlooked. In the first place, the jurists usually would not admit that they were abandoning established legal principles. Secondly, their struggles arose in individual situations that conflicted with principles, and it is the latter that are habitually stressed.

It would be wrong to pass over such struggles in silence—especially since they often incidentally reveal the jurists' concern with principle—and in this chapter I wish to bring forward some instances where the jurists endeavored to take account of social reality.[1]

The first examples concern the private-law delict of *furtum*, theft. The problem relates to ameliorating the consequences when certain parameters are fixed by early governmental intervention, such as by statute or edict, and these parameters (which cannot easily be altered by subordinate lawmakers such as jurists) are left unchanged by the government for centuries.

By an early date it was established that the physical act that was needed for the commission of *furtum* was a wrongful touching, *contrectatio*.[2] There was no need, as in English larceny, for an asportation. At the same time, the award in the *actio furti* to the victim was fixed as a multiple of the value of the object stolen. This conjunction caused problems in a number of distinguishable situations, namely:

When what was touched could be regarded as a unit but what was removed was only a fraction: for instance when someone took a bushel from a large heap of grain, or sucked up through a straw a little of the wine that filled the hold of a ship.[3]

When a container that was too heavy to move was broken into, with a view to removing only part of its contents.[4]

When there was no intention to keep the thing but only to use it temporarily: for instance, to use a borrowed object in an unauthorized way, or to introduce one's mares to another's jackass.[5]

When the person from whom the thing was taken was not the owner or when more than one person could be plaintiff in the *actio furti*, such as a person who had a life rent and the bare owner.[6]

The problem is not that "wrongful touching" is inappropriate as the constitutive act for theft—in fact, it is very appropriate for a system that did not punish attempts—but that it is inappropriate when coupled with an award to the plaintiff that was fixed by law as a multiple of the thing stolen. When a thief drank a cupful of wine from the cargo contained in the hold of a ship, he might actually have deprived the owner of one ten-thousandth part of the cargo. To make him liable, if he were caught in the act, to pay four times the value of the cargo seems harsh, especially since, if he had carted off the lot, he would be liable to no different penalty. Of course, if he had been fortunate enough to find a ship in which the cargo of wine was being carried in amphorae and he had broken into one jar to drink the same amount, he would have been liable only to pay four times the value of the wine in the amphora. If the award in the *actio furti* had been based on a different standard, such as a multiple of the plaintiff's interest, or been fixed at the discretion of the judge, the jurists would not even have been faced with the difficult philosophical question about the nature of a thing.

How were the jurists to deal with this problem? Could they have approached it by defining the object stolen in terms of the intention of the thief? Theft from an agglomeration would then be of only what the thief intended to have for himself. But this approach, if it had been taken (and it was not), would have been unsatisfactory for at least two reasons. First, with regard to the agglomeration it would have involved either a circularity of reasoning (a thief steals what he intends to steal) or a definition in terms not of touching but of asportation (a thief steals from the heap or hold what he takes away from the heap or hold). Secondly, with regard to temporary wrongful use, one would have to define what was stolen as no longer the physical object—that is, when another's horse was ridden farther than was bargained for, what was stolen would not be the horse but the use of the horse. But then the wrongful constitutive act would again not have been touching because one cannot touch the use of something. The easy solution to the problem thus did not lie in this direction. The easy solution would have been to change the method of calculating the award in the *actio furti*—to a multiple of the loss inflicted on the victim plaintiff, but that was an approach not readily available to the jurists since the method of calculation was fixed by the Edict. In this case, as often, there was no governmental intervention to ameliorate the law.

The Roman law of theft as it is presented in the sources is reasonably cohesive, but there are texts where the legal ruling seems out of line. It is revealing to look at these from the perspective of the award to the plaintiff in the *actio furti*.

D.47.2.39 (Ulpian, *On Sabinus*, book 1): It is true that if someone carried off another's prostitute slave this is not theft. For it is not the act that is examined but the cause of the act, and the motive here was lust, not theft. And, therefore, even a person, who broke down a prostitute's door on account of lust, and thieves, not brought in by him but acting independently, carried off the prostitute's property, was not liable for theft. . . .

D.47.2.83.2 (Paul, *Opinions*, book 2): Whoever carried off another's female slave who was not a prostitute on account of lust will be liable to the *actio furti*, and if he kept her concealed will be punished by the penalty of the *lex Fabia*.[7]

When these texts, admittedly by different jurists, are placed side by side, the contrast is striking. To take away another's female slave to gratify one's lust is (for Paul) theft if the slave was not a prostitute, but not theft (for Ulpian) if she was a prostitute. If the results stem from the intention of the wrongdoer and relate to the absence of an intention to make a gain, then we might have expected the converse results. After all, where the slave was a prostitute, the wrongdoer could presumably have gratified his lust if he had been willing to pay. The wrongdoer had the indirect intention to make a gain of the money he should otherwise have paid.

But the problem does not directly lie with the absence of the *animus lucrandi*, intention to gain. Intention to make a gain was usually interpreted widely. Thus in a different fragment of his text just quoted, *h.t.* 83pr, Paul holds it is theft for a fuller or tailor to wear clothes he had taken in to clean or mend. Gaius held in *h.t.* 55.1 that there was theft if someone lent without authorization something he himself had borrowed, "for it is a type of profit to exercise generosity out of another's property and to put someone under an obligation to do a good turn." Thus, the main problem is not why Paul held it was theft to carry off another's nonprostitute slave because of lust, but why Ulpian held such behavior was not theft when the slave was a prostitute.

There have been many approaches to the crux, and they have centered on *D.*47.2.39pr because it is Ulpian's position that is hard to justify. O. Karlowa suggested that for Ulpian there was no theft of the prostitute because she was available for the satisfaction of all men's desires, and so to take her because of lust was not contrary to the wishes of the owner, which was another requirement for *furtum*.[8] To this it is reasonable to respond with critics that, on that approach, to take a horse from a livery stable to ride for a while would not be theft either.[9] In either case, it would be against the wishes of the owner to take the slave prostitute or horse without an intention of paying. For Jolowicz, the text of Ulpian is interpolated, that is, altered, at some subsequent date, probably at the compilation of the *Digest:* "Our passage must be interpolated: the statement introduced by *et ideo* ["And, therefore,"] does not follow from what precedes." But, for a start against this suggestion, it is not easy to see how the first part of the text could have read in any other way that would have allowed *et ideo* etcetera to follow. Any argument here should be rather that it is the statement introduced by *et ideo* that has been altered. Further, that statement *does* follow from what precedes. It is another example of a proposition held by some jurists that if one person deliberately acts in a way that injures another, and as a result some third person is enabled to commit theft from the second person, the first is estopped from denying that he was an accomplice.[10] Ulpian, we know, was interested in the proposition.[11] Thus, what follows *et ideo* supports the notion that the first part of the text is genuine Ulpian: otherwise the substance of these two parts of the text would have to have been interpolated.

If, however, we now look at the issue between Ulpian and Paul from the perspective that sometimes the award in the *actio furti* could seem inappropriately large we may have a solution. If it had been held that there was *furtum* of a slave prostitute when she was carried off out of lust, the award in the action would have been twice the value of the prostitute. But what the owner has been deprived of is simply fees for her services. And the victim, as brothel keeper or pimp, is not a particularly worthy person to receive an exaggerated award. It should not therefore be a surprise that Ulpian was unwilling to grant the pimp the *actio furti*.

Another text has been allowed to obscure the issue:

D.47.10.25 (Ulpian, *On the Edict*, book 18): If a female slave was debauched, the action for insult (*actio iniuriarum*) will be given. Or, if he hid the slave or did anything else with the intention of stealing, the action for theft (*actio furti*) also. Or if he debauched an immature girl, some think an action on the *lex Aquilia* is also available.

Here we have another text of Ulpian that is believed to contradict, or be out of harmony with, the one we have been examining and hence is often thought interpolated. But we may take it as it stands. On this basis there are two open possibilities. First, we might take as a unit the passage "Or, if he hid the slave or did anything else with the intention of stealing," so that the hiding was done with the intention of stealing and more than mere lust was involved. That is, for improper sex with the slave woman, the correct action for the owner was the *actio iniuriarum* against the wrongdoer. Secondly, we might notice that the slave is not described as a prostitute and conclude that Ulpian's position was that to take another's slave woman for lust was theft if she were not a prostitute, but not theft if she were. Ulpian's position would then seem to be difficult to defend on legal logic, but where he would be out of line would be in holding that *furtum* had not been committed when the slave was a prostitute. And it is precisely in this holding that I would claim Ulpian was allowing social reality to impinge on the fabric of the law: pimps were not to be entitled to massive legal awards.

It is important to notice that a great part of the problem with this issue for modern scholars is precisely that they are so accustomed to the jurists' attachment to principle that they do not consider other possibilities.[12]

A further text of Ulpian, which I have discussed fully elsewhere, probably shows that jurist taking a similar approach and may even bolster my interpretation of D.47.2.39.[13]

> D.47.2.52.20 (Ulpian, *On the Edict*, book 37): If someone drives off my jackass and puts him in among his mares for breeding purposes only, he is not liable for theft unless he also had the intention to steal. I also wrote this back to a question from Dalmatia, from Herennius Modestinus, a student of mine, the issue being of some stallions which someone was reputed to have turned in with his own mares for the same purpose. I said he was only liable for theft if he had acted with the intention of stealing; if not an action on the facts (*actio in factum*) would lie.

The problem in the text is that the wrongdoer intended to make a gain from his behavior, which ought therefore to constitute *furtum*. The classicality of the text is much disputed and interpolations are often suggested, but I need not here repeat my arguments for its genuineness. All that need be noted is that one can account for the aberrational nature of the text if we are prepared to admit that Ulpian could have felt that the measure of damages in the *actio furti*—a multiple of the value of the jackass—was excessive, since the loss to his owner was slight. The action on the facts could well give him sufficient redress.

The instances discussed on theft related to problems arising from the state's failure to introduce reform. Now I wish to consider difficulties caused by the jurists' conceptualization, this time of the contract of mandate. The first text is *D*.17.1.6.6 (Ulpian, *On the Edict*, book 31):

> The question is put in the thirteenth book of Julian's *Digest:*
> If a principal instructed his procurator to take a certain sum
> of his money and lend it at his [the procurator's] risk on the
> terms that he would pay only a certain rate of interest to the
> principal; if he was able to lend at higher, he himself would take
> the profit; he seems to have taken the money as a loan. Clearly
> if the administration of all the principal's affairs were mandated
> to him, he would also be liable to the action on mandate, just
> as a debtor is usually liable in mandate who looked after his
> creditor's affairs.[14]

The problem is one that, as we have already seen, has parallels elsewhere in Roman law because of the nature of the formulary system of procedure. As was noted earlier, for a *formula* to be available, for example on a contract of sale or on a contract of deposit, there had to be a valid contract of the right type and not just a transaction that approximated to sale or deposit: if there was no contract of sale there would be no *actio empti* and no *actio venditi*, and if no contract of deposit, no *actio depositi*. This approach created problems whenever an arrangement did not fall firmly within the bounds of a recognized contract.[15]

Here A asked B to take his money, lend it out at B's risk on the understanding that B would repay it to A plus interest at $X$ percent but could keep any interest above *X* percent. The question is, what kind of a contract is this?

It is not ordinary *depositum*, because in deposit the recipient cannot make use of the object deposited. It also does not have the usual characteristics of *mandatum*, mandate, because the recipient (who would be the mandatary) is to act at his own risk.

Julian's approach is that the contract is *mutuum*, loan for consumption, with an agreement for interest whose legal basis is not stated or examined.[16] In result-oriented jurisprudence, the opinion is valuable, but the decision is not straightforward theoretically. There are three problems for holding that the transaction is *mutuum*. First, that is not how the principal expressed his wishes, and he does not seem to have intended to create the contract of *mutuum*. To this one should probably respond that it is the facts of a case, including the intention of the parties, that create a contractual obligation, but the intention does not determine which contract it is.[17] Secondly, for *mutuum*, ownership should be transferred to the recipient, the person described as procurator, and this does not seem to be the intention. Thirdly, with *mutuum*, since ownership is transferred to the recipient he should have the right to decide what to do with the money, but here he is to take the money to use it in a specified way.

The arrangement, in fact, has also some similarities with the so-called *depositum irregulare*, where money is deposited on the basis that an equivalent amount is restored and the recipient becomes owner. Such an arrangement was not uncommon, though its legal status in classical law is not certain.[18] Into that status we need not go here; it is enough to know that there are texts stating that when the money is used, the contract becomes *mutuum*.[19] On this basis the decision in the present text would be rather more understandable. Still, a *depositum* is also not what was intended, so it is hard to believe *depositum irregulare* was what was under consideration as a *mutuum*.

The text continues that if general administration had been mandated to the procurator he would also be liable to the *actio mandati*. On one level there is no problem here. Though the specific arrangement for lending out the money constituted *mutuum*, not *mandatum*, nonetheless if it were acted upon by the procurator as part of his general administration, then within the scope of that administration he would also be liable to the *actio mandati*.[20] On another level, the point of the text, as its context suggests, is that some degree of remuneration was permitted to the procurator. In essence, *mandatum* was gratuitous, but if some types of reward were agreed on, the procurator could bring an action *extra ordinem*.[21] So the text tells us that where an arrangement enables a procurator to make a profit if he lends out at a greater rate of interest, the arrangement still falls within the scope of *mandatum*.

The second text is the following fragment *D.*17.1.6.7:

> A certain Marius Paulus had given a verbal guarantee for Daphnis, having agreed upon a reward on account of his guarantee, and under the name of another he took an undertaking that he would be paid a certain amount from the outcome of the lawsuit. He was ordered by the praetor Claudius Saturninus to pay a larger amount into court, and the same Saturninus forbade him from court pleading. It seemed to me that he had guaranteed he would pay a judgment debt and was in the position of one who had bought up the lawsuit, and wanted to recover from Daphnis by the action on mandate because he had suffered condemnation. But the Deified Brothers [the emperors Antoninus Pius and Lucius Verus] very properly declared in a rescript that he had no action because of his sharp practices because, having made an agreement for payment, he proceeded to this kind of a buying up of the right of action. Marcellus, however, says about a person who gave a verbal guarantee when he had accepted payment that if the agreement indeed was that he should guarantee at his own risk, he had no action: but if it was not so agreed he does have an *actio utilis*. This view is consistent with utility.

The text presents the facts in a very abbreviated form, and it is best approached in four stages.

At stage one, Marius Paulus gave a verbal guarantee on behalf of Daphnis and received a financial remuneration from him for doing so.

Marius Paulus, under another name, then took an undertaking that he would receive a certain quantity from the outcome of the lawsuit. This can only mean, since Marius Paulus is described as *redemptor litis* (purchaser of the lawsuit), that Marius Paulus took the undertaking from the creditor and that it was to the effect that he was to act as procurator for the creditor on a basis akin to a contingent fee. In the standard situation of *redemptio litis*, which was considered to be contrary to good morals, a lawyer would pay a plaintiff for the right to act as his procurator in the lawsuit, on the understanding that he, the procurator, would keep any money obtained in the action from the defendant. Here Marius Paulus seems to have bought, and to be acting on account of, only a share of the proceeds. The conclusion that Marius Paulus's wrongdoing involved acting as a law agent is strengthened by the fact that part of Marius Paulus's punishment was a prohibition against acting as advocate.

Marius Paulus's knavery was discovered, and punished by the praetor Claudius Saturninus. Inter alia, Paulus was ordered to pay a larger amount into court.

Stage two represents Ulpian's reconstruction of what happened next. The creditor's action, we see, was in fact brought not against the principal debtor but against Marius Paulus, the guarantor. Only this can explain Ulpian's reconstruction. For Ulpian, Marius Paulus, who had been ordered to pay a greater amount, was at the same time a guarantor for payment of the judgment debt and a *redemptor litis*, acting as procurator for the creditor. And then he wanted to bring an *actio mandati* against Daphnis because of his condemnation in the lawsuit.

There is an obvious problem here irrespective of Marius Paulus's sharp practices. Mandate is essentially gratuitous, and so, though normally a verbal guarantor who paid the creditor would have an *actio mandati* against the principal, in this situation there was or should be no mandate since Marius Paulus had been paid by Daphnis to give the guarantee. That this was the prime interest of Ulpian in the case will become evident when we examine stage four.

At stage three in the text it appears that Daphnis's response to Marius Paulus's attempt to make him pay for his loss, through the use of the *actio mandati*, was to ask the Deified Brothers for a ruling. Their response was a rescript to Daphnis to the effect that Marius Paulus had no right to an action because of his sharp practice *"quia mercede pacta accesserat ad talem redemptionem"* (because he had acceeded to that redemption when a reward was agreed upon).

The sharp practice was not that he had received payment for giving a verbal guarantee. That was permitted, as is shown at stage four of this text. Nor was it that he was a *redemptor litis*, undertaking the risk of the lawsuit in the hope of a larger sum for his efforts. Such an arrangement was void as being contrary to good morals,[22] but it would not block the procurator's other legal rights.[23] The sharp practice specifically was having an interest in both sides of the lawsuit and in fraudulently hiding this fact: he was the defendant (but with a hope of recovering any sum that he was condemned to pay from Daphnis); and under a false name he was the procurator for the creditor, under the Roman equivalent of a contingent fee arrangement. No wonder the emperors refused him any remedy against Daphnis!

In stage four Ulpian discusses what for him was the basic topic of interest in the convoluted facts, and he hangs his treatment onto an opinion of Marcellus. The issue was what rights against the principal debtor a verbal guarantor had who took payment for his guarantee. It depends, we are told, on the intention. If the intention was that the guarantor was to guarantee at his own risk, then he had no remedy against the principal debtor. But if that was not the intention, he had an *actio utilis*.

It is this second alternative that really concerns Ulpian in book 31 of his commentary on the Edict, which is specifically devoted to mandate. Marcellus's ruling was to the effect that where the verbal guarantor gave his undertaking because he received payment, there was no contract of mandate. Ulpian apparently accepts Marcellus's opinion.

These two texts concern an important issue in Roman law, namely, whether a particular bargain between parties counts as a contract and, if so, which one. The bargains involved are at the outer limits of specific contracts, and discussion of them helps to fix the boundaries of Roman legal concepts.[24] Hence comes, as I have already emphasized, the high degree of conceptualization. The issues in these texts are discussed in the context of the contract of mandate where a reward was offered, though the contract was defined as being gratuitous.

In *D*.17.1.6.6, the arrangement was that A should take B's money and lend it out at interest at B's risk on the understanding that B was to pay A a particular interest and retain any amount he obtained above that sum. The approach taken for the situation kept it out of the sphere of *mandatum* and treated it (rather clumsily from a theoretical point of view but in a way that was socially useful) as a *mutuum*. No legal basis is stated or examined for any obligation on B's part to pay the stated rate of interest to A. The theoretical clumsiness disappears to a limited extent if the arrangement is still classed as giving rise to a *condictio* on *mutuum* but falling within the recognized category of *depositum irregulare*. Yet that can scarcely have been the approach.

When the general administration of B's affairs had been entrusted to A, this particular bargain would fall under the general administration agreement and so would also give rise to an *actio mandati*. Thus, B could sue A by the *actio mandati* both for his capital and the stated amount of interest. But, and this is the reason for Ulpian's treatment of the issue in this context, A would be legally entitled to retain the extra interest. In other situations, too, we know that a breach was made in the concept of *mandatum* as being essentially gratuitous, in order to allow the *procurator omnium bonorum* to receive a financial reward.

In *D*.17.1.6.7, the basic ruling is that an arrangement that C is to receive a reward for verbally guaranteeing D's debt falls outside of the contract of mandate. Thus, if C repays the debt, he has no *actio mandati* against D. Still, the situation is sufficiently meritorious that C will be allowed an ad hoc praetorian remedy, an *actio utilis*. When in the overall context C has been fraudulent in another regard and has been legally punished for it, he will also not be granted an *actio utilis* against D. It would, no doubt, have been more difficult to refuse C a regularly constituted contractual action.

I have discussed these two texts on mandate at considerable length. They illuminate an important issue. The juristic drive for conceptualization made for sharp divisions in the law, and so when a situation fell outside of a particular classification a worthy person might seem to be bereft of a remedy. The jurists at times struggled to ameliorate the legal position: they might grant an ad hoc remedy, recognizing that the basic rules were not entirely appropriate; or they might even extend the boundaries of the concept, by way of exception.

# 9 Legal Isolationism: II

In a famous dictum, thinking of the common law, Oliver Wendell Holmes claimed: "The life of the law has not been logic, it has been experience."[1] As a generalization the statement is unsatisfactory in two regards. First, as we have seen, logic or at least a specific style of legal reasoning was a marked feature of Roman law; and experience, important though it undoubtedly was for developing Roman law, did not dominate. The other regard is the subject of this chapter. As a general dictum I would prefer "The life of the law has not been logic and it has not been experience. It has been borrowing." I have argued repeatedly that in the Western world, law has mainly changed through borrowing. But to this proclivity to borrowing Roman law is a remarkable exception.

Before we come to the main issue I must mention a particular problem for the early period. A well-known crux is the accuracy of our sources for early Roman history. I am very ready to believe that the Rape of Lucretia and the Duel of the Horatii and Curiati have no basis in fact, but are legends. Yet the fact remains that the legal aspects of the episodes are essentially plausible for archaic Rome. It may be that in large measure knowledge of legal institutions and rules derived from a more accurate tradition than did much of the rest of early Roman history.[2]

In his account of the making of the *Twelve Tables* Livy relates that a mission was sent to Athens with orders to copy down the famous laws of Solon and to learn about the institutions, customs, and laws of other Greek states.[3] Now this is the kind of story that could be entirely legendary, and its truth has been much doubted by many scholars.[4] If there was any such embassy, it has also been suggested, it would have been to Magna Graecia. Whether the mission was real or legendary its purpose in both cases would be the same: another delaying tactic on the part of the patricians. For that a mission to Athens would be more appropriate than one to Magna Graecia.[5] There is nothing in the story that favors fact or fiction.

But here is the issue. From our much later perspective we know just how common and normal borrowing is.[6] The notion of such a mission to Athens is entirely plausible. But then there is the fact, as I shall claim, that it is hard to find traces of Greek influence in the *Twelve Tables*, and later the Romans certainly seem to have been averse to borrowing. What are we to make of this?

One possibility is to say that there was no mission, hence the absence of evidence for Greek influence on the code. But then it is hard to understand how the tradition could have arisen, because the Romans were indeed so little interested in borrowing law. The other possibility is to suggest there actually was such a mission and that (as was certainly later the case) the Romans found little they wished to adopt. This second possibility seems rather more plausible to me. But no matter which possibility is correct we can draw an important conclusion. If there was an embassy, then since there was so little Greek influence we have strong evidence of the Romans' inherent opposition to legal borrowing. If there was no embassy when a set of laws was to be promulgated, we have evidence in a different form of indifference to other people's law.

In the *Twelve Tables* themselves, as has frequently been claimed, there is remarkably little internal evidence for Greek influence.[7] Three instances are usually adduced. According to Gaius, the provision in the code regulating boundaries was "in a kind of a way modeled on a law of Solon."[8] This is rather indefinite and the provision of Solon, which he quotes, has nothing whatever to do with the action for regulating boundaries, but deals with the issue of how much space at the edge of one's land should be left free from certain operations.[9] Gaius also claims that the provision that members of societies could make their own rules "appears to have been adopted from a law of Solon,"[10] but the similarities are not precise and are not striking. Cicero claims that the *Twelve Tables'* provisions regulating over-luxurious mourning derive from Solon,[11] but the scope of the Roman rules is not at all clear and at the very least has no exact correspondence with the Athenian doctrine.[12]

For the influence of Greek legal rules on Roman legal rules later in the Republic, only two instances are commonly adduced, and neither is persuasive.

In some Greek systems, earnest money was used to bind a contract of sale: if the buyer failed to fulfill his agreement he forfeited the earnest money; if the seller reneged he had to return the earnest and as much again. Earnest money thus had a legal function. This was certainly not the case with *arra*, earnest money, in classical Roman law, where earnest had purely a social function. When the buyer failed to fulfill the contract it was simpler in practice for the seller to retain the *arra* as if it were liquidated damages than to bring the action on sale. *Arra* appears at Rome as early as the plays of Plautus, and it is sometimes claimed that at that time it functioned with legal effect as in Greece, and not with purely social effect as it did in later Rome. But no legal function can be demonstrated for *arra* in Plautus, and it is simpler to believe that its purpose then, as later, was purely social.[13]

No other principle and no detail of law seem to have developed from a Greek example unless it is true, as some scholars assert, that the praetorian *actiones iniuriarum* (which at first covered physical assault and later also defamation) owe something, whether in the substantive law or in the flexible pecuniary condemnation, to the Attic δίκη αἰκίας or the Alexandrian ὕβρις. There are certain similarities between the Greek and Roman law in this area, but also serious divergences, and I doubt whether a case has been, or can be, established in favor of Greek influence.[14] But even if one accepts that the praetorian *actiones iniuriarum*—as opposed to the older civil law remedies— were subject to Greek influence, this would still not mean that the substance of Roman law in the late Republic was much influenced by the Greeks.

Another instance has been adduced but, to my knowledge, only by Jolowicz and Nicholas.[15] They point to the aedilitian edict on sales of slaves in the marketplace, and they adduce Fritz Pringsheim[16] and Contardo Ferrini[17] in support. But in neither Pringsheim nor Ferrini is there any claim that the Romans borrowed here and, though there are resemblances between the Greek and Roman provisions, they are no greater than could result from two systems dealing independently with the same problem. Moreover, Jolowicz and Nicholas fail to take into account that there was an earlier aedilitian edict on the subject,[18] and they do not address the issue of which of these aedilitian edicts is supposed to be the result of borrowing. If it is the former, then the Romans borrowed a basic idea and improved on it. If the latter, then the basic idea was Roman, and foreign influence added refinement.

This nonborrowing from Greek law in the later Republic must be stressed because this is the period of greatest Greek influence on other aspects of Roman life, such as literature, philosophy, rhetoric, and architecture. Though the time has been called "The Hellenistic period of Roman jurisprudence,"[19] that is emphatically a misnomer if we simply look at the borrowing of rules.

For the continuance of nonborrowing in the Empire we should first consider a surprising case—surprising because no borrowing occurred:

> G.3.134: Moreover, an obligation by writing seems to be made by what the Greeks call "chirographs" and "syngraphs," that is, if someone writes that he owes or will give; provided, of course, there was no stipulation on that account. This type of obligation is particular to foreigners.

The Romans had no written contract in the sense that it was the written agreement that created the obligation. (The so-called contract *litteris* was not a way of creating a new obligation but of transforming an existing obligation into one of another sort.) Unless because of the subject matter the agreement fell within a specific type of contract, such as sale or hire, an agreement could only be made legally binding by the use of the stipulation. And stipulations were often used for a whole agreement whose substance was sale, or for particular terms of such agreements. Yet stipulation as a general contract had serious limitations. Above all, because it was oral, it could not be made at a distance; the parties had to be face-to-face. The problem was compounded because Roman law, as we shall see, had no doctrine of agency. It is beyond doubt that a contract with the scope of stipulation, but valid when and because it was reduced to writing, would have been extremely useful. The Romans were well aware that such a contract could exist elsewhere, as the passage of Gaius shows. Am I mistaken in detecting a certain smugness in his remark that such written contracts are particular to foreigners?

To remain with contracts, another striking failure to borrow is the absence of any real law of agency. The contract of mandate does not fit the bill. When by a mandate A asked B to buy something for him from C, and B fulfilled the mandate, there was a contract of mandate between A and B, and a contract of sale between B and C; but there was no contract between A and C. Yet the Romans were well aware of the possibility of direct agency since it had existed in various forms from an early date in Roman Egypt; and the papyri show that there it was widely used.[20]

Nonborrowing from Augustus onwards may be approached in a different way.[21] A standard modern treatise by Jolowicz and Nicholas stresses the influence of Greek law. They point to the increase in the use of writing and declining formalism.[22] I can find no sign of any decline in formalism in the principate. And if there was an increase in the use of writing, that was only to be expected in a more developed nation and is itself no sign of Greek influence, and would not affect the substance of the law. For an impact on the substance of the law they adduce only two instances of Greek influence. First, they point to a constitution of A.D. 200 that reads: "Although it was not added to the document (that you inserted in your petition) that a stipulation was taken by him to whom the promise was made, nonetheless if the business was conducted between persons present together we must believe there was a preceding stipulation and the promise followed."[23] They comment: "The stipulation has therefore become in practice a written contract, save that it is capable of being upset by proof that the parties could not have exchanged an oral question and answer."[24] This, I suggest, goes rather too far. The constitution does not show that, in practice, the *stipulatio* had become a written contract: parties may usually have performed the oral formalities. What must rather be stressed is the restricted value of the writing. The parties must still have been present together at the time of the promise. The great advantage of a proper written contract, that it could be made between parties who were distant from one another, was not granted.

Their second instance concerns the *exceptio non numeratae pecuniae*, the defense that money was not paid, which is first evidenced in a constitution of A.D. 215.[25] We know earlier, from Gaius, that when a stipulator took a promise for a sum of money on the understanding that he would advance the money to the promisor, and he failed to make the advance but still sued on the stipulation, then he could be rebutted by the defense of fraud.[26] But the burden of proof would be on the defendant, and he would have grave difficulty, especially if the fradulent lender had insisted on being given a written document acknowledging the indebtedness. This was the problem that the *exceptio non numeratae pecuniae* was meant to remedy. If the stipulator sued and the promisor put up this defense, the burden of proof was on the stipulator to show that he had actually given the money. I can see no influence of Greek law in this. Jolowicz and Nicholas relate this to the time when the *constitutio Antoniniana* had made all the free inhabitants of the Empire Roman citizens, and they claim: "Now that there was but one system of law for almost all of the inhabitants of the empire, there was a danger that the Greek view of documents as in themselves binding (abstract), and the *exceptio non numeratae pecuniae* was intended to counteract this danger."[27] This time there is no claim of influence of Greek law on the Roman development, which is purely original.

Thus, in the principate, too, borrowing from Greek law was minimal. I know of no instance where a jurist bolsters his opinion by saying "And this is also the law at X." Such an argument was outside the parameters of Roman juristic reasoning. But why was there such an absence of borrowing? Part of the answer is that borrowing usually occurs in the context of law reform. And in their writings the Roman jurists, as will emerge in subsequent chapters, were for the most part simply not interested in reform.

# 10 Conservatism and Absence of System

In chapter 7 I pointed to the extreme conceptualization of Roman law arising from the operations of the jurists and their relationship with the praetor's Edict. Now we have to consider an equally striking feature that seems at odds with this conceptualization, namely, the repeated failures to arrange legal rules and institutions in even a moderately systematic manner. There was an absence of system that at times came close to chaos. In large measure, this was due to conservatism, and though absence of system and conservatism are not the same it is convenient to treat them together at this point.

The *Twelve Tables*, as I have previously emphasized, were published around 451 B.C., and a monopoly of their interpretation was given to the College of Pontiffs. This interpretation is expressly termed *ius civile*, civil law, by Pomponius.[1] Around three and a half centuries later, long after the pontiffs had lost their monopoly, there occurred a significant event. The same Pomponius records: "After that group [i.e., of early jurists], Quintus Mucius, son of Publius, and *pontifex maximus*, was the first person to set out the *ius civile* by classes (*generatim*), by arranging it in eighteen books."[2] As well as being *pontifex maximus*, Quintus Mucius was consul in 95 B.C. The monopoly was gone, but at the beginning of the first century B.C., interpretation was still in the hands of the same aristocrats.

The structure of much of Quintus Mucius's *Ius Civile* can be restored,[3] and there are possibly surprising omissions. What does it contain? The answer is the interpretation of the *Twelve Tables*, of statutes that modified the *Twelve Tables*, and of limited matters even in the Edict where these could be attached by attraction to specific provisions of the *Twelve Tables*. Omitted are those parts of very early law that were not treated in the *Twelve Tables* (it will be remembered that the codification was not comprehensive and there had to be a particular reason for any clause being inserted), subsequent statutes that did not relate to matters dealt with in the *Twelve Tables,* and most of the edictal innovations.[4] This conception of civil law, especially as excluding much nonedictal law, can scarcely be rationally defended.

Quintus Mucius's approach entails internal oddities. Thus, *stipulatio,* the oldest Roman contract, is not discussed because it was not in the *Twelve Tables,* presumably because the law relating to it was already settled. But sale, *emptio venditio,* was dealt with, though that contract owed its entire existence to its forms of action being set out in a clause of the Edict, probably in the later third century B.C. Presumably it was brought in by attraction to *mancipatio,* the formal mode of transfer of ownership: at any rate its context in the *Ius Civile* is property law. Partnership, *societas,* another consensual contract, is discussed, presumably because it derived from the ancient *ercto non cito,* which was the joint ownership by the heirs of an inheritance until it was divided. But sale and partnership are not treated together in the same context as if there was a connection between them. The other two consensual contracts, hire, *locatio conductio,* and mandate, *mandatum,* are omitted, because there was nothing in the code to which they could be attached.

Quintus Mucius dealt with the *lex Aquilia* of about 287 B.C., which concerned damage to property including slaves because that statute replaced provisions of the *Twelve Tables* on injuries to slaves. He apparently did not deal with the *lex Cincia* of 204 B.C., which forbade gifts above a certain amount, or the slightly later *lex Plaetoria,* which dealt with fraud on a minor, because neither gifts nor minors were treated in the code. Again, he did not deal with the *lex Appuleia de sponsu* (after 241 B.C.) or the *lex Furia* (perhaps around 200 B.C.) or the *lex Cornelia* because they all concern personal guarantees that were created by *stipulatio,* and *stipulatio* was not regulated by the *Twelve Tables.* This last example brings out just how blinkered Quintus Mucius's approach was. He was closely following the *Twelve Tables.*[5] Yet long before his day the notion of *ius civile,* as distinct from praetorian law, was surely much wider. If it was not, then the durability of the narrow notion of *ius civile* is even more remarkable.

The important point, of course, is that Quintus Mucius did write the commentary. The narrow notion of *ius civile* does not appear after him, but his *Ius Civile* created its own tradition. About a century and a half after its appearance Sabinus wrote his famous commentary on the civil law. Not a single fragment of that has survived, but its arrangement can largely be reconstructed since Pomponius, Paul, and Ulpian all wrote extensive commentaries, "On Sabinus," and it emerges that Quintus Mucius's *Ius Civile* was the model for Sabinus and therefore for Pomponius, Paul, and Ulpian. Mucius omitted a treatment of hire and partnership, so did Sabinus, and therefore did Pomponius, Paul, and Ulpian. There is no indication that the real contracts were dealt with by Quintus Mucius, though loan for consumption (*mutuum*), which was actionable by the *condictio*, may well have been treated within the discussion of that action. Likewise there is no treatment of the other three, *depositum* (deposit), *commodatum* (loan for use), and *pignus* (pledge) by Sabinus, or by Pomponius, Paul, and Ulpian in their commentaries on Sabinus, or even by Gaius in his treatment of contracts in his *Institutes*.[6]

This treatise of Quintus Mucius highlights, and in part was responsible for, another aspect of legal conservatism: The treatise is restricted to civil law and does not deal with the provisions of the praetor's Edict. This may or may not have been a reasonable course for Quintus Mucius since we cannot tell the extent of the Edict in his day. It certainly contained edictal clauses and forms of action for situations where the praetor was making changes in the law, but what we do not know is whether it also contained model *formulae* for civil law remedies where the praetor had made no change in the law. These may have been assumed to be known.

But certainly in a time shortly after Quintus Mucius such civil law remedies were set out in the Edict. By that stage, then, in the words of Fritz Schulz: "The contents of the praetorian Edict can be summed up as constituting the praetor's programme of office: he is announcing to the public, at the beginning of his term, how he intends to exercise his office."[7] From the moment, whenever it was—maybe even from the outset—that the Edict contained *formulae* from the civil law where the praetor was not changing the law, there was in reality no difference between civil law and edictal law. There was only one system of courts: that of the praetors. There was no separate system of civil law courts. Where there was a difference between traditional civil law and edictal law, the latter prevailed. So in actuality there was only one system of law, that set out in the Edict and as it was interpreted by the jurists. There were large-scale commentaries "on the Edict" just as there were "on Sabinus." But this separation was unnecessary. Commentaries on the civil law should have been subsumed into the commentaries on the Edict. Though it is true that some subjects, such as marriage and paternal power, *patria potestas*, are not the subject of *formulae* in the Edict (since they would scarcely be directly the subject of an action), they were fit and proper subjects for a commentary on the Edict. Marriage law is vital, for instance, to the action for recovery of dowry, the *actio rei uxoriae*, because there could be no dowry without a valid marriage. *Patria potestas*, in its turn, is a matter of essential knowledge for understanding such edicts as those on intestate succession, and for the *actiones adiecticiae qualitatis*, actions against the *pater familias* for contracts made by persons in his power or ownership.

The continued division of major treatises into two separate kinds was confusing and unnecessary. But there is something more to the issue, which makes the continuance more unreasonable: in the commentaries it was impossible to keep civil law and praetorian law apart. For the commentaries on the Edict, all the civil law was relevant since, as I have said, model remedies were set out in the Edict. It is not surprising that in the *Digest* the main treatment of some fundamentally civil law institutions is taken from commentaries *ad Edictum*: for the *vindicatio*, Ulpian 16 *ad Edictum*; for the *condictio*, Ulpian 26, 22, and 17 *ad Edictum*; for the *lex Aquilia*, Ulpian 18 *ad Edictum*. The civil law commentaries, of course, did not need to treat the Edict in the same way; and, after all, they did not even treat all of civil law. But praetorian law could not be totally excluded. Even where a civil law remedy was left unchanged in the Edict, the praetor might at times have granted an ad hoc remedy on the facts where none was appropriate at civil law, or an analogous action. Such ad hoc reme-

dies, whether termed *actiones utiles* or *actiones in factum*, were then
treated in the civil law commentaries.

So far as we can tell, the earliest Roman work to combine civil
and edictal law was the elementary textbook the *Institutes* of Gaius,
which was written about A.D. 161.[8] Thus it was probably prepared later
than the writings of Pomponius but considerably earlier than those
of Ulpian and Paul. What makes the conservatism of Ulpian and Paul
in this regard truly remarkable is that each prepared a major commentary *ad Edictum* and another *ad Sabinum*, when the two works
rationally and systematically could have been combined. If the *Regulae* of Ulpian are really by that jurist, which has been doubted,[9] then
he knew the *Institutes* of Gaius on which the *Regulae* are modeled.

None of the above, though, should be taken to imply that the Edict
itself set out the actions in a systematic way. The arrangement of the
Edict can very largely be reconstructed from the *Digest*, in fact from
the fragments in it originating in the large commentaries of Ulpian
and Paul *ad Edictum*.[10]

The scheme was one that grew up gradually, especially in the last
two centuries of the Republic. Many clauses were put in place by the
power of attraction. Thus, the *actio Serviana*, which was given to the
pledge creditor for the recovery of pawned property, is found among
the interdicts as a result of attraction to the *interdictum Salvianum*,
which allowed a landowner to poind for unpaid rent the property that
the tenant had brought onto his land.[11] In contrast, the three major
delicts, damage to property (*damnum iniuria datum*), theft (*furtum*),
and assault and defamation (*iniuria*), are dealt with in widely separated parts of the Edict, even though *iniuria* was based on an edictal reform of provisions of the *Twelve Tables* and *damnum iniuria
datum* was a reform by statute (*lex Aquiilia*) of the same provisions.[12]
Theodor Mommsen sets out the order of the clauses and comments:
"Diese Ordnung oder Unordnung ist die des julianischen Edicts" (This
order or disorder is that of Julian's Edict).[13] Yes, indeed. The great
Julian was instructed by Hadrian (A.D. 117–38) to put the Edict in
permanent form, and the disorder that remained is the result. Julian
does not appear to have done much.[14] Yet by Justinian he is termed

"*edicti perpetui suptilissimus conditor*" (the very subtle framer of the perpetual Edict)[15] and by others he is praised for the arrangement of the Edict.[16] This laudation suggests a lack of understanding by the Romans and early Byzantines of the nature and value of system.

Moreover, to compound the confusion, the commentaries on the Edict of the great jurists Pomponius, Paul, and Ulpian follow the disordered lack of arrangement of the Edict. On one level this is understandable. Yet there is such a lack of system that the significant thing is that no improvement was sought. Of course, the above also entails that the overall arrangement of the *Digest* and *Code* is poor. This has long been known.[17]

This very sharp contrast in intellectual quality between the superbly high level of conceptualization and the low level of systematization demands an explanation. The first part of the explanation is prima facie obvious: the jurists were very interested in interpretation and equally uninterested in systematization.

But this explanation only demands further explanation. Why should that have been the case? The fundamental clue is that there is no praetor who is famous for the changes he made in his Edict. There were many praetors who became famous for various reasons, and some praetors were celebrated jurists: Appius Claudius Caecus; P. Sempronius Sophus; Ti. Coruncanius; Q. Mucius Scaevola (praetor, 215 B.C.); P. Aelius Paetus; Sex. Aelius Paetus Catus; M. Porcius Cato (Censorius); Q. Fabius Labeo; P. Mucius Scaevola (praetor, 179 B.C.); T. Manlius Torquatus; P. Cornelius Scipio Nasica Corculum; M'. Manilius; M. Junius Brutus; P. Mucius Scaevola (praetor, 136 B.C.); P. Licinius Crassus Mucianus; Q. Mucius Scaevola (consul, 117 B.C.); C. Marcius Figulus; P. Rutilius Rufus; C. Flavius Fimbria; Q. Mucius Scaevola (consul, 95 B.C.); L. Licinius Crassus; C. Aquilius Gallus; Ser. Sulpicius Rufus; P. Orbius; P. Alfenus Varus; to mention only those of the Republic.[18]

Quintus Mucius Scaevola, who was consul in 95 B.C. and therefore praetor before that, was the most famous jurist of the Republic, living, indeed, just when the development of the Edict was at its most active. As a jurist he was, as we saw, the first to arrange the civil law *generatim*.[19] As praetor he is not known for innovations. We do not know: either he was an innovative praetor or he was not. Either way the significance is the same. If he was innovative it is significant that he was not awarded fame for it. This would indicate that there was little interest in law reform and a praetor did not receive acclaim for it. If he was not innovative, then the important fact would be that the great jurist Quintus Mucius Scaevola was not interested in law reform.

Thus, the explanation we have been seeking is to be found in the fact that the Romans were not interested in systematizing the law, nor in law reform, nor in legal innovation as such. But they were interested in legal interpretation. And the historical reason for that takes us back almost to the beginning of this book, namely, the granting of a monopoly of interpreting the civil law to the College of Pontiffs, which resulted even later to prestige being generally awarded for giving legal opinions.

That is to say that the Romans who created law did so for prestige and not at all because they cared about law in the round. The point I want to make is not simply that an elite performs the public service it does for the reward of fame, but that in this instance the interest in law was limited to one aspect of the law job, and all others were neglected, because only that one aspect of law produced the appropriate prestige. It is truly astounding that Roman law developed to the point where it could be the source of much borrowing.

# 11 Conservatism and Tradition

The Romans have been the most innovative of all Western people in developing private law, yet from the promulgation of the *Twelve Tables* around 450 B.C. to the codification of Justinian there occurred no great event that changed the course of private law. The most important private-law statute, the *lex Aquilia,* does not qualify because its primary purpose was to modify the measurement of damages but not the substance of the law in the *Twelve Tables* on physical injury (including death) to slaves. The tool most used for innovation was the praetor's Edict, but the Edict was a matter of gentle accretion. There are no known great innovating praetors. The final redaction of the Edict under Julian resulted in no great change (see chapter 6). Nor is there a great reforming emperor. The closest is Augustus with his social legislation, but that was restricted to marriage and manumission.[1] Significantly there is no agreement among modern scholars as to the overall purpose of these laws. Nor do we find a jurist who greatly changed the course of legal development. Augustus's creation of the *ius respondendi* by jurists, whatever it was, did not mark a new beginning. The Valentinian Law of Citations of A.D. 426 simply gave the last four great jurists, plus the institutionalist Gaius, supreme authority when there had been no subsequent intervention by an emperor (see chapter 12). When around A.D. 235 the great jurists stopped writing books, this did not herald a speedy decline in standards. Classical jurisprudence did not die out about the middle of the third century, to be restored to some extent after the economic, social, political, and military catastrophes by Diocletian (284–305).[2] The rescripts of the intervening emperors show the continuance of high legal standards.[3] The move of the hub of Empire to Constantinople and the acceptance of Christianity as the state religion did not lead to quick and sweeping changes in such central matters as slave law and marriage.

Nor do the collections of imperial rescripts, so noted a feature of postclassical law, represent a break. By their writings, the classical jurists kept the people (who wanted to know) abreast of the law, including imperial pronouncements, and at least one, Papirius Iustus, produced a collection of rescripts.[4] When the jurists stopped producing books around A.D. 235, the need to know the latest rescripts led to the unofficial collections of them, the *Codex Gregorianus* probably of 291 and the *Codex Hermogenianus* of 295. The only official collection before Justinian was the *Codex Theodosianus* of 438, and this expressly followed the pattern of the unofficial codes.[5] It is quite typical of Roman legal thinking that Justinian's first reform project, which resulted in the *Codex* of 529, was nothing other than an updated collection of imperial rescripts.

The Roman approach was essentially atheoretical. Their greatest achievement was the high degree of conceptualization, but this was primarily the result of jurists working within the Roman court system to determine which action or remedy was appropriate. Borderline situations were much discussed. Even when the jurists discussed hypothetical, even unlikely situations, as they often did, this aim remained the same. With this narrow focus, the jurists were unconcerned with overall systematization, hence the poor arrangement of legal materials in general even as late as Justinian's *Digest*. But, having said that the jurists were essentially atheoretical, I must insist on their remoteness from practice and from actual happenings in court. Though we know from Cicero that the jurists occasionally appeared in the courts as orators, their reputations as jurists depended entirely on their work of interpretation. Hence we also find no trace in their writings of advice on dodges and devices intended to take advantage of procedural loopholes.

Law is fundamentally a conservative discipline. Innovative as the jurists were in developing individual concepts such as possession and the contract of sale, determining the requirements for the commission of a theft (*furtum*), establishing the scope of actions under the *lex Aquilia*, and so on, they yet failed to stand back to see the bigger picture. Thus, they never asked questions such as "Why must mandate be gratuitous?" (see chapter 8) or "Why do we, unlike the Greeks, have no general contract created by writing? Why do we not want one?" They did not set about creating a general theory of contract. They were, in fact, very much tethered to the legal tradition that they themselves created.

No better illustration of this exists than the work for which they are most famous, the development of contract law.

The immediate thrust of the next part of this chapter is to account for the recognition by the Roman state of the individual types of contract, such as deposit and sale; to show why they arose individually in the chronological order that they did; to indicate why the dividing lines between one contract and another are as they are; and to explain why other contracts, such as a general contract in writing, did not arise or, as in the case of barter, arose only late and with unsatisfactory rules. It is apparent that although economic or social reasons favored the introduction of each type, it was the legal tradition that determined the nature, structure, and chronology of every contract. The basic structure of Roman contract law then remained long after there was any societal justification for the divisions. It is enough here to give some major examples.[6]

It is often said that the Romans never developed a system of contract but only individual contracts,[7] and the attempt is sometimes made to explain in economic terms why each contract arose when it did. Such attempts are doomed to failure. No investigation into contracts one by one and separately can make sense in economic terms of the order of their appearance. For instance, deposit, which had to be gratuitous, appears in the fifth century B.C., loan for consumption—also only gratuitous—in the third century B.C. at the latest, but barter, insofar as it ever was a contract at all, had to wait at least another few hundred years; and all this while there was no contract of sale until about 200 B.C. Again, there was no specific contract for reward for looking after a thing, for reward in return for another's use of one's property, or for reward for one's services until the introduction of the contract of hire sometime close to 200 B.C. Even then there was only such a contract if the corresponding prestation was in coined money.

In these circumstances, the early dating, before 123 B.C.,[8] of the invention of a contract of mandate, where someone agreed to act gratuitously for another—and the essence of the contract was again specifically that the performance was to be gratuitous—seems unlikely if the need for the contract is to be explained on economic grounds.

The truth is more complicated, but if one is prepared to grant legal tradition an important role in legal development, then the unfolding growth of Roman contracts is straightforward and simple to explain. The starting point is that from very early times, even before the *Twelve Tables*, the Romans did have a method—the *stipulatio*, in fact—by which parties could agree to create any obligation that was not positively unlawful. If one dares to speak anachronistically, one can say that in very early times the Romans did have a general theory of contract, not a law of individual contracts. The question to be resolved, then, is how this general approach to contracts came to be lost. The clue to the development lies in a strange fact that needs an explanation: apart from the very special and complex case of partnership, all Roman contracts either have a money prestation or no prestation. In this latter category are two kinds of contract: they may either be gratuitous of necessity or they are unilateral (in which case they may in practice be matched with another contract). What does not exist, apart from that late and uncertain instance of barter, is a Roman contract where goods or services are proffered in return for goods or services. What is striking, moreover, is that in deciding which contract is involved, the touchstone is whether performance is necessarily (so far as the contract goes) for nothing or whether the performance is for money. For instance, the three distinct contracts of *depositum, commodatum* (loan for use), and *mandatum* all become hire (*locatio conductio*) if payment in money is promised. What is so significant about a prestation in coined money that a Roman contractual type must either contain it or be gratuitous? The solution to the problem of development, I submit, is that in most cases an individual type of Roman contract arose subsequent to *stipulatio* when, for whatever reason, a *stipulatio* was inappropriate or inefficient for that type of situation and when there was a societal need. Thus, almost every subsequent contractual type is a derogation from *stipulatio*. It should be noted that a legal remedy on an agreement is needed not in accordance with the frequency of important transactions but in accordance with the frequency of their going wrong.

The origins of the *stipulatio* (also known as the *sponsio*) are obscure and may have involved a libation or an oath, but they need not concern us now, nor should further conclusions be drawn from any hypothesis as to origins.[9] What matters is that the *stipulatio* was well developed before the time of the *Twelve Tables*, under which the contract was actionable by the form of process known as *legis actio per iudicis postulationem* (G.4.17a), the action of the law by requesting a judge. It was a formal, unilateral contract in which the promisee asked, "Do you promise [whatever it might be]?" necessarily using the verb *spondere*, and the promisor immediately replied "*Spondeo*" (I promise), using the same verb. Later, other verbs could be used, but *spondere* could only be used by Roman citizens. The content of the promise was judged only by the words used, and the contract would remain valid and effective even if the promise was induced by fraud, was extorted by fear, or proceeded on an error. *Stipulatio* could be used for any lawful purpose: to promise a dowry, make a sale (when mutual *stipulationes* would be needed), engage one's services,[10] and so on. But when an agreement was not cast in the form of a stipulation, then, no matter how serious the intentions of the parties and no matter how important the subject matter of the transaction, there was no contractual obligation and no right in any disappointed party to bring a contractual action.

*Stipulatio*, by skillful modernization, could have become the root of a flexible, unitary contractual system. Writing, perhaps incorporated into two documents, could have been adopted as an alternative to the oral question and answer, or agreement (however it was proved) could have become the basis of a contract; remedies for fraud, intimidation, or error could have been made inherent in the contract; and implied terms could have been developed for specific types of factual situations. Instead, a number of other individual contracts arose, each defined in terms of its function. This definition by function, and not by form, separates them sharply from stipulation. They might even appear to be lesser breeds, particular rather than general. Each of the contractual arrangements, however, whether loan for consumption or sale, could be cast in the form of one or more *stipulationes* and then would be that type of contract.

One early contract was *mutuum*, loan for consumption. *Mutuum* was provided with the rather strange action known as the *condictio*, which lay when the plaintiff claimed that the defendant owned a thing that he was legally bound to deliver to the plaintiff. Many scholars believe *mutuum* to be very old, with a prehistory before it came to be provided with the *condictio*, and if so, the general argument of this chapter is strengthened. But much that is peculiar about the *condictio* is explicable, as we shall see, if we link the introduction of that action with the creation of *mutuum* as a legal institution. The form of action, the *legis actio per condictionem*, was introduced by the *lex Silia* when what was claimed was a determinate sum of money, and by the *lex Calpurnia* when what was claimed was a definite thing (*G*.4.19). It is usually held that the *lex Silia* came first, on the basis that otherwise there would be no need for a law specifically covering money.[11] David Daube, as we shall see, adds a new dimension. In any event, whatever the priority of these two statutes may have been, the remedy of the *condictio* is old. As early as the composition of the *Rudens* by Plautus, who died in 184 B.C., the classical procedure by *formula* could be used for the *condictio* as could the archaic procedure by *legis actio*.[12] And there would be little point in setting up fresh *legis actiones* after *formulae* came into use.

The peculiarities of the *condictio* are that it was abstract in the sense that the plaintiff did not set out in the pleadings the grounds of his case; that it was general in that it could be brought any time a nonowner believed that the owner of money or of a certain thing was under a legal obligation to give it to him;[13] and that, apart from exceptional cases, there had to be a preceding delivery of the thing to the defendant by the plaintiff. Thus the *condictio* could be brought both where there was and where there was not a contract.[14] The generality coupled with the abstraction requires explanation, and the simplest explanation is that the *condictio* was originally envisaged for a concrete situation so obvious that it did not have to be expressly set out— and then was found to be extendable to others.[15] The most obvious concrete situation is *mutuum,* which in fact has always been treated as the primary use of the *condictio.* Loan for consumption would need to be given legal effectiveness when there was a breakdown in neighborly relations, when one friend failed to repay a loan; in an early agricultural community a loan of seed corn to be repaid after the harvest would be a common case. No stipulation would have been taken precisely because it is morally inappropriate for one friend performing an amicable service to demand a formal contract from another.[16] Where the loan was commercial, a stipulation would have been taken (to cover interest as well), and there would be no need for a specific contract of *mutuum.* We now see also why the action on *mutuum* was for the principal only and did not extend to interest: friends do not demand interest from friends.[17] The breakdown in neighborly relations might be related to an increase in Rome's size.

Another early specific type of contract, I believe, was deposit. The jurist Paul tells us: "On account of deposit an action is given by the *Twelve Tables* for double, by the praetor's Edict for single."[18] It has long been held—by me as well as by others—that the action for double under the *Twelve Tables* being penal was not necessarily based on any concept of contract and was closer to delict,[19] and the further suggestion is then sometimes made that the delict is akin to theft.[20] But what must be stressed at this point is the very restricted scope of the action. It lies, if we believe Paul, where a thing that was deposited was not returned. According to Paul's words, it does not lie, nor does any similar ancient action that we know of, where a thing that was hired out or lent for use was not returned, nor even, deposit being necessarily gratuitous, where a fee was to be paid for looking after the property. Moreover, apart from questions of contract, there seems little need for the action. The owner would have the normal action (of the time) claiming ownership, the *legis actio sacramento in rem,* and he would have the action for theft, at least if the depositee moved the thing (and it would be of little use to him if he did not). There seems little reason to single out this particular situation for a specific action based on the notion of delict.

What then would impel the desire for a specific action? Deposit differs from hire of a thing and loan for use, first, in that the object deposited is being taken out of circulation—no one can use it, and certainly not the depositee—and, second, in that it is precisely the recipient who is bestowing the favor. It follows that the depositor is in no position to demand that the recipient formally promise by contract to restore the thing: the depositor cannot reward the depositee for his good deed by showing doubts about his honesty. Again, the reason the depositor is willing to have his property out of circulation for a time is often that he finds himself in an emergency and cannot look after the property himself—as a result of earthquake, fire, collapse of a building, or shipwreck—and here too he is in no position to demand the formality of a stipulation from his helper. But the depositor is particularly vulnerable to fraud, and it is reasonable to give him a forceful remedy with penal damages. In the late Republic the praetor issued a complicated edict on deposit[21] whose main clauses gave an action for double damages against a depositee who failed to return property entrusted to him in what has come to be called *depositum miserabile*—deposit made as a result of earthquake, fire, collapse of a building, or shipwreck—and an action for simple damages in other cases. Arguments have been produced both for the proposition that the *Twelve Tables'* provision applied only to *depositum miserabile*[22] and also for the proposition that it applied to deposits of all kinds. The arguments seem inconclusive, though I tend to favor the second and more usual view; but in either eventuality the argument given here for an early specific action in fraud would fit. The strength of feeling that the depositor should have an action in the event of fraud would be intensified if, as seems likely, deposits were frequently made in temples or with priests.[23]

One of the great Roman inventions—it is now widely accepted that there were no foreign models[24]—is the consensual contract, a contract that is legally binding simply because of the parties' agreement and that requires no formalities for its formation. There were four of these, and it is generally presumed that the contract of sale, *emptio venditio*, was the earliest. It seems to have been fully actionable by around 200 B.C.[25] There have been numerous theories to explain the origins of consensual sale.[26] Some, such as the hypothesis that at one time the agreement became binding only if the buyer had given the seller an earnest of his payment of the price, or only if the seller had delivered to the buyer, are now seen to lack support from the sources. Other explanations, such as that of Theodor Mommsen, that state contracts (for example, the public sale of booty) provided the example or model,[27] are concerned with the issue of what gave the Romans the idea that agreements without formality might be actionable, but they provide no other insight into the transformation of private bargains into contracts of sale that, though made by private individuals, were enforced by the courts. There may be more than one root in the development of the consensual contract. But whatever economic or social pressures one wants to postulate, whether one says consensual sale was wanted because (as some think) of an expansion of foreign trade and the need for contracts that could be made at a distance, or because (as others hold) of a need for a formless contract to accommodate foreign merchants unfamiliar with Roman law formalities, or because (as still others argue) of a growing awareness of the worth of good faith in contract law for dealings with both Romans and foreigners,[28] the same conclusion holds: consensual sale as a separate contract arose in part because of the inadequacy of the *stipulatio* for the task. Of one thing there should be no doubt. Before the introduction of the consensual contract, parties to a sale-type transaction who wanted legal enforcement of their agreement made their arrangements in the form of stipulations,[29] and further development would not have occurred if this way of making arrangements had been satisfactory.

My own version of the origins of consensual sale and the connection with *stipulatio*[30] derives from the observation of two defects in the contract of sale that were there initially and continued to exist for centuries; namely, that the contract did not contain any inherent warranty of title or against eviction nor any inherent warranty against latent defects. Yet buyers did want the protection of warranties for such matters, as hundreds of texts on the actual taking of warranties by *stipulatio* show. And the notion of inherent warranties was not foreign to Roman lawyers, because they had already existed for centuries in the *mancipatio*, the formal method of transferring certain types of important property. The absence of inherent warranties would make the consensual contract far less valuable commercially. Whenever merchants wanted warranties—and the evidence shows that they often did—the parties had to be face-to-face to take a stipulation: hence the contract could not be made by letter or by messenger. Certainly one could send a dependent member of one's family to take or give the stipulation, but that in itself would often be inconvenient and expensive.[31] The centuries-long absence of inherent warranties, the strong Roman desire for warranties, and their knowledge that warranties could be implied demand an explanation that I believe can be found only if we postulate an origin for the contract where the deficiencies were not so obvious.[32]

If we go back beyond the origin of sale, the parties to a sale-like arrangement who wished a legally binding agreement would, as I have said, conclude their business by stipulations. They had no alternative. All terms, given the nature of *stipulatio*, would have to be spelled out. The buyer would promise payment on a fixed date, with interest if he delayed. The seller would promise that he would deliver the thing on a fixed day, that he would pay a penalty if he delayed, that the buyer would not be evicted from the thing, and that the thing was free from hidden defects. Each *stipulatio* was unilateral, but the parties would want their rights and duties to be reciprocal: hence the obligation to fulfill each *stipulatio* would have to be made conditional upon the fulfillment, or the readiness to fulfill, of the other. To make matters worse, this conditional reciprocity would have to be framed so as to take account of a partial but not complete failure to perform. For instance, if a sold slave was found to be suffering from some relatively unimportant defect, the buyer might want to keep the slave but pay only a reduced price. The drafting and taking of the stipulations would be extremely cumbrous and complex, and often it would happen that the parties' intentions would be frustrated. So far we are on sure ground. What follows is a conjectural, but I think plausible, account of how the praetor, the magistrate in charge of the law courts, dealt with the problem. At some point a praetor accepted that he ought to grant an action in accordance with good faith to cover accidental interstices in stipulations concerned with a sale.[33] Above all he would seek to make the obligations reciprocal. In accordance with the Roman tendency to see law in terms of blocks (see chapter 13), the strict-law *stipulatio* and the new action based on good faith would be kept separate. But the position would be reached that provided there was a sale-type situation and at least one *stipulatio*, there would be an action to give the buyer or the seller an action against the other for an amount equal to what ought to be given or done in accordance with good faith.

The separate contract of sale was in the process of being born. But what would be the content of the necessary stipulation? In the simplest possible sale-type transaction there would be, immediately upon agreement, a handing over of the money and a handing over of the thing. The stipulation wanted would cover only continuing obligations, and they would be only of the seller and would consist only of a warranty against eviction and latent defects. We know from the republican writer Varro[34] that these warranties were contained in a single stipulation. Eventually, an action on *emptio venditio* would be given even when no stipulation was taken, but because of the way the contract emerged, the action long provided no remedy if the buyer suffered eviction or the object contained hidden defects, so long as the seller acted in good faith. Heavy stress was placed on good faith in *emptio venditio* whether as a result of the way the contract emerged or, as many think, as part of the pressure for recognizing the contract. This suggested development has one further feature that renders it plausible: It avoids any sudden leap forward in legal thinking; it is bedded firmly on how parties to a sale-type transaction would conduct their business and the gradual response of those in charge of lawmaking to the problems that arose.[35]

A second consensual contract, hire (*locatio conductio*), has more obscure origins, but the usual assumptions are that its beginnings are closely connected with those of sale and that sale was the more important case; either the example of sale was followed for hire, which is thus a later contract, or the impetus for recognizing a contract of sale impelled also, and simultaneously, the recognition of the less significant *locatio conductio*. The need to attach legal importance to good faith in contracts would, for instance, be one joint impelling factor.[36] If one grants priority to sale, whether in time or legal importance, then one fact emerges unequivocally for hire, though strangely it appears never to have been noticed either by Romans or by later scholars. *Locatio conductio* is a residual category for all types of bilateral agreements that are not sale and where the prestation of one of the parties has to be in money. This and this alone can account for the peculiarity that at least three very different contractual situations are included within it: the use of a thing for a time in return for money, providing one's labor for a time in return for money, and the assignment of a specific task to be performed in return for money. In each of these situations the obligations of the party who is acting in return for money are very different. Any doubts that *locatio conductio* is a residual category must disappear when one notices that in the corresponding situations where no money is to change hands, this one contract is replaced by three: mandate, deposit, and loan for use.[37] It is in the highest degree illuminating for the force of legal tradition in legal development that such a figure as *locatio conductio* came into being, remained unchanged in its scope throughout the Roman period, and still flourishes in countries such as France, Chile, and Argentina as one contract.

As a further indication that one need not, even within the Western tradition, draw the line between one type of contract and another exactly as it is usually drawn, it is worth observing that in the second century B.C. at Rome, an agreement to allow another to pasture his flock on one's land for the winter in return for a money payment was regarded as sale of the fodder.[38] Classical Roman and modern law would treat the agreement as hire. The republican position was perfectly sensible and would have remained so in classical law, given the fact that sale did not involve a requirement to transfer ownership but only to give quiet possession—in this case for the duration of the agreement. The standard warranties in sale against eviction and hidden defects would have been perfectly appropriate.

A third consensual contract, mandate (*mandatum*), was in existence by 123 B.C.[39] and is different in its raison d'être from the two just examined. Mandate is the agreement to perform gratuitously a service for another. It is thus not a commercial contract but an agreement among friends. It is thus again precisely the type of situation where a stipulation could not be demanded, either from the friend who was asked to perform the service or by the friend for repayment of his expenses. That the contract came into existence at all is a tribute to the great weight the Romans placed upon friendship: friends were expected to do a great deal for one another. It may seem surprising that such a distinction is made between agreeing to act gratuitously for another and acting for reward, but the Roman attitude that found labor degrading is probably a sufficient explanation. It is that, at least, that led to the view that performance of *artes liberales* could not be the subject of *locatio conductio*.[40]

A similar explanation can account for the emergence of *commodatum*, a gratuitous loan for use, as a separate contract, probably around the beginning of the first century B.C.:[41] a friend who lends gratuitously to a friend cannot demand a formal promise for return. The same holds for the remodeled obligation of deposit probably around the same date.

Only one further standard Roman contract, *societas* (partnership), will be dealt with, and its origins and growth are unique. The oldest Roman partnership, *ercto non cito*, is very old and came into being when a head of family died and his estate went to his *sui heredes*,[42] that is, persons who were subject to his paternal power and on his death came to be free of any power. They were immediately partners in the inheritance and remained so until the inheritance was divided. Since in early Rome persons in the power of another owned no property, the *sui heredes* had nothing until the inheritance came their way; hence *ercto non cito* is a partnership of all the property of the partners. This is not a contractual partnership, but persons who wished to set up such a partnership were later allowed to do so before the praetor by means of a *legis actio*, the archaic form of process.[43] Eventually the praetor gave an action on a consensual contract of partnership, perhaps around the time when he created the consensual contracts of sale and hire. But this consensual contract of partnership was modeled on the old *ercto non cito*: significantly, the praetor set out in his edict only one *formula*, a model form of action, and that was for a partnership of all of the assets of the partners. Hence the primary type of consensual partnership was not a commercial arrangement between merchants—they would want a much more restricted partnership—but between close relatives and friends, probably wishing to engage in a communal agricultural enterprise.[44] Rome had long been commercially active; a business partnership would clearly have been economically useful, but because of legal history and legal tradition the primary instance of consensual partnership was not mercantile. Whether from the outset, as certainly later, there could also be partnerships of a restricted kind cannot be determined.

This origin of partnership in succession, and not in business, accounts for a significant peculiarity in consensual partnership. A Roman heir was liable for the debts of the deceased, even if they exceeded the assets. Coheirs would be liable for debts in the same proportion as they inherited. Hence the jurist and pontiff Quintus Mucius Scaevola claimed that it was contrary to the nature of partnership that it be so set up that one partner was to take a greater share of any eventual profit than he would take of any eventual loss.[45] Mucius's view was expressly based on the nature of partnership as he saw it, not on fairness. Though Servius Sulpicius broke away from this approach and successfully argued that such a partnership, and even one where one partner was entitled to share in the profit but not in any loss, was valid because that could be a fair arrangement if his services were valuable, yet Sabinus and Ulpian held that such an arrangement was valid only if in fact it was fair.[46] This is the sole instance in classical Roman law where a voluntary contractual arrangement entered into without error, coercion, or fraud was valid only if there was an equivalence of contribution and reward.[47] It owes its existence entirely to the internal logic of the legal tradition, and not at all to economic, social, or political pressures. It is this same legal logic and the piecemeal development of Roman contracts, and not societal forces, that prevented the necessity for equivalence from spreading to the other bilateral contracts or from being extinguished for partnership.

The force of this internal legal logic is apparent in another failure in development. The contracts of deposit, loan for use, and mandate grew up one by one, but once they were all in existence there was no reason for not subsuming deposit and loan for use under mandate, except that they were in fact thought of as separate institutions. It was no obstacle that deposit and *commodatum* required delivery of the thing for the creation of the contract. The practical effect of the law would be unchanged if these contracts were incorporated into mandate; so long as nothing had been done on a mandate, either party was free to revoke or renounce unilaterally.[48] There might even be doubt at times, as Pomponius discovered, over whether a particular arrangement was mandate or deposit.

But the impact on legal development of the lawyers' ways of looking at problems is even clearer when we look at contracts that did not develop or developed only partially or developed late. To begin with, it is prima facie astonishing that the Romans never developed a written contract that would take its place by the side of *stipulatio* as a second contract defined by form, not by function. Such a contract would obviously have been very useful, above all for situations where the *stipulatio* would have been the obvious contract except that the parties could not easily be present together: these situations would include sales where warranties against eviction or latent defects were wanted. Again, a contract whose validity depended on the existence of writing would usually be easy to prove. In fact, other contracts, including *stipulatio*, were often reduced to writing partly in order to provide proof[49] and partly to ensure that the terms were not forgotten. Nor can the Romans have been unaware of the possibility of the usefulness of written contracts; they had been standard even in classical Athens.[50] And the jurist Gaius in the second century A.D. was well aware of the existence of Greek written contracts and of the contrast between them and the Roman literal contract.[51] The absence of such a contract demands an explanation, and it cannot be either economic or social. The most plausible explanation, I suggest, is that originally stipulation was the only contract, at a time when writing was not widespread. The habit of looking at *stipulatio* as *the* contract was so ingrained that other contracts arose as exceptions to or derogations from it only when *stipulatio* was obviously inappropriate. The idea of creating a new type of contract defined by form, which would be used in all situations where *stipulatio* could be used and in other situations where it could not, just did not occur to the Roman lawyers.

It is equally astonishing that no contract of barter developed until the Empire at the earliest. Until the introduction of coined money around 275 B.C.,[52] a barter-type situation, often where one party was to give an amount of uncoined metal, must have been the most common type of commercial transaction. Even afterward barter would be a frequent transaction. Yet barter, *permutatio,* as a legal institution came centuries later than the contract of sale, and it was never fully accepted into the Roman system of contracts.[53] As a contract it was unsatisfactory: it required for its formation delivery by one party, and an action for nonperformance lay only for the value of the delivered goods. Contrast this with the contract of sale, which required only the agreement of the parties, and where the action lay for a sum of money equal to what the defendant ought to give or do in accordance with good faith. Nor can one say that the all-purpose *stipulatio* made a contract of barter unnecessary, since the *stipulatio* required an oral question and answer and hence required the contracting parties to be face-to-face. The only way two merchants in different places could make an agreement for a barter situation was for one of them to send to the other, often at considerable expense and inconvenience, a dependent member of his family, such as a son or a slave, to take delivery or engage in mutual *stipulationes.* To say that Roman merchants did not engage much in barter is to forget that the introduction of coined money into Rome came relatively late; and to say that the Roman merchants would not find the law relating to barter inconvenient is to render inexplicable the introduction of such a splendid contract as sale.

The individual Roman contracts emerged, certainly because of societal needs, at a pace and with characteristics dictated by legal reasoning. Nothing illustrates this more clearly than the dispute already discussed between the Sabinian and the Proculian schools of jurists as to whether the price in a contract of sale could consist of a thing other than coined money.[54] Law was being treated as if it were an end in itself. This makes evident the extent of legal blindness. Apart from instances where it was morally impossible to demand a stipulation, the only derogations from *stipulatio* that were allowed to create a contract were those that involved an obligation to pay money: sale and the residual category of hire. It took even sale a very long time to break loose from the shackles of *stipulatio.*

Perhaps as early as the first century A.D., the Roman jurists began to devise remedies to plug gaps in the contractual system;[55] the remedy for barter seems to have been one of them. The jurist Paul in the second or third century A.D. eventually stated that an action would be given on any agreement of the following types provided the plaintiff had performed his side of the bargain: "I give to you in order that you give, I give in order that you do, I do in order that you give, I do in order that you do."[56] Thereafter, any agreement containing bilateral obligations that was followed by performance by one party gave rise to an action. It is sometimes said that this was a step toward a general theory of contract. This seems incorrect. Each individual type of contract remained, each with its own major quirks. There was still no general contract law.

Finally, we should return to the oldest contract, *stipulatio,* which despite its long history never developed to its proper extent for reasons to be associated with the legal tradition. It is perhaps to be expected that a very early contract is rigid, that the promisor is bound by what he says, and that the reason for his promise—even error, fraud, or intimidation—is irrelevant. But once it came to be accepted, especially for the consensual contracts, that the obligations could be based on good faith, then only lawyerly conservatism and tradition would keep *stipulatio* a contract of strict law. There are societal advantages for the law to take good faith into account for contracts, and there is no social class of cheats. But no remedy was provided with regard to *stipulatio* for extortion or fraud until the first century B.C. Remedies for extortion were introduced by a praetor named Octavius around 80 B.C. and for fraud by Aquilius Gallus apparently in 66 B.C.[57] What concerns us are the special defenses, *exceptiones,* of extortion or fraud, which could be raised when an action was brought on a *stipulatio.* The point of an *exceptio* is precisely that the defendant is not denying the validity of the plaintiff's case. He is merely claiming that there is another fact that ought to be taken into account. In other words, extortion or fraud did not invalidate a *stipulatio.* It remained valid, but its effects could be negatived by the use of the defense. *Stipulatio* always remained at this primitive level. Nor should it be thought that the distinction between invalidity and blocking by an *exceptio* is insignificant: if the defendant failed to plead the *exceptio* expressly at the appropriate time, he could not plead it later and would lose his case if he tried. No explanation for retaining a stipulation as valid but rendering it ineffective is satisfactory other than that of lawyers' ideas of what is appropriate in law.

The main thrust of this part of the chapter has been that it was Roman legal thinking, based on a tradition rooted in *stipulatio* as the original contract, that above all dictated the origins and nature of Roman contracts.[58] Though *societas* did not develop as a derogation from *stipulatio*, the mature contract, in its origins and nature and also in a unique and important rule, equally demonstrates the enormous role of the legal tradition in legal evolution. None of this, of course, excludes the influence of economic forces or of the politics of power. But this input of forces outside the legal tradition did not have a commensurate outcome. Nothing illustrates this more clearly than the relatively early actionability of contracts of *depositum, commodatum,* and *pignus,* on the one hand, and the late appearance and continuing unsatisfactory state of *permutatio,* on the other. It is not just that the first three, individually and collectively, were of much lesser commercial importance than barter; it is also that they were scarcely needed in view of existing actions in property and delict, whereas attempts to engage with legal protection in barter at a distance were fraught with inconvenience and expense. And it is surely hard to believe that the Roman merchants and others who engaged in barter had less political clout than the persons who deposited their property or lent it or used it as security for a loan.

The approach, blinkered by tradition, was of course not restricted to contract law. Examples abound. Thus, an important issue in all legal systems is to what extent, in what ways, and with what remedies may an owner of land be restrained by his neighbor from using his land in a way that is otherwise lawful in order to avoid causing a financial loss or reducing a financial benefit to his neighbor, as a result of diminishing or increasing the flow of water to the neighbor's land. The problem is that almost any agricultural, domestic, commercial, or industrial use of water by one landowner will have an impact on other landowners. The *Twelve Tables* contained one provision (in Table 7.8c) with the wording "*si aqua pluvia nocet*" (if rainwater does damage). Under the Edict, the remedy was given only if the flow to the neighbor's land was increased as the result of human labor. The remedy was the restitution of the status quo ante, and damages were allowed only for loss that arose after the action was brought.[59] The *Twelve Tables* provided no remedy for the possibly even more damaging situation where the result of human labor was the diminution of a supply of water to a neighbor, and the action under the Edict did not apply to this case. This position remained unchanged even in the time of Justinian. Similarly, the law developed no compromise position to regulate competing claims for too much or too little water.[60]

The same conservatism is to be found in the frequent absence of reform when the existing law was clearly unsatisfactory. An example from theft, *furtum*, is set out at the beginning of chapter 8. A simple alteration in the calculation by imperial fiat would have solved many problems. Again, the jurists concentrated their interest—a further case of juristic isolationism—on *iudicia legitima*. Gaius describes actions as either *imperio continentia*, dependent on the *imperium* (authority of the magistrate), or *iudicia legitima*, statutable judgments.[61] He defines the latter: "Actions are statutable which take place at Rome or within the first milestone of the city, between parties who are all Roman citizens and before a single judge."[62] The distinction did not depend on other characteristics of the action; a praetorian ad hoc *actio in factum* was a *iudicium legitimum* if it had these features, an action on sale was not if anything was lacking. We need not consider here the history of the distinction;[63] what matters is that with the expansion of Rome there ceased to be any point to it but it nevertheless continued throughout classical law, and that the classification of an action had important consequences. Thus, a *iudicium imperio continens*, because it rested on the magistrate's *imperium*, ended when he demitted office: there was no termination date for a *iudicium legitimum* until the *lex Iulia iudiciaria* provided that it had to be completed within eighteen months of *litis contestatio*. Again, the *adiudicatio* in a divisory action gave full civil law ownership if the action was a *iudicium legitimum*, but otherwise it gave only bonitary ownership.[64] (In the three divisory actions, *actio familiae erciscundae*, the action for dividing an inheritance, the *actio communi dividundo*, action for dividing common property, and *actio finium regundorum*, action for regulating boundaries, the judge after giving judgment had to go a further step and determine in an *adiudicatio* how the property had to be divided.) The result in the *iudicium imperio continens* is bizarre, especially when the property had previously been held in civil law ownership and all the parties were citizens. Further, a woman needed the authority of her *tutor* in order to be a party to a *iudicium legitimum*;[65] and in such an action between a *tutor* and his ward, a *tutor praetorius* (a praetorian tutor) had to be appointed.[66] A final important difference to be mentioned is that if a party to a *iudicium legitimum* underwent *capitis deminutio*, the action was lost, to the benefit of the other party.[67]

Such examples can be multiplied, but it will be enough here to discuss one more, the *lex Aquilia*, the primary authority on damage to property, and we need only consider chapter 1. The statute was passed in its final form around 287 B.C., but chapter 1 must be earlier. It provided that "Whoever wrongfully killed another's male or female slave or four-footed beast of the kind called *pecus* let him be ordered to pay to the owner whatever was the highest value in the past year."[68] Various problems became apparent.

The first problem was that the action was restricted to the owner, but it came to be recognized that others, such as the possessor in good faith, usufructuary, and the pledge creditor, had an interest in the slave or animal worthy of protection. The solution came to be that the praetor gave such persons an ad hoc remedy, termed *actio utilis* or *actio in factum*. This approach might have been reasonably satisfactory in general practice, but there are at least two clear difficulties. In Roman actions there was a decisive moment at an early stage of the proceedings, called *litis contestatio*. If, after that stage, the plaintiff withdrew or lost his case, he was not allowed to bring a further action on the same facts. Thus, if a plaintiff sued as owner for the killing of his slave, and after *litis contestatio* it emerged that he was not owner but only a possessor in good faith (who believed he was owner), he lost his *actio legis Aquiliae*; and because he had already sued as owner he was barred from suing again by an *actio in factum* as a bona fide possessor. A further problem was that there might be two persons with a right to some remedy on account of a wrongfully killed slave. One person might have a usufruct and another be the owner. Depending on their respective ages, the usufructuary might well have by far the more valuable right. The usufructuary would have a praetorian ad hoc remedy, the owner the *actio legis Aquiliae*. But the *actio legis Aquiliae* lay to the owner not for a sum calculated on his interest in the slave, but for the highest value the slave had had in the past year, so he might recover many times his interest. A cautious person would be well advised to stay far from a slave in whom more than one person had a real right.

Closely related to this last issue was another obvious defect in the statute. As I have stated, the owner's *actio legis Aquiliae* lay for the highest value the slave had had in the past year. Probably the reason for this was a seasonal fluctuation in the value of agricultural slaves: an owner was not to suffer loss because he had to buy a replacement at spring planting time for a slave killed in early winter. But the approach had known and obvious problems. Suppose an artist slave lost his thumb by someone's carelessness, and the owner recovered substantial damages under chapter 3 of the *lex Aquilia*, and another person negligently killed the slave within a year. The owner could now recover in the action on chapter 1 the highest value of the slave in the past year, even if the slave had come to be worth less than 1 percent of his previous value and even though the owner had already received full compensation for the earlier damage.

A further defect in chapter 1 was that the jurists came to draw a distinction in the wording of the statute between "killing," *occidere,* and "furnishing a cause of death," *mortis causam praestare.* The reason for the distinction is not known. A common suggestion that it relates to the Roman view of causation[69] may be discounted since a similar distinction is not made with regard to murder in the *lex Cornelia de sicariis et veneficiis,* the Cornelian law on assassins and poisoners, of 81 B.C. The distinction appears to have been made at the end of the

Republic or beginning of the Empire, probably with the intention of narrowing the scope of the *actio legis Aquiliae;* for *mortis causam praestare* an ad hoc remedy was given.[70] Fine lines were drawn. For Labeo, it was killing if a midwife administered with her own hands a drug to a woman from which she died, but it was furnishing a cause of death if she gave the substance to the woman for her to take for herself.[71] If a man pushed another who fell onto a slave who died, the first is not liable to an *actio legis Aquiliae* because he did not kill, nor is the second, who did nothing unlawfully. The first was liable to an *actio in factum.*[72] To lock up someone's slave or herd animal so that he or she died of starvation was not to kill but only to furnish a cause of death.[73] Some situations gave rise to disputes. For Celsus it amounted to killing to thrust someone off a bridge into a river so that he died, whether he died from the impact or was drowned after being exhausted by the current.[74] But Gaius saw this as an instance of furnishing a cause of death though he does add, "although it is not difficult to recognize here that he caused the loss by his own body inasmuch as he thrust him in."[75]

Similar problems existed for chapter 3 of the statute. Indeed, the jurists had difficulty in understanding the wording relating to damages.[76] What is in issue is, of course, simply that despite all defects the *lex Aquilia* was never replaced by better legislation or rescript.

# *12* A Central Indefiniteness

In previous chapters I have stressed the high degree of conceptualization and the small extent of systematization in Roman law. These two characteristics do not present a paradox. The conceptualization was the result of the jurists working within the Roman system of actions: the boundaries of an institution had to be delineated so that it could be known whether an action (or other remedy), and which action, would lie. This was very much within the scope of the jurists' primary interest, interpretation. A need for systematization did not force itself upon the jurists' attention and, because of past history, there was no prestige in systematizing. A third characteristic is somehow related to these two: at the heart of the system is a certain indefiniteness, almost an unwillingness to be precise about legal growth and change.[1]

A first manifestation of this is an unwillingness to proffer definitions, even an aversion to it. The famous account is Javolenus's: "Every definition in civil law is dangerous; for it is rare that it may not be overthrown."[2] This seems an accurate statement of the jurists' viewpoint, and definitions are rare. Many texts examine the boundaries between sale and hire, and between sale and barter, but none defines sale, hire, or barter.

A true juristic definition, however, is that of *tutela*, guardianship:

D.26.1.1pr (Paul, *On the Edict*, book 30): Guardianship is, as Servius defines it, a force [*vis*] and power [*potestas*] over a free person given and permitted by the civil law, for the protection of one who, on account of his age, cannot protect himself of his own accord.[3]

It is remarkably unhelpful: We do not know the difference between force (*vis*) and power (*potestas*); the phrase *vis et potestas* appears in other contexts but does not seem to be technical; the extent of this authority is not set out in the definition; and, above all, the powers and duties of the guardian related to the property of the ward and not directly to his or her person.[4] *Potestas* here has none of the force of *patriapotestas*.[5]

We should also regard as an attempt at definition Quintus Mucius's account of *penus* (stores).

> Aulus Gellius, *Noctes Atticae*, 4.1.17: For I hear that Quintus Mucius used these words to explain *penus*: "*Penus*," he said, "is what is to be eaten or drunk, which was prepared for the use of the father of the family himself, or the mother of the family, or of the children of the father, or of the household which he has around him or his children, and which is not engaged in work[6]   as Mucius said, ought to be regarded as *penus*. For what is prepared for eating and drinking day by day for lunch or dinner are not *penus*; but rather those things which are collected and stored for use during a long period are called *penus* because they are not ready at hand, but are kept in the innermost part of the house (*penitus*).

Frequently a legacy was left of *penus*, stores, so it was important to determine what was included in the definition. That this is one of the few surviving definitions by a republican jurist is striking for a number of reasons. First, it is not a definition of a legal institution or even of a technical term. Rather, it is an attempt to define the objects that would be contained within a generic term. The purpose of the definition is certainly legal—to establish what is within the scope of the legacy—but *penus* is no more a technical legal notion than is *supellex*, furniture.[7] Second, the reason for the definition is identical with that which drove the jurists toward conceptualization. Just as one had to discover the exact boundaries of sale and hire to know which action was available, so one had to discover the boundaries of *penus* to know what was contained in the legacy. There is no abstraction here for theoretical purposes. Thirdly, it is not an analytical definition but a definition by enumeration, a listing of what is contained within the term.[8] Mucius also uses etymology to explain the scope of *penus*.[9]

(Incidentally, the legacy of *penus* would have been a very fit subject for chapter 5 on legal isolationism, on the exclusion of nonlegal circumstances. Legacies of *penus* were common. But why? Why should stored food and drink be an appropriate object for a specific legacy? There seems to have been an original connection between *penus* and *di penates*, the household gods. Indeed, the name *penates* signifies the deities who live in and rule over the storeroom.[10] It is thus plausible to suggest, as Ormanni has,[11] that the original purpose of the legacy was to enable the legatee to carry out the family religious rites without personal expense. But of this religious background to the legacy there is no expression in the numerous texts.)

A second manifestation of imprecision at the center concerns the sources of the law. Gaius writes:

> G.1.5: An imperial constitution is what the emperor ordains by decree or edict or letter. It has never been doubted that this has the force of statute since the emperor himself receives his sovereign power by statute.

Again, from Ulpian:

> D.1.4.1pr (*Institutes*, book 1): A decision given by the emperor has the force of a statute: This is because by the royal statute that is passed concerning his authority the people commit to and into him its own entire authority and power. 1. Whatever therefore the emperor has determined by a letter and his signature, or has decreed on judicial determination or has pronounced on an interlocutory matter or has prescribed by an edict is undoubtedly a law. These are what we commonly call *constitutiones*.

A decision of the emperor has the force of statute. But how has this come about, and what is its theoretical basis? Because a person receives his power by statute, it does not follow that he has lawmaking powers. Again, Gaius's claim that it was never doubted that the emperor could make law is rather surprising since Augustus had been offered such power and had refused.[12] As for Ulpian we have one *sena-tus consultum* conferring power upon an emperor, Vespasian, and that does not, as it stands, confer lawmaking powers.[13] The powers just came into being, without legal intervention but no doubt because of personal authority and military might, and they were accepted. But the powers were not examined, with the consequence that rules did not really exist for determining when a writing of an emperor was to have lawmaking force, and to what extent. The powers and their application might even be questioned by an emperor. It is recorded of the emperor Opilius Macrinus (217–18):

> In law he was not without astuteness: to such an extent that he laid down that all the rescripts of the old emperors were to be abolished so that decisions would be given on the basis of law, not rescripts. He said it was wrong that the wishes of Commodus and Caracalla and men lacking in skill be laws when Trajan never gave replies by letter lest decisions which seemed to be given on account of favor be extended to other actions.[14]

No doubt, there was a general reluctance to discuss the emperor's powers since to discuss might appear to question. But that does not explain why the jurists do not discuss their own powers to make law.

We have already examined the jurists' lawmaking powers. Apart from the monopoly of interpretation given to the College of Pontiffs it rested on no state authority. Twice during the empire it was bolstered by state intervention, by the *ius respondendi* (the right to give replies) and the Law of Citations. For the former we have two basic texts:

> *D.*1.2.2.49 (Pomponius, *Manual*, sole book): It may be observed in passing that before the time of Augustus the right of deliver-ing replies publicly was not granted by leaders of the state, but persons who had confidence in their own learning gave replies to those who consulted them. Nor did they always give their replies under seal, but often they themselves wrote to the judges, or had those who consulted them testify as to their opinion. The deified Augustus was the first to lay down, in order to give greater authority to the law, that they might give replies on

his authority. And from that time this began to be sought as a favor. Therefore, the excellent emperor Hadrian, when men of praetorian rank sought from him that they might be permitted to give replies, wrote back to them that this was not usually asked for but was simply performed and, therefore, he would be delighted if anyone had faith in himself that he prepare himself for giving replies to the people.

The second text comes from Gaius's account of the sources of law:

G.1.7: The replies of the jurists are the propositions and opinions of those to whom it is permitted to build up the law. If the propositions of all of them agree, what they so hold has the force of law. But if they disagree, the judge is permitted to follow whichever opinion he wishes. This is declared by a rescript of the deified Hadrian.

The translation of these texts may be open to doubt, and their general lack of precision has created much dispute as to the meaning of the *ius respondendi*.[15] It does, however, appear from the text of Pomponius that Augustus gave selected jurists the right to utter *responsa* under his authority and seal. Since Augustus was careful not to give himself legislative powers, it seems unlikely that he declared these *responsa* legally binding, but in practice they would be very highly persuasive. Nor can we tell whether this *ius publice respondendi* involved giving *responsa* to a judge nor whether all jurists with the right had to be consulted. The reason for the right, according to Pomponius, was to give greater authority to the law, and it would indeed make the opinions of the chosen jurists more authoritative. In addition, the skillful granting of the right could bring legal developments by juristic opinion much more under the control of the emperor. Greater precision is not possible for the period, partly because of some confusion in the surrounding fragments of Pomponius. *H.t.* 2.48 seems to say that Sabinus was an *eques* (a knight) and was the first to give *responsa* publicly, and this advantage, once it came to be granted, was given him by Tiberius; and *h.t.* 2.50 repeats that Sabinus was given the right by Tiberius to issue *responsa*. Perhaps the texts mean not that Sabinus was the first jurist to be given the *ius respondendi* but that he was the first *eques* to be so privileged; after all it would be surprising if Augustus had not named anyone after creating the *ius*. If this view is correct, then we have additional point to Pomponius's claim that Augustus's intention was to increase the authority of the law; after a century of legal domination by *equites* and the confusion of long years of civil war, legal authority was to be returned to senatorial jurists.

Hadrian's reform is not clear. Pomponius's account is taken from his one volume of Roman legal history, and it is reasonable to treat his statement as referring to something significant rather than to an isolated episode that had no further consequences. It is also reasonable to hold that he and Gaius are concerned with the same rescript. I believe the most obvious interpretation, then, is that Hadrian was simply refusing to make anyone a grant of *ius respondendi*. The *ius* in effect was abolished, with a consequence like that set out in *G.1.7*. Only when all influential jurists were agreed was a judge actually bound because only then was the law settled. It may be relevant here that under Hadrian the *concilium principis* (the emperor's council) became a standing organ of state with permanent salaried members, including a number of leading jurists, and imperial rescripts became a major source of law.[16] Other interpretations of Hadrian's activity do exist, but the main significance of the ambiguity here is surely that it reveals how unimportant the *ius respondendi* was. The need to be more specific was not felt. Indeed, Sabinus is the only jurist whom we know did have the *ius respondendi*. If Hadrian's reform had made the *ius respondendi* more important, then the grant of the right would mark a decisive step in a jurist's career—just as decisive, though not similar to, receiving a doctorate at a German university or "taking silk" at the English bar—and we would surely expect the event to be recorded for some jurists.[17] A further argument from silence may possibly have some validity. Suetonius, the biographer of the Roman emperors, takes a particular interest in and frequently mentions legal changes for which an emperor was responsible. Yet he does not mention Augustus's introduction of the *ius respondendi*, which is surprising if the innovations had great importance.

The second type of state intervention, that contained in the Valentinian Law of Citations of A.D. 426, was along very different lines:

> *Codex Theodosianus*, 1.4.3 (Emperors Theodosius and Valentinian, Augusti, to the Senate of the City of Rome):
> After other matters.
>
> We confirm all the writings of Papinian, Paul, Gaius, Ulpian, and Modestinus so that the same authority attends Gaius as Paul, Ulpian, and the others, and readings from his whole corpus may be cited. We also declare to be ratified the learning of those persons whose treatises and opinions the above-mentioned have incorporated in their own works, such as Scaevola, Sabinus, Julian, and Marcellus, and all whom they cite, provided however they are confirmed, on account of the uncertainty of age, by a collation of the codices. Where different views are produced the greater in number of authors prevails, if the number is equal, the authority of that party prevails in which Papinian, man of splendid intellect, shines forth. Just as he overcomes individuals so he yields to two. As was previously enacted, we order to be invalidated the notes of Paul and Ulpian made on the corpus of Papinian. Where their opinions cited in court are equal and their authority is thought to be equal, the decision of the judge decides whom he ought to follow. We order that Paul's Sentences also are to be valid. (6 November 426)

Thus, the constitution made the writings of five classical jurists—Papinian, Paul, Gaius, Ulpian, and Modestinus—primary authorities and also provided for the production of the works of other jurists cited by them. The constitution is often regarded as evidence of the low quality of legal talent in the early fifth century: "Such mechanical treatment of legal authorities shows clearly the low level to which jurisprudence had sunk, and, if it was necessary, justifies the strictures which Theodosius, in the introduction to his Code, passes on the lawyers of his own age."[18] But the Law of Citations tells us nothing about the state of jurisprudence at the time when it was passed; above all, it does not rank the old, classical jurists favorably against contemporaries.

With the complete bureaucratization of leading jurists came an end to their writing of legal books. Instead they were concerned with issuing imperial rescripts and with other official legal business. Changes and advances in the law were now to be found in the rescripts, and it can scarcely be doubted that in the main these were the work of jurists and not of the emperor. But when an issue arose before a court and the opinions of Papinian, Paul, Gaius, Ulpian, and Modestinus were ranged all on one side and an imperial rescript was on the other, the latter would prevail. Any one senior but anonymous postclassical jurist writing in an official capacity therefore ranked higher than the combined weight of all five classical primary authorities. The issue addressed by the Law of Citations was rather different. If no rescript relevant to a case could be found, juristic writing would be treated as valuable, but the old problem still existed of determining which jurist had the greatest authority. There is more to the solution of the problem than the no mean virtue of establishing certainty in the law, though for their achievement here the originators of the Law of Citations deserve some credit. Notably, Modestinus was included as a primary authority, though his present reputation is not so high as that of others such as Julian and was also unlikely to have been so in antiquity. The explanation is that Modestinus, Paul, Ulpian, and Papinian are the last of the great classical jurists. The aim of the originators of the Law of Citations, that is to say, was to make authoritative not so much the best of classical law but the best of classical law at its apex, at the end of its development. The inclusion of Gaius as a primary authority might seem to contradict this, but his belated fame rested on his *Institutes.* The elementary principles of law go out of date more slowly than do details.[19]

Thus, the Law of Citations does not give authority to future opinions of jurists but establishes a ranking of past jurists for future cases. Together with the old *ius respondendi* it represents the sum of official intervention to determine the weight of juristic authority. This degree of intervention to achieve certainty may not be much, though it is greater than any that will appear again for juristic opinions in later Western tradition.

A similar vagueness surrounds the lawmaking power of the publicly elected magistrates. Gaius relates:

> G.1.6: The magistrates of the Roman people have the right of issuing edicts. Very extensive law is in the Edicts of the two praetors, urban and peregrine, whose jurisdiction is held in the provinces, by their governors; likewise in the Edicts of the curule aediles whose jurisdiction is held in the provinces of the Roman people by the quaestors; for no quaestors are sent to the provinces of Caesar and hence this Edict is not set up there.

And Pomponius:

> D.1.1.7.1 (*Definitions*, book 2): Praetorian law is that which the praetors have introduced for the public interest to aid, correct or supplement the civil law.

But strictly the magistrate could not make law. He was not granted the right to change existing law or innovate.[20] Simply his right to declare how he would enforce the law in his court went unchallenged. And the old civil law existed side by side with praetorian modifications, though it would not operate in practice. An instructive example of this occurs in G.3.223f, where Gaius sets out the civil law penalties for *iniuria*, assault and verbal outrage, and then explains that they are obsolete and will be replaced by praetorian remedies. But no Roman discussion of this dichotomy between theory and practice is known. The Romans, it seems, were just not interested in the theory of lawmaking.

This indefiniteness at the center of things, the reluctance to offer definitions and the lack of interest in setting out the scope of lawmaking powers, has always in part the same motive: to preserve flexibility in legal development. When an institution is not defined, its boundaries can be subtly moved. When lawmaking powers are not delineated, the lawmakers are less restricted.

The high degree of conceptualization in setting out boundaries between institutions was forced upon jurists by their own role and the structure of Roman proceedings. There was no corresponding pressure to systematize the legal materials, and little systematization occurred. Precision was wanted for many things but was avoided at the very core of the system to give flexibility of development. But there is another reason for this absence of definition and lack of precision on the sources of law: these are not matters of interpretation, and it is on interpretation of law alone that the jurists focused.

This concentration on interpretation had another impact on the central indefiniteness, one that also has wide-ranging implications for other chapters and might even have justified a chapter to itself. The jurists were eager to put forward their opinion on a particular matter. No doubt they wished their opinion to prevail, but they wanted it to prevail because of their authority or the force of their arguments. They had, however, little interest in having the view they espoused adopted for reasons not directly attributable to themselves. They were fundamentally indifferent to law reform. Hence basic legal issues might remain long unresolved. This indefiniteness is not incompatible with the high degree of conceptualization. They have in fact the same origin in the jurists' desire for prestige, which depended on interpretation. No prestige was won for an interpretation that became the law because the jurist persuaded the emperor to issue a rescript. The interpretation had to stand on its own merits.

This indefiniteness, and other things, will be seen when we consider some of the recorded disputes between the Sabinian and the Proculian jurists. Thus, property was divided into *res mancipi* and *res nec mancipi*, the former being Italic land, slaves, rustic predial servitudes, and animals commonly broken to draft or burden, such as oxen, horses, mules, and asses.[21] There was a dispute, with the Sabinians holding that the animals were *res mancipi* from birth, the Proculians from the time they were broken in, or if they were too wild to be tamed from the age at which they were usually broken in.[22] The distinction affected the mode of transferring ownership since *res mancipi* could be transferred only by the formal *mancipatio* or *in iure cessio*.[23] The basis of the dispute is unknown.

Again, when one person made a new thing out of materials wholly belonging to another (without his consent), the Sabinians held that it belonged to the owner of the materials, the Proculians that it belonged to the maker.[24] Again, the basis of the disagreement is unclear.[25] On the view that the new thing belonged to the maker, compensation might be owed to the owner of the materials, even when the maker acted in good faith. But clear evidence is lacking.[26] But even if compensation was due to the owner of the materials, that would not render the dispute insignificant. The issue is again the nature of Roman actions. If the owner of the materials brought the *vindicatio* claiming to be owner of the made thing and the judge held he was not its owner, he lost his case and could not sue by another action on the same facts. If he sued by the *condictio*, which was available only to a nonowner, and the judge found he was owner, he again lost the case and could not sue again.

Further, a *stipulatio* on behalf of another was void (unless to benefit the person in whose power the stipulator was), but if I took a stipulation for delivery to me and another, the Sabinians held that the whole was validly promised to me, the Proculians that half was promised to me and that the rest of the stipulation was void.[27]

A person executing a mandate was not to go beyond the terms of the mandate. If someone was instructed to buy a farm for another and bought it for more than the amount authorized, the Proculians held he had an action against his principal up to the amount that had been fixed; the Sabinians held that he could not proceed against the principal at all.[28]

According to the Sabinians, males reached puberty when that fact could be proved by physical examination; the Proculians held that puberty was to be judged solely by age, fourteen years. The matter was important. Guardianship of males ended on puberty, and the youth also acquired the right to make a will. If a *paterfamilias* appointed a *suus heres* his heir "if he reaches puberty," with a substitute heir if the child did not—the so-called *substitutio pupillaris*—then on the child's death before puberty the substitute would become heir by the will; if the child died after puberty the estate would descend to his heirs on intestacy.

These examples of school disputes, with no resolution over centuries, could be multiplied. But the best illustration of a central indefiniteness caused by the jurists' lack of concern for law reform is to be found in Justinian's *Quinquaginta Decisiones*, the *Fifty Decisions*. For more than a year after the promulgation of his first *Code* in A.D. 529 Justinian undertook no new law-reform initiative, but then he promulgated a series of constitutions to settle remaining juristic controversies and to abolish obsolete law. Some of these, whether published together or not, were known as the *Fifty Decisions*. These constitutions are best regarded as preliminary to the work collecting and abridging the writings of the jurists for the *Digest*.[29] However that might be, the important thing for us in this context is that many of the constitutions were to resolve juristic disputes that had been in existence three centuries before and had never been settled. Not even one of the great bureaucratic jurists such as Paul, Ulpian, and Papinian, with access to the ear of the emperor, had wished the disputes resolved by imperial diktat. The approach to law reform and legal certainty of the classical jurists was very different from that of Justinian's bureaucrats.

# *13* Legal Isolationism: III

The treatment of private law by the Romans as something apart from the practical concerns of public life was so endemic that this chapter, the third on the subject, will consider four aspects of the phenomenon.

First, we have already seen that there was very little influence from other legal systems, including Greek law, and that the jurists had a restricted view of legal reasoning. Now we must notice that even in the Hellenistic period of Roman civilization, the later Republic, there was very little impact from Greek philosophy, and the jurists took little account of it in their reasoning.[1]

The opening issue is whether in the later Republic there was any legal rule or principle whose substance was based on Greek philosophical opinion. At the very most only two texts, a remarkably small number, can even be brought into discussion.

D.33.10.7.2 (Celsus, *Digest*, book 19): Servius admits that the opinion of him who left the legacy ought to be looked at to see in which category he was accustomed to place objects. But if he was accustomed to ascribe things to furniture about which there is no doubt but that they are in another category, such as silver dining vessels, or cloaks and togas, it should not on that account be held that these things are included in a legacy of furniture: for words ought not to be interpreted according to the opinions of individuals but from common usage. Tubero says that this is not quite clear to him. For what is the point of words, he says, unless to show the intention of the speaker. Indeed I do not judge that someone says what he does not mean, especially if he used the word in its usual sense: for we use words as our servant. Moreover, no one should be thought to say what was not in his mind. But even if the reasoning and authority of Tubero move me greatly still I do not dissent from Servius that no one can be considered to have said that for which he did not use the correct word.

Thus, there was a dispute between Servius and Tubero on the extent of legacies of "furniture." For Servius, although the intention of a testator was relevant, it was not solely relevant. Things which commonly were considered in one category were to be put in that category in evaluating a legacy even though the testator was accustomed to put them in a different category. Tubero was not so sure: the purpose of words is to give the intention of the speaker.

Part of the education of Romans of the wealthier kind was some Greek philosophy, especially Stoic, but with some admixture of Epicurian or Platonic-Aristotelian. For some scholars, notably Johannes Stroux,[2] the *usus communis*, common opinion, of Servius was the χοινὴ συνήθεια (common custom) of Greek linguistic theory, and in fact of the Stoics. But Franz Horak demonstrated that on this point the Stoics would not rely on the common opinion but would hold that words express the essence of things.[3] Tubero's reasoning can be related to no philosophical school.

Perhaps there is a substratum of Greek philosophy in Servius's argument, but if so it is indistinct. The issue, though, is one that would have to be discussed in any relatively sophisticated legal system and—independently of any philosophy—the approaches of Servius and Tubero are the two commonsensical ones. The Stoic doctrine, it should be noted, would have been of no help in deciding the legal problem.

The other text is *D.*50.16.25.1 (Paul, *On the Edict*, book 21): "Quintus Mucius says that by the term 'part' something indivisible is meant; for what is ours as a share is not a part but a whole. Servius, not inelegantly, says that both are meant by the term 'part.'" It is perhaps not too fanciful to imagine that somewhere behind Quintus Mucius's argument lurks some philosophical reasoning; but if so it cannot be discovered. There is no known forerunner, direct or indirect, for Mucius's opinion.[4] I would suggest, indeed, that an idea akin to Mucius's never existed in Greek philosophical writings: the situation that concerned the jurists was of little interest to the philosophers. A *pro indiviso* share (which Mucius considers a *pars*, part) can, of course, normally be converted into a *pro diviso* share (which Mucius considers a *totum*, a whole), though the steps to do so have not been taken. In most cases whether a share is construed as *pro diviso* or *pro indiviso* will depend entirely upon the wording of the conveyance or will and not at all upon the subject matter involved. This is a world away from Greek discussions of the smallest possible unit and of its indivisibility. I submit that at the most the influence of Greek philosophy on this idea of Mucius was the recollection that what was separable from a whole might itself be considered a whole.

Closely related to the foregoing is the situation where a legal decision is supported by an argument from Greek philosophy and where, in fact, the decision could have been suggested by the philosophical theory. There is only one instance but, as it happens, it provides the clearest evidence of the jurists' acquaintance with philosophy.

> D.5.1.76 (Alfenus, *Digest*, book 6): The case was put that some judges who were appointed to the same suit were excused after the case was heard, and others were put in their place; and the question was raised whether the change of individual judges caused it to be the same matter or another judgment. I replied that not only if one or two but even if all the judges were changed, nonetheless it remained the same matter and same judgment that it was before. Nor was this the only example of a thing being considered to remain the same when its parts were changed, but there were also many others. For even a legion is regarded as being the same though many of its members had died and others were put in their place. And the people is thought to be the same now as it was a hundred years ago, although none of them are now alive. Likewise a ship, if it was often repaired to such an extent that no plank remained that was not new, nonetheless is thought to be the same ship. But if anyone thought a different thing was made when its parts were changed, it would be the

case on that reasoning that we ourselves would not be the same people that we were a year ago because, as the philosophers say, we are composed of very small particles [*particulis minimis*] which leave our body every day and others take their place from outside. Therefore, a thing whose appearance remained the same was considered to be the same.

Alfenus holds that a lawsuit remains the same lawsuit if one or all the judges appointed to it are changed, and he supports his decision by claiming that, for instance, a legion remains the same though many of the individual soldiers have been changed, a people is regarded as the same people as it was a century before, a ship is the same ship even if it has been so often repaired that no single timber remains unreplaced, and he ends by a *reductio ad absurdum:* otherwise we would not be the same persons that we were a year ago. The ship example, as has been recognized, comes from the thirty-oared galley of Theseus, which was preserved at Athens until the very late fourth century B.C. and whose timbers were replaced from time to time. It was, as Plutarch relates,[5] a standing illustration for the philosophers in the question of growth. But as Horak reminds us,[6] Plutarch makes it clear that while some philosophers regarded the often-repaired ship as the same vessel, others did not. Alfenus for his own purposes has given only one view as if it were accepted dogma. The question involved is of the kind that interested both the Stoics and the Peripatetics, whose doctrines cannot be sharply distinguished.[7] In Alfenus's *reductio ad absurdum* there is probably a reference to the atomic theory both in the idea that the human body (like other things) is composed of numerous minute parts and also that these are in constant motion. We cannot, however, be certain that Alfenus is referring to the atomic theory. The change of matter in a living body is an obvious fact for everybody, not only for atomists. And for everyone it is due to the addition and subtraction of "very small particles": only the atomists would say that these were the "smallest possible particles." Alfenus's words "*particulis minimis*" might mean "atoms," but equally need mean only "very small particles." The atomic theory, though properly associated with Epicurus and his school,[8] also goes back to Democritus and Leucippus.[9] According to Servius, *In Vergilii Eclogas* 6.13 and the *scholia veronensia In Vergilii Eclogas* 7.9, Alfenus had been a pupil of Siron the Epicurean. The statement that we are not the same persons we were a year ago seems to be Alfenus's own contribution for the purpose of making the *reductio* even more striking. What some philosophers seem to have said is that a man is not the same today as he was yesterday.[10] Such a view used in legal argument would have received little sympathy from the republican lawyers, and Alfenus rightly prefers to talk of a year, whether he knew of the philosophers' similar argument about a day or not. From the arguments concerning the ship and from the apparent use of the atomic theory the conclusion is unavoidable that Alfenus was more concerned with having his opinion on the legal case accepted than he was with the purity of his philosophical position and, further, that he reached his conclusion not on philosophical considerations but on commonsense grounds and that philosophy merely provided him with subsequent justifications. If this view is correct, the text would demonstrate the jurist's knowledge of general philosophical learning but not that this learning contributed to the development of the substance of the law.

Less directly, Greek thought could have helped in the development of the substance of the law if, as a result of proper understanding of the dialectical method, institutions were placed in genera, species were observed, and the proper distinctions within an institution were drawn and applied. Organization and ordering of concepts is, to some extent, natural to the human mind and is not specifically Greek. The Code of Hammurabi provides one example of what had been achieved in the organization of legal material without the help of Greece. But the Greek contribution was the double invention of $\gamma\acute{\varepsilon}\nu o\varsigma$, genus, and $\varepsilon\hat{\iota}\delta o\varsigma$, species. A genus contains classes of items possessing common structural characters, and it is divided into species where the classes are marked off from each other by the differences existing between them.[11] The conception of genus and species does appear very clearly in Cicero,[12] but it cannot be emphasized too strongly that there is no sign of species in this context[13] in republican juristic thought. Certainly we are told that Quintus Mucius distinguished five genera of *tutela*[14] and different genera of possession,[15] and Servius three genera of *tutela* and four genera of *furtum*.[16] But the drawing of these distinctions could easily have occurred without the influence of Greek dialectics; and without the further division of a genus into its species the essential Greek contribution is lacking. It is not indicative of strong Greek influence on Quintus Mucius and Servius that they use the word "genus" in this connection,[17] given that the word had been used to mean "kind" since at least the time of Terence.[18]

Again it has been argued that the Stoic theory of etymology—that the word shows the reality of the thing named—influenced the republican jurists.[19] And indeed, as we saw in the previous chapter, we do find the jurists concerned with etymology: Quintus Mucius with *postliminium*[20] and *penus;*[21] Servius also with *postliminium*,[22] *testamentum*,[23] and *vindicia;*[24] Alfenus with *urbs;*[25]. Ofilius with *tugurium;*[26] and Trebatius with *sacellum*.[27] But in Greece itself, long before the Stoics and any Hellenistic theory of language, attempts were being made as early as Homer to use etymology to clarify the meaning of obscure words.[28] And in the republican jurists' attempts to use etymology to show the meaning of a word there is nothing that points specifically to Stoic doctrine[29] or to the teachings of any other school. Proof of Greek philosophical influence is accordingly nonexistent.[30] The very most that might be legitimately claimed is that the Roman jurists learned from the Greeks (directly or indirectly) that to know the etymology of a word might help in elucidating its meaning.[31]

To sum up: there would appear to be remarkably little evidence to support a hypothesis that Greek philosophical thought had much influence on the development of the substance of the law in the later Republic. The jurists gave no religious dimension to private law; nor did they make much use of philosophy.

My point, of course, is not that the republican jurists were unaware of Greek philosophy but that they failed to make constructive use of it. A most revealing text is *D.*50.16.124 (Proculus, *Letters*, book 4) from the early Empire. Juan Miquel has clearly shown that it proves that Proculus was well versed in Stoic logic.[32]

These words "one or another" are not only disjunctive but also belong to subdisjunctive speech. It is disjunctive when, for instance, one says "It is either night or day"; if one is postulated, the other must be excluded. So in a similar construction a word can be subdisjunctive. There are two kinds of subdisjunctive; one when of two possible conclusions, both cannot be true and neither need be true, as when we say "Either he is sitting down or he is standing": for just as no one can do both at the same time, so one could be doing neither, for example, a person lying down. The other kind is when of the possible conclusions one must be true and both can be true, as when we say, "Every animal either acts or suffers"; for there is none that does not act or does not suffer; but one can both act and suffer at the same time.

That is all that we have of the text of Proculus. No practical use is made of this demonstration of awareness of logic's terminology.[33] Perhaps Proculus did make use of his exposition to settle a point in law, but then it is significant that Justinian's compilers should have cut it out. Moreover, any practical use for law that could be derived from the exposition could be made by anyone who had no exposure to Stoic logic. One does not need a training in logic to make the distinctions found in the text.[34]

But the most surprising failure of Greek philosophy to penetrate the substance of Roman law relates to natural law. Our evidence for the juristic approach to natural law is later than the Republic.

D.1.1.1.3 (Ulpian, *Institutes*, book one): Natural law is that which nature taught all animals: for that law is not particular to the human race, but is common to all animals that are born on the land and in the sea, and to birds. Hence comes the union of male and female that we call marriage, hence the procreation and upbringing of offspring. For we see also that the other animals, even wild beasts, are marked by knowledge of that law.[35]

The notion of natural law appears in various guises among Greek philosophers. Aristotle drew a distinction between natural law, which had the same validity everywhere, and conventional law, which varied from place to place.[36] But nowhere is there anything akin to Ulpian's proposition that natural law was common to humans and animals alike. As has been often observed since, Ulpian (who is accepted by Justinian) is not describing law of a particular type, but instinct.[37] Whether or not the jurists themselves knew the distinction between law and instinct, they chose this definition precisely to make the idea of natural law meaningless, to cut out any relevance of philosophical notions of the nature of law.[38] The approach of the jurists to law was entirely positivist.

If there had been any influence of Aristotelian philosophical classification of law, then his natural law would be *ius gentium* in one sense of that term, namely, the law that is found everywhere.[39] But no conclusions are ever drawn by the Romans from that term. The classification here is classification for its own sake.

The second aspect of isolationism to be dealt with in this chapter is that Roman legal rules and institutions often developed a life of their own, and little regard might be given to their purpose. We will discuss the phenomenon specifically in the light of only one topic, the infamous *senatus consultum Silanianum* of A.D. 10. This provided, among other things, that if an owner was murdered in his own home all of the slaves residing with him were to be questioned under torture and then executed. Ulpian explains the rationale:

D.29.5.1pr (*On the Edict*, book 50): Since otherwise no home can be safe unless slaves are compelled to guard their masters, at the risk of their own lives, both from members of the household and from outsiders, *senatus consulta* have been introduced concerning the public questioning of those who have been killed.

Naturally, *senatus consulta* require interpretation, and this one had spoken of the killing only of owners. But who is an owner? Ulpian held that a possessor in good faith was not an owner.[40] This goes against the rationale of the *senatus consulta* that was given by Ulpian himself. A possessor in good faith is someone who received a slave thinking that ownership was being transferred to him. For the issue in the text to be relevant, the slave must have been residing in the home of the possessor in good faith who was killed. If a slave should be under a duty to guard the life of his owner, one would suppose he should be bound to protect someone who was to all intents and purposes the owner. Similarly, Ulpian held that a person who had a usufruct in a slave was not to be treated as owner.[41] Again, the situation is that the slave was residing with the usufructuary, who surely was entitled to security in his own home. Likewise, Ulpian held that a son given in adoption was not owner.[42] But, again, for the issue to be relevant, the son must have been killed in his natural father's home. Also for Ulpian, if a son or daughter were killed, the slaves of the mother were not covered by the *senatus consulta* even though the children were resident with the mother. Perhaps the most striking case is in *D.29.5.10pr* (Paul, *On the senatus consultum Silanianum*, sole book):

> If a disinherited son was murdered before the inheritance of his father was accepted, the case is to be looked at according to how the facts turned out, so that if the inheritance was accepted the slaves are considered as if they belonged to someone else; but if the will has been avoided, everything is done as if he were owner because they would have been his if he had lived.

In Roman law, an heir (under a will or on intestacy) who was neither a slave of the deceased nor a free person in the deceased's power who became *sui iuris* on his death became owner of the inheritance only when he made a formal acceptance. If he refused to accept the inheritance, the will was voided and the inheritance descended according to the rules of intestate succession, or if there was no will the inheritance went to the next nearest heir. If there was an intestacy or a will and the nearest heir was a direct descendant of the deceased who became *sui iuris*, such as a son, then the heir became heir at the moment of death (unless he abstained from the estate). In other situations the heir became heir only from the moment at which he accepted the inheritance. In the case decided by Paul a father died leaving a will in which he appointed an outsider to the family as heir and disinherited his son. Then the son was murdered, obviously in the paternal home. What was to happen to the slaves? Paul's opinion was that one should adopt a wait-and-see approach. If the heir under the will accepted the inheritance, nothing was to happen to the slaves. Their ownership was in suspense between the testator's death and the acceptance of the inheritance. If the testamentary heir refused the inheritance, the will failed, the disinherited son would be regarded as heir from the moment of the father's death, and the slaves would be treated as if they were his from that time and hence at the moment of his murder. Thus they would be questioned under torture and executed. The reasoning is legally irreproachable.

The point I wish to stress is twofold. First, the jurists use an approach to interpretation that gives a term the meaning it would bear in other contexts even though this failed the rationale of the statute. Second, not only did this interpretation prevail but over five centuries later the *senatus consultum* was still in force unchanged, and so was the interpretation.

The third aspect of isolationism to be dealt with in this chapter is the astonishing concentration of interest by the jurists on conditions at Rome. We know from Cicero that, in addition to the Edicts of the urban and peregrine praetors and of the aediles, governors issued Edicts for their provinces.[43] A provincial Edict existed also in the Empire. But the outsider jurist, Gaius—and his outsider quality will be discussed again in appendix B—was the sole jurist to write a commentary on the provincial Edict, in thirty-two books. It has been suggested [44] that Callistratus's commentary on the *Edictum monitorium*—and what that Edict was is unknown—was also on the *Edictum provinciale*. If it were, and we cannot assess the plausibility of the suggestion, then it is important to notice that Callistratus himself seems to have been a provincial, indeed from the Greek-speaking eastern part of the Empire.[45] There is no other text in the *Digest* that clearly refers to the *Edictum provinciale*. We have no information on whether the provincial Edict was ever stabilized. Indeed, so fixated were the jurists on Rome that Gaius himself in his *Institutes* makes no mention of the provincial Edict in his discussion of the sources of law. His express concern was the *iura populi Romani*, the law of the Roman people.[46] Perhaps not surprisingly, the untenable suggestion has been made that there was no such thing as the provincial Edict.[47]

Another aspect of this concentration on Rome, the *iudicium legitimum*, was discussed in chapter 11. This type of action was focused on by the jurists, and one requirement was that it be heard in Rome or within one mile of the city.[48]

To come to the final aspect of isolationism in this chapter, I observed in an earlier work[49] that it was fundamental for the later spread of Roman law that, as it appears in the sources, it divides naturally into self-contained and self-referential blocks. This division is found not only in the legal institutions and concepts but also in the four individual parts of Justinian's *Corpus Juris Civilis.* Transmission has often been of individual blocks, not of Roman law itself. The important unit for transplanting and for affecting the recipient system is the block, not the individual rule.

In that book I described the blocks in order to show how they enabled Roman law to be the object of borrowing. Here I use some of the same material, but my purpose is different: to demonstrate that the blocks were not the result of any deep-laid plan.

Although all legal institutions in any developed system can be regarded as blocks, the Roman law blocks are markedly different. To begin with, substantive law is treated in the *Corpus Juris* quite separately from procedure. The Roman jurists discuss whether an action will lie on particular facts but have no interest in what happens when the case comes to court. If it were not for the survival of book 4 of the elementary *Institutes* of both Gaius and Justinian, in each case primarily dedicated to procedure, it would not be possible to reconstruct in any measure the course of legal proceedings, whether in the archaic, classical, postclassical, or Justinianian periods. Again, the texts ignore the difficulties of proof. The jurists set out a factual situation and declare the legal decision that should flow from the facts. There is normally no indication that in practice the facts may be in dispute and that sufficient evidence may be lacking.

All this comes in the first instance from the fact that the jurists really had no interest in what went on in court. Their reputation resulted from their skill in determining legal issues, not in separating fact from fiction, not in winning a lawsuit for a client. It also derived in large measure from the need for conceptualization, as already

discussed, deriving from the Roman court system and the close interaction between praetor and jurist.

But though conceptualization resulted from the system of actions,
the Romans gave a lowly significance to the actual pleadings. For instance, in the *Digest* title on the acquisition of ownership, the actions
relating to ownership can scarcely be said to be prominent; the reader
has to wait until the twenty-eighth text of the title before one makes
its appearance.[50] Again, there was a special procedure, by interdict, to
protect possession. But the procedure is not mentioned at all in the
main *Digest* title, 41.2, "On the Acquisition or Loss of Possession."
Indeed, that title is devoted to setting out the circumstances in which
a person acquires, retains, or loses possession. One would never know
from it that legal protection does not always go to the present possessor; yet some interdicts protect existing possession, some are for the
recovery of lost possession, and still others are to enable someone to
possess although he has never had possession. In short, Roman substantive law as it appears in the *Corpus Juris* has to be understood
independently of the forms of process. This resulted from the jurists'
concentration of interest.

Likewise, the blocks of one institution or concept are kept rigorously separate, and even over a long period of time there is often no
real movement toward integration or amalgamation. Thus, in a sense,
it is entirely right that the Romans never developed a general theory
of contract but only individual types of contract. The block is the
individual type. There is no sign that the Romans even groped toward
a general theory. It is often wrongly claimed that the introduction
of the so-called "innominate contracts," perhaps as early as the first
century A.D., was "an enormous advance towards a general theory of
contract."[51] The jurist Paul in the second or early third century stated
that an action would lie on any agreement of the following four types,
provided the plaintiff had fulfilled his side of the bargain. "I give that
you give, I give that you do, I do that you give, I do that you do."[52] On
this basis an action will lie on any agreement that seeks to impose
obligations on both parties, provided that one party has performed his
side of the bargain. Although the existence of a remedy in these circumstances fills in gaps in the Roman contractual system and makes

the law of contracts much more satisfactory, it is not a step toward a general view or theory of contract. Each individual type of contract, such as stipulation, loan for use, or loan for consumption, sale, hire, or mandate, remains intact with its own *sui generis* body of rules. This also was the direct consequence of the Roman system of actions and the juristic emphasis on interpretation.

Though contracts could be distinguished from other branches of the law and though contracts were classified, according to the requirements for their formation, as verbal, literal, real, or consensual, yet for a Roman jurist it was unthinkable, as we have seen, to write a commentary on the law of contracts or even on the law of a group of contracts, such as the consensual contracts. The same is equally true of other fields, for instance of delicts. Similarly, for the Romans there was no such topic as family law; but the various subjects that might be comprehended under that head—husband and wife, parent and child, guardianship, owner and slave—were kept quite distinct. In harmony with this approach, praedial servitudes were treated independently of land ownership.

Likewise emerges the characteristic that to a surprising degree the blocks are self-referential. Rarely are arguments drawn by analogy from one block to another—from, say, sale to hire, or from acquisition of possession to acquisition of ownership.

Again, the Roman sources treat law quite unhistorically. The *Code* does arrange the constitutions within each title in chronological order, but there is otherwise no indication that the passage of time and new ideas have any effect on attitudes to legal rules. Roman jurists cite other jurists as authority with no apparent awareness that some authorities lived centuries earlier than others. Justinian's *Digest*, too, includes texts by jurists of six centuries before, and their opinions are referred to in no way differently from those of their successors. The legal rules thus appear independently of time. With few exceptions, of which the outsider Gaius is the best example, the Roman jurists were uninterested in and unmoved by history. With their isolationism they had little feeling that law was a societal tool, to be changed when society changed or used to mold society.

For subsequent generations the most striking blocks are the individual parts that together make up the *Corpus Juris,* namely, the *Digest, Code, Institutes,* and *Novellae.* But the important separation, that of the *Digest* and the *Code,* was the result of an absence of planning. The *Code* was simply the continuation of a previously existing tradition of collecting and publishing the imperial rescripts that were still useful. To collect and abridge the writings of the jurists was a later ambition.

Finally the *Corpus Juris* is in large measure devoted to private and criminal law, with public law decidedly secondary. This trait, too, corresponds to the interests of the classical jurists.

# 14 "Law Keeps Out"

A feature, perhaps, of all legal systems is that "law keeps out" of certain areas, usually because the subject matter for a variety of reasons is thought unsuitable for public regulation. The most noticeable example for twentieth-century Britain is the immunity from liability in tort and contract of trade unions after the Trade Disputes Act of 1906.[1] The point is that law and legal processes are not judged to be a satisfactory means of resolving such disputes in modern Britain.

The phenomenon becomes obvious only when one looks at an alien system, either because that system regulates some aspect of life that one's own does not, or because it scarcely regulates some matters that our own takes cognizance of.

For the first branch of this phenomenon, the most obvious example is Prussia's *Allgemeines Landrecht für die Preussischen Staaten* of 1794. The second title of part two concerns the rights and duties of parents and provides, among other things:

s.61   Children owe both parents respect and obedience.

s.67   A healthy mother is under the obligation of suckling her child herself.

s.68   How long she must keep the child at the breast is determined by the father's decision.

s.69   He must, however, submit himself to the ruling of experts if the health of the mother or child would suffer from his decision.

s.76   If the parents are devoted to different religious confessions, then until the fourteenth year is complete, sons should be educated in the religion of the father, daughters in the religious confession of the mother.

s.77 Neither of the parents can bind the other, even by contract, to set aside these legal rules.

s.109 The settling of the future mode of life of sons depends in the first instance on the judgment of the father.

s.121 Children are bound in accordance with their strength to provide a helping hand to their parents and their business and trade.

s.122 But time necessary for their teaching and education should not be taken from the children in that way.[2]

Such regulation of domestic life by law in the Anglo-American world would be greatly resented.

For the second branch of the phenomenon, the absence of legal regulation of some aspects of life, the most obvious example is Roman private law.[3] As we have already seen, throughout the whole history of Rome from city-state to world empire, under pagan deities and Christian god alike, no form was prescribed for the celebration of marriage. Consent of the parties was required and no doubt it was advisable to have evidence of it, but no form of proof was established by law. Less surprisingly perhaps, no register of marriages was kept.

Again there was at no time an official hearing for granting a divorce. Divorcing was at the wishes of the spouses, and no grounds were needed for it. It may be that in very early Rome, specific grounds were necessary, but more plausibly, I believe, a husband who divorced his wife without being able to allege one of the specified grounds was subject to penalties.[4] In any event, there was complete freedom to divorce from the late third century B.C. Later, when the Empire became Christian, penalties were imposed for divorce except for a specified reason or, at other times, where the reason was insufficient. Still, the divorce itself was valid.[5] Nor does it appear that any particular formalities were essential to carry through a divorce. Certainly, a particular verbal formulation was standard from early days, but nothing proves it was obligatory. Likewise, Augustus seems to have strengthened evidentiary requirements without imposing the necessity of a particular form.[6]

A second extreme instance where law keeps out is testate succession. In the Western world typically there have been restrictions on testacy. At some times and some places, wills could not be made at all; at others wills were restricted to the distribution of movables. Even when wills can be made it is standard that the law insists that a minimum proportion be left to certain persons such as a spouse or children. But at Rome there was complete freedom of testation. Testacy was permitted from the earliest times, and land as well as movables could be devised by will. There was no legal requirement that a minimum proportion be left to a spouse or children.

Such legal rules that did exist on disinherison were intended to prevent a testator from omitting an heir by accident, not to restrict the right to disinherit. Thus, an actual son whom the testator did not wish to be heir had to be disinherited by name; otherwise the will was absolutely void.[7] Other *sui*, such as daughters and grandchildren, if they were not to be heirs, could be disinherited by a general clause: "Let all others be disinherited." In the absence of such a clause, the will was not void, but the *suus* or *sua* passed over was entitled to the same share as any *suus* or *sua* who was instituted heir, or to half the estate if an extraneous person had been appointed heir.[8]

To this freedom to disinherit there was one massive exception, but it is an exception that proves the force of the notion that law keeps out. Persons who felt that they had not been appointed heir unjustly and who had no other remedy available could bring the *"querella inofficiosi testamenti,"* the complaint of the unduteous will, and if they were successful the will would be declared void. Thus, possible claimants were *sui* who had been disinherited by will; ascendants who had not been appointed heirs; and brothers or sisters, provided in this case that the person named as heir was regarded as base. But the important thing was how the *querella* came into existence. It was not a product of state intervention, whether by statute or edict, nor does it seem to have been a development of the jurists. Rather, it was the result of a court, in this case the centumviral court, responding to individuals' desires. A person who would have been heir on intestacy but was excluded by the will or given only a small share brought the ordinary action to claim an inheritance, the *petitio hereditatis*, asserting that the will was void on the ground that the testator was insane. The argument must have been that no sane testator could have passed over the plaintiff while instituting the heir that he did.[9] At times the court would accept such a plea, and eventually the action became standard. What we have here is an instance where the state practiced "law keeps out," but citizens wanted legal regulation and it was introduced by a dodge.

Contract law may also be cited for "law keeps out." For an agreement to fall within the scope of a particular type of contract, such as sale or deposit, it had to have the substantive characteristics of that type or have the formalities of *stipulatio*. But within these bounds, the parties were largely free to make their own terms. Naturally one could not contract to be free from liability for fraud, but otherwise the parties could modify responsibility. Thus, in deposit, the depositee was liable only for fraud since he could not profit from the transaction, but if they wished the parties could validly agree that the depositee would be liable also for negligence. In the bilateral contracts, with the exception of partnership,[10] there was no necessary correspondence between the prestations on either side.

Thus, in classical Roman law in the contracts of sale and hire there was no notion of a just price. The price had to be seriously intended, but there was no requirement that it should correspond in value in some way to the thing sold or hired, or the services provided. This is very explicitly set out in the *Digest:*

D.19.2.22.3 (Paul, *On the Edict*, book 34): Just as in the contract of sale it is naturally permitted to buy for less what is worth more and to sell for more what is worth less, and thus to take advantage of one another, so that is the law in the case of hire.

D.4.4.16.4 (Ulpian, *On the Edict*, book 11): Likewise, Pomponius says with regard to the price in sale that the contracting parties are naturally permitted to take advantage of one another.[11]

A change of some kind occurred at some time after the classical period to introduce in some cases rescission of a contract for gross inequality of exchange—*laesio enormis* or enorm lesion, as it is called in Scots law. There are only two relevant texts, and since they also bring out points treated in earlier chapters I will discuss them in the round. Both texts appear in Justinian's *Code*, both are rescripts attributed to the emperor Diocletian, and both were ostensibly issued on account of a sale.

> C.4.44.2: If you or your father sold a thing of a higher price for a lower price it is equitable that you either recover the farm you have sold, after restoring the price to the buyers, with the assistance of the judge's authority or, if the buyer so chooses, you recover what is lacking from the just price. The price is considered too little if one-half part of its true price was not paid.

> C.4.44.8: If your son sold your farm on your instructions, fraud from the guile and ambushes of the buyer must be proved or fear of death or imminent torture of the body shown if the sale is not to be regarded as valid. The mere fact that you show the farm was sold for a slightly too low price has no force for setting aside the sale. Clearly, if you had considered the substance of the contract of buying and selling, and that the buyer comes to the contract hoping to buy more cheaply, and the seller to sell more dearly; and scarcely after much argument, with the seller reducing a little what he asked for, the buyer adding a little to what he offered, do they agree to a settled price; then you would truly see that neither good faith which protects the agreement of buying and selling nor any reason allows a contract definitely agreed on whether at once or after much haggling over the price to be set aside: unless less was given than half of the price that was just at the time of the sale, when the choice previously given to the buyer must be observed.

The two rescripts, of A.D. 285 and 293 respectively, are virtually the only evidence for *laesio enormis* in the Roman legal sources, and they seem to be contradicted by rescripts of only a few years later.[12] Since these two texts are so close together in date, and since they say the same thing about the law, and since there is no other legal evidence, we cannot plot the historical development of *laesio enormis*. At most we may say, in view of what seem to be the contrary texts in the *Digest*, that the doctrine does not appear to have been known to the classical jurists. To complicate the issue, from the time of Christianus Thomasius (1655–1728) the claim has frequently been made that the rescripts are interpolated and that the doctrine is due to Justinian. In this instance the issue of interpolation is of relevance to us. Interpolations are changes made subsequently by another person to juristic texts or imperial rescripts. They may affect the substance or only the form. With these rescripts we can produce arguments both in favor of and against substantive interpolation, but none is conclusive.[13]

What would be needed in order to identify the source of inspiration is some peculiar detail or details in the scope of *laesio enormis* (or in the format of the rescripts) that corresponds to the same peculiarity or peculiarities in the source. But here the rescripts let us down completely. Like the great generality of rescripts addressed to private individuals, these are concerned with providing an answer to the particular problem of the questioner. They do not, and are not meant to, delimit the rule. Both rescripts concern the same situation: sale of land at a low price. To that situation they return answers. But the scope of the rule is not set out. We might ask, as have many others, whether the rule applied to the sale of movables? To a sale for too high a price? If so, how was "too high" to be calculated? Did it apply only to sale or also to other contracts? To bargain situations outside of the field of contract? To any seller no matter what his social position? To a seller who knew the value of the land? Where rescission on the ground of lesion was expressly excluded by the terms of the contract? One might even ask how the true value was to be calculated. Certainty in answering most of these questions is beyond our reach. Part of the problem is the absence of information on the source of the doctrine. It could be suggested that the source is to be found in one of four possible elements: the legal tradition, moral or philosophical opinion, general social or economic conditions, or a particular political or historical event. The first may be discounted in this instance since the classical jurists seem not to have said anything that points toward the doctrine; the fourth may perhaps be ignored in the absence of any suggestions as to the particular event. But the second and third have been thought relevant; and different answers are plausible for the scope of *laesio enormis* depending on whether the origins of the doctrine are moral and philosophical or social and economic.[14]

For instance, on the former hypothesis, the issue is one of fairness, and we would expect that the doctrine would apply to movables as well as to land, to instances where the price was too high as well as too low, and to other contracts as well as to sale. On the second hypothesis one might easily argue for the restriction of the doctrine to the too-cheap sale of land. In a preindustrial society, it can be claimed, land is the main economic asset and (as under the feudal system) demands particular rules. Economic conditions may force a landowner to sell a particular plot and take whatever bargain he can make, but no one—except in very special circumstances—is forced to buy a particular plot of land.[15] We are in a vicious circle. If we do not know the causes of *laesio enormis*, we cannot discover its scope; if we do not know the scope of *laesio enormis*, we cannot discover its causes.[16]

The two rescripts illustrate vividly themes of earlier chapters: the continuing habit (this time, of emperors) of giving a legal response on facts as stated, but without investigating the accuracy of the facts; the absence of interest in setting a legal ruling in its social context. But here our concern is with "law keeps out," and the significance of the rescripts for this does not depend on whether the rescripts were issued by Diocletian or Justinian. If they are Diocletianic, state intervention in private bargains is not only postclassical but was rapidly deemed a failure; if they are Justinianian, then state intervention with private bargains occurred only at the very end of Roman legal history.

A final extreme illustration of "law keeps out" may be chosen from the law of slavery. Slavery, after all, was of vital economic importance, but it was not much regulated by law. The phenomenon is again most easily shown when Rome is contrasted with another society, this time English-speaking America.

English slave law possesses a public dimension that is in sharp contrast with Roman law. Apart from ordinary criminal law, the state and the other citizens at Rome were not much involved with the slave and the owner. For example, no one could interfere with a slave except at the master's instigation. If the slave ran away, his capture was the master's business. No citizen group was organized to find the runaway. On recapture, it was the master's business to decide whether and how severely the slave was to be punished. It was up to the master to decide what clothing the slave wore, how he was to be educated, the training he was to receive, and the work he was to do. The slave could make contracts with the master's permission, could live wherever the master wished, could indulge in whatever activities (that were otherwise lawful) that the master allowed. In contrast, in English America one might almost say that a slave belonged to every citizen: at least he was subordinate to every white. Thus a slave off a plantation could be stopped by any white and questioned about his activities. Citizens were organized by law in patrols to recapture runaways. Penalties were laid down for each offense of running away; if within a certain time the master did not inflict them the state would. The government declared that only appropriate clothing was to be worn, and it might even determine what clothing was appropriate. The state intervened in the education of slaves even to the extent of prohibiting teaching them to read or write. Slaves could not buy and sell as their master wished, they could not live apart from the master whenever he wished, they could not keep horses, cattle, and pigs; they could not, even if the master would allow it, hire out their time. These rules did not apply at all times and in all colonies or states, but they do give the flavor of the general law.[17]

# 15 Simplicity and Economy of Means

In this last chapter I use "simplicity" and "economy of means" to describe two distinct yet related phenomena. By "simplicity" I want to indicate the clarity, distinctness of forms, sharpness of focus, and paucity of types in Roman law. By "economy of means" I want to point out how one institution or form could be used for more than one purpose.

Nothing better illustrates simplicity in law than the Roman *stipulatio*. At an early date, before the *Twelve Tables*, it was the oldest and only Roman contract. It could be used to make actionable any bargain that was not void at law. It was formal, but the formalities were remarkably simple. It was an oral promise in response to an oral question; hence the parties had to be face to face. No time interval could elapse between question and answer, and in substance the answer had to correspond to the question. In the early days, only one verb, *spondere*, to promise solemnly, could make the contract legally binding: "*Spondesne?*" "*Spondeo.*" (Do you solemnly promise? I solemnly promise.) It was so simple that it was of necessity unilateral, but often it would be matched by another *stipulatio* taken from the promisee. Since this is possibly or probably the sole Roman institution that required a very particular formulation and since *spondere* is etymologically related to the Greek σπονδή, a libation, I have suggested an early connection with Roman religion.[1]

Thus, originally if an agreement was made in the form of a *stipulatio* or *stipulationes* there was a contract or contracts; otherwise there was none. Indeed, that was the point. The formalities showed the parties that the promisor was agreeing to be bound: they certainly did not serve to provide evidence for a court of a contract since the *stipulatio* required neither witnesses nor a writing. This simplicity was in the contract from the beginning and was not the result of juristic striving.

A second early example of simplicity that does not derive from juristic conceptualization comes from the Roman idea of heir, *heres*, and the inheritance, *hereditas*. The heir or heirs succeeded not only to the deceased's liabilities and assets but also to the performance of his private *sacra* or religious duties. It is probably the heir's obligation to perform the *sacra* that led to the introduction of the first Roman will, that before the *comitia calata*. Though there is no evidence, it is plausible that the will was only allowed when the testator had no *suus heres*, that is, someone in his power who would become independent on his death.[2] (Likewise, the early form of adoption, *adrogatio*, of a male *sui iuris* took place in the *comitia calata* and was allowed only when the adopter had no *suus heres*. Thus, the adoptee would be the adopter's heir on intestacy with an obligation to perform the *sacra*.[3]) This early connection with religion explains much of the simplicity of the Roman law of succession. The heir stepped into the place of the testator; hence there was no need, as there was in English law, to develop a law of executry.[4] Likewise, we have here the origin of the rule, which also made for simplicity, that no one could die partly testate, partly intestate.

An innovation that will be discussed subsequently in this chapter in connection with "economy of means" was the mancipatory will, the *testamentum per aes et libram*. In my view, originally and still at the time of the *Twelve Tables* it could not be used to appoint an heir, but only to appoint legatees and guardians to children and women.[5] This will was not created by any official act, but came about because individuals acted in this way and their behavior was ratified by the *Twelve Tables*.

Later, the *testamentum per aes et libram* became a true will, and an heir could be appointed under it. This led to the disappearance of the *testamentum comitiis calatis*, but not because of any desire for simplicity. Rather the *testamentum comitiis calatis* could not survive the competition because it was public, it required a legislative act, and the *comitia calata* met only twice a year for willmaking.

A text of Gaius, *G.2.117*, indicates but does not prove that in early times only one formulation, *"Titius heres esto"* (Let Titius be my heir), was a valid institution of a heir.[6] If this is correct, then I would link the requirement, as was the case with *stipulatio*, with the original connection with religion. As I have just mentioned, the heir was liable to perform the *sacra* of the deceased. As is well known, Roman religion was replete with verbal formalism.[7] In contrast, the awarding of a legacy did not involve a rigorous formulation.[8]

Simplicity is, indeed, a marked feature of Roman private law, as is clearly seen if one contrasts it with medieval English or German law.[9] I have put the above examples first because they did not derive from the jurists' drive toward conceptualization observable in other contexts, for example, in the rigid separation of one type of contract from another. But what has to be stressed is that neither these examples of simplicity nor those resulting from conceptualization seem to derive from any particular desire for simplicity for its own sake.

An even more striking example of simplicity of private law that was not brought about by any juristic desire for it is that almost no distinction existed at law between one citizen and another. Naturally, the legal status of women differed from that of men, that of persons in paternal power from those free of it, and that of juveniles from adults. But virtually no distinction existed at private law between patrician and plebeian; between senator or *eques*, knight, or proletarian; between a freedman and a freeborn citizen; and between the adherents of one religion and another. Certainly, the *Twelve Tables* forbade intermarriage between patrician and plebeian, but that was the work of the second set of *decemviri*, who had turned tyrannous, and the rule was abolished as early as the *lex Canuleia* of 445 B.C.[10] By the *lex Julia de maritandis ordinibus* of 18 B.C. Augustus forbade senators, their children, and their descendants in the male line intermarrying with freed persons, actors, and actors' children.[11] The prohibition did not even extend to senators marrying the children of freed persons. And freed persons owed certain private-law obligations to their patron but not to other citizens.[12] But that closes out the private-law differences between citizens until at least the end of the classical period. Despite the simplicity, the apparent egalitarianism before the law is entirely misleading. Vast differences, of the most fundamental kind, between one social group and another were enshrined in public law.[13] The explanation of the difference between public law and private law goes back to the *Twelve Tables*, as I claimed in the second chapter. What the code contained was virtually only private law. Egalitarianism before the law is an illusion for Roman law; but private law, from the fount of the *Twelve Tables*, has all the appearance of it and thus contributes to simplicity.[14]

For "economy of means" I want to discuss above all the great success story of *mancipatio*, the formal mode of transferring those important things designated as *res mancipi*. Its form for the classical period is described by Gaius in his *Institutes*, 1.119:

> Now *mancipatio* is, as we said above, a sort of imaginary sale, and it, too, is peculiar to Roman citizens. It is performed thus: not fewer than five witnesses who are Roman citizens above puberty plus one other who holds a bronze scale and is called a *libripens*, are summoned and brought together, and the person who takes by the *mancipatio*, holding the bronze, speaks thus: "I declare this man is mine by the law of the citizens, and let him have been bought by me by this bronze and this bronze scale." Then he strikes the scale with the bronze and he gives the bronze, as if in the place of the price, to the person from whom he is receiving in *mancipatio*.

In *G.1.121*, Gaius tells us that the object to be mancipated must be present, unless it is land, which is regularly mancipated at a distance. The ceremony, whose antiquity is well attested, obviously derives from an actual sale before the time of coined money, when copper or bronze as the price was actually weighed on the scale. Which things were *res mancipi* in Gaius's time are explained by him in *G.2.14a–17*:

> 14a. There is also another division of things: for they are either *res mancipi* or *res nec mancipi*. *Res mancipi* are land and houses on Italic soil, likewise slaves and those animals that are usually broken to draft or burden, such as cattle, horses, mules, and asses: likewise rustic praedial servitudes. For urban praedial servitudes are *nec mancipi*. *Nec mancipi* are also stipendiary or

tributary lands. 15. A question is raised as to the meaning of our statement that those animals that are usually broken in are *res mancipi*, because they are not broken in at the time of birth. And the leaders of our school think they are *res mancipi* as soon as they are born. But Nerva and Proculus and other leaders of the other school hold that they do not become *res mancipi* unless they are broken in and if, because of too much wildness, they cannot be broken in then they come to be *res mancipi* when they reach the age at which they usually are broken in. 16. Likewise wild beasts are *res nec mancipi*, such as bears, lions, likewise these animals which are almost in the category of wild animals, such as elephants and camels; and it does not matter that these animals too are broken in to draft or burden, for their very names did not exist in the time when it was settled which things were *res mancipi* and which *res nec mancipi*. 17. Also *nec mancipi* are almost all incorporeal things, with the exception of rustic praedial servitudes, which, it is settled, are *mancipi* although they are in the category of incorporeal things.

Three peculiarities in the list may help to establish the original list of *res mancipi* and explain the classification. First is the dispute between the Sabinians and the Proculians over cattle, horses, mules, and asses, the Sabinians including all such, the Proculians only those broken in or of the age at which they were usually broken in. Second is the inclusion of land, which is thought not to fit particularly well into the ceremony, which involves a grasping by the hand.[15] Third is the inclusion of rustic praedial servitudes, which were incorporeal rights and did not involve (in classical law at least) the legal right of ownership. A fourth peculiarity—much discussed by scholars—is less obvious at first sight: the inclusion of horses may be odd, since unlike the other animals classified as *res mancipi*, horses were not much used for agricultural work.[16] Until the invention much later of the horse collar, horses had little pulling power. (A further, revealing, point appears incidentally. Gaius shows that the classification has no surviving rational value. Elephants and camels are not *res mancipi*, not because they lack the characteristics of the objects of that class, but because they were not known when the classification became fixed. Gaius betrays no disquiet at this lack of fit.)

But one undoubted fact, as far as I am aware never adduced, may prove helpful—namely, that what counted as *res mancipi* would have developed at a very early date, before Rome became a literate society. It appears that "oral cultures tend to use concepts in situational, operational frames of reference that are minimally abstract."[17] Using this notion to guide us, it would appear that (along with slaves) cattle, horses, mules, and asses were all original members of the grouping and that the Proculian view corresponded to the original classification: these were the major animals that worked with man or were worked by man. The Sabinian view that all such animals, whether broken in or not, were *res mancipi* corresponds to the notions of classification of a literate culture.[18]

The remote origins of the classification probably cannot be determined. It may be that originally there was no rigid distinction between *res mancipi* and other things: there was only the feeling that for greater security, important things should be transferred before witnesses. What these things were gradually became fixed, as did the details of the required ceremony. An alternative thesis might be that some things were conceived of as being more "family" property than other things[19] and were at first inalienable or (both at first and later) alienable only publicly. In either eventuality, slaves, horses, cattle, asses, and mules are an obvious unit. Greater precision is not needed here.

Italic land is also classified as *res mancipi* along with these animate beings, though it is (to us) obviously different in nature. Whether or not it was always so classified—perhaps not, if, as is sometimes claimed, land in early times was not in private ownership—cannot, I think, be established, but the application to it of the ceremony of *mancipatio* is our first glimpse of pragmatism in this context. *Mancipatio*, as a ceremony, involved in its developed form a grasping in the hand that is not entirely appropriate for land. One may conclude either that land was added to the list of *res mancipi* after the form of the ceremony was fixed, or that as the class of *res mancipi* emerged and as the details of the form of transfer were recognized as necessary, one ceremony alone became acceptable for the transfer of all *res mancipi*, though it was not always wholly appropriate. In either case, it was opportunistic either to classify land as *res mancipi* or to treat *mancipatio* as appropriate to it.

But a much more flagrant case of opportunism appears in the classification of rustic praedial servitudes as *res mancipi*.[20] The four original praedial servitudes were *iter*, a right of passage, *actus*, a right of driving beasts, *via*, a right of having a "paved" road, and *aquae ductus*, a right of aqueduct. These servitudes are of extreme economic importance in a primitive agricultural community. Farming neighbors will obviously want to make use of them, and they will come into existence in practice by consent, even without legal recognition. But nonetheless the need for legal protection will soon be felt. How are neighbors to create such rights? Some form will be needed. In the absence of official intervention, recourse could be had to the ceremony of *mancipatio*.[21] *Traditio* (delivery), the standard method of conveying *res nec mancipi*, could not be used, not just because of its informality but also because it required physical delivery of the thing to be transferred.[22] There is no alternative to *mancipatio*. And eventually the courts will recognize that servitudes have been created. A purely pragmatic solution was found. But, as a consequence, praedial servitudes, though incorporeal rights, were classified as *res mancipi*.

Failure to appreciate Roman legal pragmatism has led most scholars to hold that the early Romans and their successors for a long time conceived of servitudes as corporeal objects, and that the holder of the servitude right had ownership of the corresponding strip of land, or alternatively that ownership of the strip of land was functionally divided between the owner of the land and the neighbor in right of the servitude.[23] Diósdi has given the conclusive arguments against such views by analyzing two provisions of the *Twelve Tables*. One provides that the owner of the land must lay a road, *via*, with stones (or, alternatively, set curbstones), and if he does not the other may drive his beast wherever he wants.[24] As Diósdi says, if the person entitled to passage had become the owner of the strip of land, the owner of the servient land would be under no obligation to pave it, nor if the owner failed to do so, would the other be able to lead his beast where he wished.[25] The other provision is even more to the point and declares that the breadth of the *via* should be eight feet on the straight, sixteen feet on the bends.[26] This provision, as Diósdi claims, would have been superfluous if *via* gave ownership, since the transfer itself would then define the territory.[27] It should be stressed that it is the fact that *mancipatio* is used to create servitudes that is the main argument for the belief that servitudes were considered by the early Romans to be corporeal things.

*Mancipatio*, with a variant wording for the nature of the taking—akin to *"fide et fiduciae"* (to my faith and trust)—was used to create real security of *res mancipi*.[28] The creditor accepted ownership of the pledged property, and, since as owner his security was great, he could allow the debtor to continue to possess and use the pledged property.

But the Romans came to use the ceremony of *mancipatio* very creatively well outside the realm of the transfer of *res mancipi*. One early variation was to permit the making of a will, the so-called *testamentum per aes et libram*, which has been discussed earlier in this book. This is described by the jurist Gaius in the mid-second century A.D., in his *Institutes* 2.104:

The proceedings are as follows: the person making the will, as in other mancipations, takes five Roman citizens above puberty as witnesses and a balance-holder and, after having written his will, mancipates his *familia* [i.e., his property considered as a unit].[29] In the *mancipatio*, the recipient of the *familia* uses these words: "I declare your *familia* and your property to be subject to your instructions under my guardianship so that you may lawfully make a will according to the public statute, and let it have been bought by me with this bronze (and as some add) with this bronze scale." Then he strikes the balance with the bronze and gives the bronze to the testator as if in lieu of the price. Then the testator, holding the tablets of the will, says: "As it is written on these tablets and in this will, so I give, so I legate, so I call to witness, and so, citizens, do you bear me witness." This is called a *nuncupatio, nuncupare* meaning to declare publicly. And by these general words the testator is thought to declare and confirm what he had specifically written in the tablets of the will.

By the second century A.D. (and, indeed, long before), this *testamentum per aes et libram*, as it is called, had become a proper will in which an heir could be appointed. This, as I said earlier, was not the original position. In early Rome before the *Twelve Tables*, as already noted, a will could be made publicly before the assembly known as the *comitia calata*, which met twice a year, on 24 March and 24 May, for the purpose of making wills. This was obviously very inconvenient, and the practice grew up of making testamentary dispositions by using a modified form of *mancipatio*. This practice was confirmed by the *Twelve Tables* in a provision (Tab. 5.3) that apparently read something like: "*Uti legassit super pecunia tutelave suae rei, ita ius esto*"[30] (As he made a legacy over his property [*pecunia*] and the guardianship of his goods, so let the law be). The provision talks of legating, not of appointing an heir; the word *pecunia* (property) does not have, as *familia* has, the implication of property treated as a unit, and it would thus seem that at that time this type of testamentary disposition did not extend, as it did later, to the appointment of the heir entitled to the estate.[31]

Although no heir could thus be appointed at the time of the *Twelve Tables*, this is, nonetheless, a very creative use of *mancipatio*. This variant *mancipatio* could be used to appoint a tutor under the will, a result very different from transferring *res mancipi*, and to transfer *res nec mancipi*. The variant shows that the wording of *mancipatio* was not absolutely fixed and that no real weighing out of copper had to be involved. There is also no evidence that the *familiae emptor* ever acquired any rights or duties as a result of the ceremony,[32] and the legatee became owner automatically on the testator's death. Hence the ceremony did not immediately transfer even *res mancipi* at the moment it was performed. This use seems to have been the result of private initiative, hence the clause confirming its legal effectiveness in the *Twelve Tables*.

But scholars seem to have difficulty in accepting the opportunism involved in this kind of development. Thus, Max Kaser talks in terms of a divided ownership between the testator and the *familiae emp-tor* and subsequently between the *familiae emptor* and the legatees.[33] None of this is justified by the sources, and such an explanation is needed only if one takes a formalistic attitude to legal development.

A further use of *mancipatio* was in marriage (*G*.1.113): "By *coemp-tio* women come into *manus* (matrimonial power) by *mancipatio*, that is by a sort of imaginary sale; thus, in the presence of not fewer than five Roman citizen witnesses above puberty, he, into whose *manus* she comes, buys the woman."[34] In early Rome, marriage was either *cum manu* or *sine manu*. The former put the wife into the family and under the power of her husband, or of his *paterfamilias* if he had one. The latter left her in her family, or *sui iuris*. *Coemptio* was one of the major ways of putting the wife into the *manus* of her husband, and it existed from an early date. Whether *coemptio* originally was a true sale cannot be established. Certainly one can draw no argument from the fact that the ceremony involved the appearance of a sale, since a similar procedure operated for adoption, which certainly did not in-volve sale and purchase. In all probability, *coemptio* was a device to extend marriage *cum manu* to segments of the population that could not make use of *confarreatio* for that purpose, which required the presence of some of Rome's highest religious dignitaries and hence was very much confined to the most powerful families.

One easily overlooked detail in *coemptio* is instructive regarding Roman legal opportunism. There is no indication that *coemptio* was restricted to situations in which a woman had a *paterfamilias*, and it would be very surprising if it were. But if the woman were *sui iuris*, there would be no one to whom the *familiae emptor* could give the copper. She would be in the *manus* of her husband and all her prop-erty would belong to him, so she should not be the recipient of the copper. The innovative Romans were unlikely to have wasted time on such an unimportant technicality.

Closely allied to *mancipatio*, probably in fact a version of it and cer-tainly an act *per aes et libram*, was *nexum*, by which a free man was bound to a creditor and was subject to his control until an amount of bronze that had been paid out was repaid.[35] *Nexum* was regulated by the *Twelve Tables* (Tab. 6.1), and probably in this context also belongs the provision (Tab. 4.2b): "*Si pater filium ter venum duit, filius a patre liber esto*" (If a father sells his son three times, let the son be free from the father).[36] If a son was mancipated—that is, given in *nexum*—three times by his father to work off a debt (or until a loan was repaid), the son would become free from paternal power. This clause came to be used pragmatically to achieve two very different ends. First was to free a son from paternal power (*emancipatio*) while his father was still alive and thus make the son a *pater* in his turn. This had numerous advantages for the son, above all in that only a person *sui iuris*, not subject to another's power, could own property.

> G.1.132: Moreover, children cease to be in paternal power by *emancipatio*. But a son passes out from paternal power by three mancipations, other descendants whether male or female by one mancipation. For the *Twelve Tables* speak of three mancipations in the case of the son alone, in these words: "If a father sells his son three times, let the son be free from the father." This is the procedure: the father mancipates the son to someone; this last manumits the son *vindicta*; on that account the son reverts into the *potestas* of his father. He mancipates him a second time either to the same or another person (but it is customary to mancipate him to the same person), and he afterward similarly manumits him *vindicta* again; and thereby he reverts again into the *potestas* of the father. The father mancipates him a third time either to the same or another person (but it is customary to mancipate him to the same person) and by this *mancipatio* he ceases to be in the power of the *pater* even though he has not yet been manumitted but is in the position of a *mancipium*.

But, of course, the person who received him by *mancipatio* for the third time would manumit the former son, who now became a *paterfamilias* in his own right. The interpretation of the *Twelve Tables*' provision as being restricted to sons, so that other descendants would be free from paternal power after one mancipation, is a minor example of opportunism intended to simplify the procedure.

The second pragmatic use of the *Twelve Tables* clause was to permit adoption of a person who was in *patria potestas*.

*G.*1.134: Further, fathers cease to have in their *potestas* those children whom they gave to others in adoption. In the case of a son, if he is given in adoption, three mancipations and two intervening manumissions are used, and they are accomplished in the same way as when a father is releasing him from *potestas* in order to make him *sui iuris*. Then either he is remancipated to the father and it is from the father that the adopter claims him as his son in front of the praetor, who, with the father making no counterclaim, adjudges the son to the claimant; or he is not remancipated to the father but the adopter claims him from the person with whom he is under the third mancipation. But remancipation to the father is more convenient. For other descendants whether of the male or female sex one mancipation is enough and either they are or are not remancipated to the father. In the provinces the same proceedings are used before the governor of the province.

We still have not finished with the opportunistic use made by the Romans of the simple ceremony of *mancipatio*. One further use may be adduced. Throughout the classical period,[37] a Roman woman who was *sui iuris* was subject to perpetual tutelage and required the authority of her tutor for various acts. But if she wished a more complaisant tutor, she could, as Gaius tells us (*G.*1.115), give herself in *coemptio* with the consent of her tutor, not for the purpose of marriage. The recipient would remancipate her to the person of her choice, whereupon, after being manumitted *vindicta* by him, she would come by matter of law under his tutelage. Until the time of Hadrian, this procedure had a particular advantage, since a woman who had not undergone *capitis deminutio*, or change of civil status, could not make a will.[38]

*G.*1.115a: Formerly, too, fiduciary *coemptio* was used for the purpose of making a will. For at that time women, with certain exceptions, did not have the right of making wills, unless they had made *coemptio* and had been remancipated and manumitted. But the senate on the authority of the deified Hadrian remitted the need of making a *coemptio*.

The uses made of *mancipatio* represent a splendid success story for legal opportunism. From being a formal, immediate conveyance of certain kinds of things, *mancipatio* became a way to create and transfer easements, to form a real security, to put a wife into the marital power (*manus*) of her husband, to adopt, to free a person from paternal power, to make a will under which even a tutor could be appointed, and to enable a woman to change her status, with the effect, *inter alia*, that she could make a will. But such juristic ingenuity needed official acceptance to be successful. Indeed, for some of the situations involved—notably adoption, emancipation, and the change of a woman's status—active state participation was required.

Opportunism by jurists can go a considerable way at times toward alleviating defects in official lawmaking. But it also pinpoints a failure by the state authorities to create the law that was wanted. Successful juristic opportunism with economy of means can only proceed out of such a failure. In addition, such successful opportunism shows a readiness on the part of the state authorities to allow others, private individuals at that, to make a considerable part of the private law. Yet the opportunistic uses of *mancipatio* have profound social and economic effects. The creation of legally recognized rustic praedial servitudes allows land to be used much more efficiently; *fiducia* has numerous agricultural and commercial advantages; *coemptio* greatly widens the social range of husbands who have wives in their power, adoption allows families that would otherwise become extinct to continue, emancipation greatly increases the number of persons who can own property, the (more or less) free power of testation is of great consequence for families and dynasties, and so even more is the power of testation accorded to women.

The uses made of *mancipatio* are by no means the only instances of legal opportunism and economy of means at Rome. Perhaps two other examples will suffice, and I wish to choose one that has already surfaced—*manumissio vindicta*. *Manumissio vindicta* existed from the very early Republic and was one of the main ways to manumit a slave; indeed, throughout the classical period, it was the main form of *inter vivos* manumission. A person who wished to free his slave would arrange for a friend to bring against him the *vindicatio in libertatem*, the claim for freedom, before the praetor. The friend thus claimed that a free man was being wrongfully held as a slave, the owner put up no defense, and the praetor declared the slave free.[39] Citizenship was acquired at the same time as freedom. The only other regular means in the Republic and early classical law for *inter vivos* freeing and giving citizenship to a slave was to enroll him on the census as a free man. This may or may not have involved a fiction, but in any event it was excessively inconvenient since the census was taken at most once every five years and after 166 B.C. was largely abandoned.[40]

My final example of economy of means is the contract of *stipulatio* with which we began this chapter, in discussing simplicity. It was, as I said, the earliest Roman contract, and the only one that could be used to make legally effective any type of lawful bargain. But it came to be used prominently in various contexts with their own particular understandings. Thus, it was used for three differing types of verbal guarantees, *sponsio, fidepromissio,* and *fideiussio.* It was used to make one specific type of promise of dowry, *dotis promissio.* It was also used to provide warranties against hidden defects and against eviction that were not provided for in the contract of sale. Thus, though a separate contract it could be used to provide for specific clauses in the context of a wider bargain.

The main point I want to establish is, of course, not that economy of means was (as, indeed it was) a feature of Roman private law, but that it was not a goal that was aimed at by the state. Rather, in the absence of reform, individuals, at times no doubt with the aid of the jurists, made creative use of existing machinery for new purposes.

We have reached the end of the last chapter, but not the end of the book. There are three appendices, termed as such not because they are unimportant, but to mark them off sharply from the rest of the book. Their force can only be felt in contrast to what has gone before.

# APPENDIX A
## Cicero the Outsider

We have recently been reminded that Cicero was "the only Roman republican social and political thinker of supreme importance, and if we are to recapture something of the experience of the Roman state, structure of rule, and cast of mind, his many works are a rich source and an indispensable guide."[1] It is this importance coupled with his knowledge of law that makes the contrast between the approach of Cicero and that of the jurists so revealing of the spirit of Roman law. In almost every particular his attitude is the reverse of that of the jurists.

Trained in the law as he was by the famous jurists Quintus Mucius Scaevola, the augur, and Quintus Mucius Scaevola, the *pontifex*, Cicero did not aim to be a jurist but an advocate.[2]

> *De amicitia* i.i: . . . Now, when I assumed the *toga virilis*, I was taken by my father to [Quintus Mucius] Scaevola [the augur] so that so far as I could and he would allow I would never leave the old man's side. And so I committed to memory many points carefully discussed by him, and many of his brief and pointed sayings. When he died I took myself to the consul [Quintus Mucius] Scaevola, whom I dare to proclaim as the most outstanding man of our state, both in intelligence and justice.

But, importantly, Cicero records a remark of Aquilius Gallus, "*Nihil hoc ad ius, ad Ciceronem*" (This has nothing to do with law, but with Cicero), when a dispute turned only on facts.[3] Cicero felt himself to be an outsider and was so regarded by the jurists. (In turn, Cicero's opinion of jurists as orators is unenthusiastic at best.[4]) In contrast he stresses the importance of oratory:

> Pro Murena 14.30: It should be granted that there are two arts
> that may raise men to the highest rank of office; the first that of
> a general, the second that of a good orator. For, by the latter the
> blessings of peace are retained, by the former the dangers of war
> are repulsed.

He relates, in the mouth of Crassus but as if it were a commonplace,
that orators lacked knowledge of the law.[5] He claims in his own voice
that orators, indeed, have no need for a deep acquaintance with law[6]
and maintains that cases were most handsomely argued by an elo-
quent man quite unversed in law.[7] Indeed, he complacently asserts
his own ignorance of the law[8] and states that the great orator Anto-
nius always despised the civil law.[9] He ridicules knowledge of law,
including that of the jurist Servius Sulpicius:

> Pro Murena 10.23: And since you seem to me to be caressing
> your knowledge of the law as if it were your little daughter, I will
> not allow you to continue in such a great error as to consider
> as something of value that trifle that you have learned with so
> much work. . . . 24. . . . There is no honor, Sulpicius, in that art
> of yours. 25. To begin with, there can be no dignity in so slight a
> science: for the subject matter is insignificant, being concerned,
> we might almost say, with spelling and division of words.

In fact, Cicero shows particular contempt for the very task most
prized by jurists, namely interpretation:

> De legibus 1.4.14: ATTICUS: . . . But please begin straightaway
> to explain what you think about the civil law. MARCUS: What
> I think? There have been the most eminent men in our state
> whose habitual function it was to interpret the law to the people,
> and give replies on it, but though they made great claims they
> spent their time on trivial matters. What subject is so big as the
> law of the state, but what task is so slight as that of those who
> give replies on legal matters. But it is necessary for the people.
> And while I do not judge those who have applied themselves
> to this task to have lacked a notion of universal law, still they
> have carried their studies of this civil law as they call it only so

far as they wished to be useful to the people. This amounts to
little with regard to learning, though it is necessary in practice.
Therefore, to what task are you calling me, or asking me to
explain. Do you want me to write tracts on the law of water
dripping from eaves or the law of common walls? Or to compose
formulas for stipulations and court procedure? These have both
been carefully written by many others, and they are also of a
lower stature than those that I think you expect from me.

Thus, Cicero is blaming the great men of the state who wasted their
time—and thought it important so to spend their time—as jurists
in interpreting the details of the actual law. Though they had some
notion of universal law, says Cicero, they were not interested in pur-
suing that branch of knowledge. His audience will want from him, he
believes, his opinion on more important matters than the interpretation of civil law.[10]

Though elsewhere he heaps praise on jurists for interpreting law to
anyone who consults them, he also makes the orator Crassus say:

De oratore 1.45.199: Indeed, for giving companionship and
grace to old age, what worthier refuge can there be than the
interpretation of law. For my part, from my youth, I laid up this
resource, not only for the practice of suits in court, but also
for the distinction and adornment of old age, so that when my
powers begin to fail (a time which already has almost come) I
might protect my home from loneliness.

Thus, interpretation of the law is to be reserved for old age and the
onset of senility, with the purpose of avoiding loneliness. Learning
the law has, of course, to be done earlier, but primarily for the sake
of appearing in court. Cicero responds to Crassus that old age might
possibly be equally redeemed from loneliness by a large fortune.[11]

Similarly, Cicero stresses the superiority of the task of the orator
and claims that a jurisconsult, who is not also an orator, is nothing
but a circumspect, sharp pettifogger, a crier of actions, a chanter of
formulas, and a catcher of syllables.[12]

Cicero's dismissal of the importance of the main work of the jurists is all the more striking in that he was aware that Roman law was so developed as to make all other systems look childish by comparison.[13]

Again, in sharp contrast to the jurists (with the exception of the much later Gaius), Cicero wanted to reduce the civil law to a system:[14]

> De oratore 1.42.190: . . . For if I am permitted to do what I have
> long planned, or if someone precedes me, burdened as I am, or
> completes the work when I am dead, first dividing the whole
> civil law into general classes (*genera*), which are very few; then
> distributing what I may call the limbs (*membra*) of those classes;
> then declaring the proper force of each by definition; then you
> will have a perfect system (*ars*) of the civil law, magnificent and
> fertile but neither inaccessible nor obscure.[15]

We know from Aulus Gellius[16] and Quintilian[17] that his book *De iure civili in artem redigendo* (On reducing the civil law to a system) was written, but it has not survived. Significantly, it seems to have had not the slightest impact on the thinking or writing of the jurists.

Likewise, in marked contrast to the jurists, Cicero took a serious interest in natural law. Indeed, though his starting point was in Stoic philosophy, he took the concept beyond what is in their writings.[18] He claimed that to know this law and justice was much more important than to know the civil law; and that the science of law should be drawn from the deepest philosophy and not, as the majority believed, from the praetor's Edict and previously from the *Twelve Tables*.[19] A clear statement is to be found in *De re publica* 3.22.33:

> True law is right reason in agreement with nature. It extends to
> all, unchanging, everlasting. It summons to duty by command-
> ing, and it averts from wrongdoing by prohibiting. It does not
> order or prohibit upright persons in vain, nor does it influence
> the wicked by command or prohibition. It is a sin to alter this
> law, nor is it permitted to derogate any part of it, nor abrogate it
> altogether. Nor indeed can we be released from this law either
> by the senate or by the people, nor is any other expounder or
> interpreter of it to be looked for. Nor will there be one law at
> Rome another at Athens, one law now, another later, but one

law, eternal and unchangeable, will contain all people and for all time. There will be one master and ruler, one god over all, the inventor, author and promulgator of this law.

Thus, natural law is of divine origin; it is independent of human promulgation and cannot be changed by human action. It is right reason in harmony with nature. It is the same law everywhere, applies to everyone, and is unchanging.[20] Elsewhere Cicero adds that natural law is common to god and man since it is based on reasoning, and therefore other animals do not participate in it.[21] Law that is contrary to natural law is, therefore, no law at all.[22] Here is a full vision of natural law, ready to pose a challenge to positive law, and it is precisely of the kind excluded by the jurists.

In keeping with this approach to natural law, and again in contrast with the jurists, Cicero stresses that there is and ought to be a connection between law and morality; and he shows a keen awareness that laws may be unjust.[23] He does not hesitate to designate as unfair some aspects of the Roman law of succession as they affect women.[24] Above all, in his theoretical writings Cicero shows a keen awareness of a philosophical dimension to law that is entirely absent from the jurists.

Finally, whereas the jurists in general concentrate on private law, the subject of most of their writings, the stress in Cicero is very different. His most sustained discussion of law is *De legibus*, of which the greater part of the first three books has survived. It is early made explicit that Cicero will be in no hurry to discuss private law.[25] In fact in book 1 he deals with natural law, in book 2 with sacred law, and in book 3 with aspects of public law, primarily with the state officials.

How many more books of *De legibus* were published is a matter of conjecture, but there must have been at least five since Macrobius refers to the fifth book.[26] The usual opinion is that there were six, since that is the number of books in his *De re publica*, and the present work contains his laws for his republic. We are, of course, most interested in his treatment of private law, but the clues are slight. Atticus is made to say that a subject remains to be discussed, namely, the law of the Roman people, and that Cicero had planned to do this. If we can take this at its face value, what had been proposed for discussion was in fact Roman private law.[27] But next Atticus goes on to say that what is missing is a treatment of the legal powers of the officials, still a topic of public law, and that these powers should be discussed. Cicero responds:

> 3.20.49: I will do so briefly if I can. For your father's friend, Marcus Junius, dedicated to him a long treatise on the subject, which in my judgment was written with skill and care. We ought to investigate and discuss the law of nature according to our own judgment, but with regard to the law of the Roman people we must follow precedent and tradition.

Marcus Junius Gracchanus's treatise was certainly on an aspect of Roman public law, so the subject that Cicero is proposing now to discuss is part of Roman public law, not as he has up to this point the *ideal* law for the ideal state. If we can assume[28] from the last sentence quoted above that Cicero regards himself as having finished his treatment of natural law and is now going to discuss Roman law, we should recall that he has never treated an ideal private law according to natural law. Perhaps the missing remainder of *De legibus* also omitted a treatment of private law, ideal or Roman?

What emerges from this, and has to be stressed for an understanding of the spirit of Roman law, is that Cicero's outlook is remarkably different from that of the jurists. That is why it is appropriate in a book of this kind to treat Cicero's views in an appendix.

# APPENDIX B

## Gaius and His *Institutes*

It must seem surprising to treat only in an appendix something Roman that was so momentous in the world's legal history as Gaius's *Institutes*, but that is the only reasonable approach. The fact is that Gaius was quite exceptional, and his work does not really correspond to the spirit of Roman law. For A. M. Honoré, "if we take the evidence at its face value, Gaius was the originator of no fewer than three types of legal literature."[1] If one does not accept Honoré's claim that Gaius's *Res Cottidianae* was a book on everyday matters addressed to the general public,[2] it would remain the case that Gaius was responsible for two types of original work. Thus, he alone of the jurists wrote a commentary on the provincial Edict. It was, at that, a largish work, in thirty books. Of the jurists, therefore, he was alone in taking a prolonged look at legal matters outside Rome. Unlike the others, he was interested in more than *iudicia legitima*. His other work of an original type, which will be our main concern here, is the *Institutes*, a teaching manual.

The *Institutes*, whatever the faults in its organization, was a wholly original attempt to set out the law in a systematic way. In his interest in systematization, Gaius was unique among the jurists. It is appropriate to list his achievements in this field. It was he who declared "All the law that we use relates either to persons or to things or to actions,"[3] and he then set out the law in these terms, dealing, consistently, with persons in book 1, things (including ownership, succession, and obligations) in books 2 and 3, and actions in book 4. The result is something remarkably more sophisticated than Quintus Mucius's *Ius Civile*, followed in arrangement as that work was by Sabinus's *Ius Civile* and the commentaries of Pomponius, Ulpian, and Paul *ad Sabinum*.[4]

Again, Gaius was the first to treat contracts and delicts, the law of obligations, as a unit. For the first time the contracts appear together and so do the delicts, which follow upon the contracts in Gaius's arrangement. Indeed, the contracts are divided into four groups, according to how they were created: contracts made by delivery, orally, in writing, or simply by agreement however that was expressed. Though in the *Institutes* he classified obligations as arising from contract or delict, Gaius went further in his *Res Cottidianae* and was well on the way to claim that other obligations arose as if from contract and yet others as if from wrongdoing.[5]

Moreover, Gaius was the first to treat together, and weave into a usually harmonious whole, both civil law and edictal law.

To understand the nature of this achievement, and Gaius's isolation, it is enough to recall the lack of systematization on the part of the great jurists long after Gaius's demise. Indeed, whether because his work was unknown to other jurists or not, he had little success in having his approach adopted. In fact, he is followed, so far as we can really tell, only in the *Regulae Ulpiani*, which is often considered not to be by the great jurist.[6]

But if Gaius was neglected by the other jurists, the *Institutes* was a great success as a teaching book; consequently more fragments of it have come down to us than of any other classical law book. The *Regulae Ulpiani* may well have been the second most popular teaching book.[7]

As part of the great compilation of Roman law, the emperor Justinian issued in 533 an elementary textbook with the force of law.[8] The *Institutes* of Justinian are modeled on, and are very much a revised edition of, the *Institutes* of "*Gaius noster*," "our own Gaius," as Justinian called him.[9] In their turn, Justinian's *Institutes* became the main model of hundreds of "institutes" of local law, primarily in the seventeenth and eighteenth centuries,[10] and they likewise were the basis, and formed the structure, of modern civil codes, such as the French *code civil* of 1804. Without a systematic work such as Justinian's *Institutes* at the center of legal education from the eleventh century onward, Roman law would have been much less approachable, and the Reception of it would have been much more difficult. But its very success has tended to obscure just what an aberrant work the *Institutes* were.

Gaius is a unique figure in Roman law: in addition to what has already been said in this appendix, he, together with Pomponius,[11] were the sole jurists interested in legal history. That he was somehow an outsider is confirmed by the fact that, of the jurists, only Pomponius appears to have referred to him.[12] It is ironical in the extreme that the one man who, different from all others, tried in a sustained way to create a systematic structure for Roman law, and who was outside of the main tradition, created a system that is so much regarded as embodying "the spirit of Roman law" but would not have been recognized by the Romans.

# APPENDIX C

## A Conclusion: The Astonishing Success of Roman Law

Paul Vinogradoff begins his celebrated book *Roman Law in Medieval Europe*[1] by claiming "Within the whole range of history there is no more momentous and puzzling problem than the subsequent Reception of Roman law." For me, there is no puzzling problem. The Reception "corresponds to the cultural norms of massive, voluntary legal borrowing."[2] Borrowing is the name of the legal game. Once law is well developed and accessible, it will serve as a quarry for other systems. Roman law as set out by Justinian was in writing and was the most detailed law available in the Middle Ages and later. Once it becomes common to borrow from a particular system, to borrow from that system becomes the right and proper thing to do. For me it is a non-Reception that would have constituted the most puzzling problem of history. We are, of course, concerned with private law, the supreme Roman achievement.

Nonetheless the success of Roman law is astonishing in a different way. The surprise is that Roman law ever reached the degree of achievement where it could be borrowed. The truth that emerges from the preceding chapters is that the Romans—and here I do not mean the average men in the street, but those powerful figures who shaped the law and society—were not really interested in law. These Romans were not interested in building up a legal system, nor in making law systematic, nor in law reform, nor in having law serve specific social aims, nor in law as contributing to order.[3] The jurists were primarily interested in interpretation according to rules they devised for themselves, and they neglected other parts of legal work. It was the conceptualization resulting from their interpretation, coupled with the *Institutes*, that made Roman law the supreme law force for succeeding centuries.

The jurists in their lives were first and foremost politicians or bureaucrats. It must be stressed that to give opinions or write books was not a profession or even a part-time job for these upper-class gentlemen but a recreation, like playing chess. But chess is not a good analogy because it has no social dimension, it is governed by fixed rules, and playing ability does not generally affect social standing. Perhaps a closer recreational analogy is with pheasant shooting as it is practiced in the United Kingdom. To shoot pheasants is already to be in a particular class though the activity is not nearly so exclusive as to be a jurist. Not everyone in that class shoots pheasants but those who do have a special regard for their fellows. Their sporting activity spills over into their social life. Again, they concentrate on shooting the birds, not on studying them in the round. They recognize, whether or not they have keepers raising birds for them, that their sport has implications both for the ecology of pheasants and other wildlife and also for the economy, but that recognition remains in the background. On one rather superficial level the sport of killing pheasants is the goal; on another it is winning the respect of one's fellows. To be considered a good shot is to receive an accolade from one's peers. To be active and skilled in raising or preserving pheasants receives no applause. Even the pleasure of eating pheasant is not important: typically, most of the bag is sold for a pittance, and anyone can buy shot wild pheasant from a game dealer for a fraction of what it cost to shoot it. Rules of behavior, of approaching the sport, develop often implicitly, and noncompliance will awaken unspoken disdain. There are good shoots and rubbish shoots. A rubbish shoot is not a shoot with few birds but one with rubbish birds—that is, the stands are so placed that the birds are not high and the hunters have considerable time to aim and fire. Pheasant shooting should not be easy. It must be a challenge. A marked feature of the sport is the kindly, gentle but watchful, unorganized training of the next generation.

The jurists came from a particular stratum of society. They concentrated on interpretation and neglected other aspects of law. They won the approbation of their fellows (and others) by proferring an ingenious opinion based on an accepted style of reasoning. It was on this basis that Papinian was the most admired jurist. Nothing else among the law jobs had this effect. Structuring the materials won no applause. Nor did simply coming up with a solution that overtly bene-fited society. Reforming the law by invoking action from the emperor was disapproved. It is no coincidence that the one jurist, Gaius, who was interested in systematizing the law was ignored by his fellows.

I have argued at various times that though law has a great impact on society, society's input into law is often very limited, and even that is filtered through the culture of the lawmaking elite.[4] Law is very much a product of this elite, who to a very great extent develop law according to cultural norms that they have made for themselves. Roman law presents an extreme example of this.

# NOTES

## Preface

1 This is so true that numerous books with a general title, such as the examples below, are confined to private law; W. W. Buckland, *Textbook of Roman Law*, 3d ed. by P. Stein (Cambridge, 1963); F. Schulz, *Classical Roman Law* (Oxford, 1951); J. A. C. Thomas, *Textbook of Roman Law* (Amsterdam, 1976); B. Nicholas, *Introduction to Roman Law* (Oxford, 1962); R. W. Lee, *The Elements of Roman Law*, 4th ed. (London, 1956); V. Arangio-Ruiz, *Istituzioni di diritto romano*, 14th ed. (Naples, 1960); M. Talamanca, *Istituzioni di diritto romano* (Milan, 1990); P. F. Girard, *Manuel élémentaire de droit romain*, 8th ed. by F. Senn (Paris, 1929); R. Monier, *Manuel élémentaire de droit romain* 1, 6th ed. (Paris, 1947), 2d and 5th eds. (Paris, 1954). This narrow focus on private law is well brought out by the fact that the first book published in any language on Roman administrative law appeared in 1992: O. F. Robinson, *Ancient Rome: City Planning and Administration* (London). Moreover the great bulk of information on the subject of administrative law is from nonlegal sources. It comes as no surprise that the great works on Roman constitutional and criminal law were written by someone much more a historian than a legal scholar: Theodor Mommsen, *Römisches Staatsrecht*, 3d ed., vols. 1–3 (Leipzig, 1887–88) and *Römisches Strafrecht* (Leipzig, 1899).

2 *Geist des römischen Rechts*, published from 1852 onward.

3 *Principles of Roman Law* (Oxford, 1936).

## Chapter 2: The Spiritual History of the Law

1 See, in general, P. S. Atiyah, *Pragmatism and Theory in English Law* (London, 1987).

2 See, e.g., Watson, *Slave Law*, pp. 102ff.

3 Suetonius, *Divus Iulius*, 42.

4 See Robinson, *Ancient Rome*, pp. 34ff.

5 Texts that touch on markets are discussed in chapter 3.

6 For the full argument see Watson, *State, Law and Religion*.

7 Instructive is, e.g., J.-L. Halpérin, "Tribunat de la plèbe et haute plèbe

(493–218 av. J.C.)," *Revue historique du droit français et étranger* (1984), pp. 161ff.

8   See, e.g., Rotondi, *Leges publicae,* p. 236.

9   See, e.g., Rotondi, *Leges publicae,* pp. 216ff.

10   4.7.2; 5.12.9.

11   See, e.g., Rotondi, *Leges publicae,* pp. 212f.

12   6.42.9ff; 8.15.9.

13   See Watson, *State, Law and Religion,* pp. 76f.

14   1.43.10, 11.

15   For this struggle see Livy, 3.9.1ff; 3.10.5ff; 3.11.3, 9, 12f; 3.15.1; 3.18.6; 3.19.11; 3.31.5ff; 3.32.1; 3.32.5ff; 3.34.6; 4.3.17; Dionysius of Halicarnassus, 10.1.1ff; 10.2.1; 10.3.3ff; 10.4; 10.51.5; 10.55.4ff; 10.57.6; 10.58.4.

16   *D.*1.2.5f.

17   For more detail see Watson, *State, Law and Religion,* pp. 75ff.

18   See Kunkel, *Herkunft,* pp. 38ff; cf. A. Schiavone, *Giuristi e nobili nella Roma repubblicana* (Rome, 1987).

19   Cf., e.g., Schulz, *Principles,* pp. 84ff. It seems proper to record here the criticism of a friend who is a skilled legal historian but with no exposure to Roman law. He considered much of the argument of the book to be circular. In his view, I defined Roman private law as jurists' law, and excluded other aspects of law as not involving the spirit of Roman law. Thus, for him, I excluded custom, downplayed legislation, *senatus consulta,* and the decrees of the emperors, and turned praetorian edictal law into the work of the jurists. For me, the criticism is illuminating for the spirit of Roman law. The most striking fact in its development is precisely the prominence of the jurists and in this it stands in marked contrast to Anglo-American law.

## Chapter 3: Public Law and Private Law: Public and Religious Dimensions

1   Cf., e.g., F. de Zulueta, *The Institutes of Gaius,* vol. 2 (Oxford, 1953), p. 5.

2   Cf. F. Wieacker, *Textstufen klassischer Juristen* (Göttingen, 1960), pp. 186ff.

3   There is no evidence that it had any impact on their thinking: see appendix B.

4   See, e.g., Kunkel, *Herkunft,* p. 14.

5   See, e.g., Kunkel, *Herkunft,* pp. 21f.

6   But they are mentioned again in Valerius Maximus, 8.12.1, which is concerned with this passage of Cicero.

7   G.2.5, 6.

8   G.2.8.

9   "Learning in the law entails knowledge of God and man," which is the translation of P. Birks and G. McLeod, gives entirely the wrong impression: *Justinian's Institutes* (Ithaca, 1987), p. 38. Though that book is the most recent translation into English it must always be consulted with caution.

10  There is an important mistranslation by Birks and McLeod of part of this text (*Justinian's Institutes*, p. 147): "*Sed de publicis iudiciis haec exposuimus, ut vobis possibile sit summo digito et quasi per indicem ea tetigisse*" ("We have not said much about crime. Our finger has pointed, like an informer's; yours have touched the subject's surface"). I would translate something like: "But we have said this much about criminal actions for it to be possible for you to have touched the subject with the tip of your finger and almost with your forefinger."

    As translators in the past have noticed, this is not a passage that lends itself to elegant translation. But there is certainly nothing in the Latin to justify Birks and McLeod's "Our finger" and "yours." If *summo digito et quasi per indicem* go together, as they seem to translate (and I would agree), then the finger mentioned belongs either to the students or to the emperor, but it cannot belong to both. *Ut vobis possibile sit summo digito . . . ea tetigisse* shows that Justinian is writing of the students' finger and not, as Birks and McLeod have it, of the emperor's. And though *index* can mean an "informer," it is surely correct in the context of *summo digito* to translate it as "forefinger" or "index finger." Also, there is probably a reminiscence here of *G*.3.54, where *index* can only refer to a finger, not to an informer.

11  *J*.1.5.1.

12  *J*.1.13.2.

13  *J*.2.1.39.

14  The contrast between his description of the subject and his partial treatment of it may mislead the unwary. Thus, Birks and McLeod mistranslate "*dicendum est igitur de iure privato, quod est tripertitum*" as "Our business is private law. It has three parts." (*Justinian's Institutes*, p. 38.) The best that can be said for them is that, without saying so, they have changed the punctuation of the Latin that they print.

15  *J*.2.1pr, 2.

16 See, e.g., Watson, *State, Law and Religion*, pp. 14ff, 21ff.

17 Whether it was a legal requirement that the wife had to be led to the husband's house is disputed. I believe *deductio in domum* was required in the Empire but not in the Republic: A. Watson, *The Law of Persons in the Later Roman Republic* (Oxford, 1967), pp. 25ff; and Treggiari thinks it was never a legal requirement: *Marriage*, p. 167.

18 Cicero, *Philippicae* 2.69; Plautus, *Amphitruo* 928, *Trinummus* 266; Seneca the Elder, *Suasoriae* 1.6; Apuleius, *Metamorphoses* 5.26; Martial, 10.41.2; Quintilian, *Declamationes* 262.6. See Treggiari, *Marriage*, pp. 441ff.

19 *D.*24.1.35; 24.2.9; 38.11.1.1; 48.5.44. See Treggiari, *Marriage*, pp. 454.

20 See for details, Treggiari, *Marriage*, pp. 461ff; Kaser, *Privatrecht* 2:174ff.

21 *Novellae* 117.10, 140.

22 One text, *D.*1.15.4, mentions that the prefect of the city had the duty to hunt down runaway slaves and return them to their owners.

23 For the American South see, e.g., Watson, *Slave Law*, pp. 63ff.

24 See, e.g., *D.*48.8.11.1, 2; 18.1.42; 48.8.4.2; *C.Th.*9.12.1, 2; *Coll.* 3.3.4, 3.4.1; *J.*1.8.1, 2.

25 *G.*1.41f; *Epitome Ulpiani* 1.14; *P.S.* 4.14.4.

26 *G.*1.38, 40; *Epitome Ulpiani* 1.13; *C.*2.30.3pr.

27 See, e.g., Watson, *Slave Law*, pp. 75ff.

28 *C.*1.13.1.

29 *C.*1.13.2.

30 See, e.g., Watson, *Roman Law and Comparative Law*, pp. 122ff.

31 In very early times only one verb, *spondere*, was effective; *G.*3.93.

32 Contrast the need for writing to prove the English covenant: see, e.g., Watson, *Roman Law and Comparative Law*, pp. 145ff.

33 *Ancient Rome*, p. 133.

34 *D.*48.10.32.1 concerns the general tampering with publicly approved weights and measures; cf. *D.*19.1.32.

35 See, e.g., Watson, *Studies*, pp. 289, 298; J. A. C. Thomas, "*Contractatio*, Complicity and *furtum*," 13 *IURA* (1962), pp. 70ff at p. 86.

36 See Robinson, *Ancient Rome*, pp. 34ff, 42ff, 48ff, 66ff, 72ff, 135ff, 158ff, 206ff. A few jurists did write treatises on aspects of public law: cf. Schulz, *Legal Science*, pp. 46, 81. But private law above all was the concern of the jurists.

37 See, e.g., Cicero, *De harispicum responsis* 9.19, *De natura deorum* 2.3.8; Sallust, *Bellum Catilinae* 12.3, *Bellum Jugurthinum* 14.19; Valerius Maximus, 1.1.8.9; Tertullian, *Apologeticus* 25.2; Polybius 6.56.6ff.

Augustine pokes fun at the notion in *De civitate Dei* 4.8; cf., e.g.,
G. Wissowa, *Religion und Kultus der Römer*, 2d ed. (Leipzig, 1912), pp.
386ff; W. H. C. Frend, *Martyrdom and Persecution in the Early Church*
(New York, 1967), pp. 77f.

38  See, e.g., K. Latte, *Römische Religionsgeschichte*, 2d ed. (Munich, 1967);
E. Simon, *Die Götter der Römer* (Munich, 1990).

39  *G*.1.144f.

40  For the ceremony see *G*.1.112; *Epitome Ulpiani* 9.1; Servius, *In Vergilii
Georgica* 1.31 and *In Vergilii Aeneidon* 4.103, 339, 374.

41  See Watson, *State, Law and Religion*, pp. 51f. If the ceremony was mentioned in the *Twelve Tables*, which is disputed, it would be only because
of the introduction of *usus*, the third mode of creating *manus*.

42  R. E. Mitchell, *Patricians and Plebeians: The Origins of the Roman State*
(Ithaca, 1990), pp. 83f.

43  See, e.g., Kaser, *Privatrecht* 1:324.

44  Aulus Gellius, *Noctes Atticae* 5.19.7–10; 15.27.3; Servius, *In Vergilii
Aeneidon* 2.156; *G*.1.101f.

45  2.25.2.

46  *G*.1.112.

47  Aulus Gellius, *Noctes Atticae* 15.27.3; Servius, *In Vergilii Aeneidon*
2.156.

48  What follows derives in large measure from Watson, *State, Law and
Religion*, pp. 44ff.

49  *G*.2.96; *Epitome Gai* 2.9.4; *D*.40.12.44pr.

50  The logic of the device is not perfect, but that is in the nature of dodges.

51  *D*.12.3.5.3; 12.3.2.

52  *D*.12.3.1; 12.3.4.2.

53  See the texts in *D*.12.2.

54  Livy, 3.31.5ff.

55  Watson, *State, Law and Religion*, pp. 21ff.

56  I am grateful to Patricia Crone for insisting on this point with me. An
example of religious values enshrined in law without being expressly
mentioned is in *C.Th*.3.8.2; cf. A. Watson, "Religious and Gender Dis-
crimination: St. Ambrose and the Valentiniani," to appear in *Law, Religion, and Society*, ed. L. Mayali (Berkeley, 1994).

57  Cf. A. Ernout and A. Meillet, *Dictionnaire étymologique de la langue
latine*, 4th ed. (Paris, 1967), p. 329.

58  *In Virgilii Georgica* 1.269.

## Chapter 4: Juristic Law and the Sources of Law

1   See, e.g., Watson, *Roman Law and Comparative Law*, pp. 97ff.

2   See, e.g., Jolowicz and Nicholas, *Historical Introduction*, pp. 479ff.

3   *C. Deo auctore* §9.

4   Contrast volume 1 (ed. S. Riccobono, Florence, 1941) and volume 2 (ed. J. Furlani, Florence, 1940) of *Fontes iuris romani antejustinani.*

5   For the meaning of Cicero, *Topica*, 5.28 and *Rhetorica ad Herennium* 2.13.19, see Watson, *Law Making*, pp. 3ff. For custom in very early Rome see L. Capogrossi Colognesi, "Les *mores gentium* et la formation consuetudinaire du droit romain archaïque (7$^e$–4$^e$ s. avant J.C.)," 51 *Recueils de la Société Jean Bodin* (Brussels, 1990), pp. 91ff.

6   *D.*23.2.39.1; 23.2.8.

7   *D.*29.2.8pr.

8   For the argument see Watson, *XII Tables*, pp. 52ff.

9   Tab. 5.3; 5.6; 8.20.

10  For the argument see Watson, *XII Tables*, p. 72.

11  *D.*28.6.2pr.

12  *D.*24.1.1.

13  *Vat. Fr.* 302.

14  *Rhetorica ad Herennium*, 2.13.19.

15  See Watson, *Law Making*, pp. 170f.

16  See, e.g., J. A. C. Thomas, "Custom and Roman Law," 31 *T.v.R.* (1963), pp. 39ff, and the works he cites.

17  Thomas, "Custom," p. 45.

18  This kind of relationship between jurist (*mufti*) and judge (*gadi*) will be familiar to students of Islamic law, particularly with regard to the extraordinary cognition.

19  This is not the same as regarding decisions as sources of law.

20  *Rhetorica ad Herennium* 2.9.13; 2.10.14; 2.13.19; Cicero, *De oratore*, 2.56.240: cf. Schulz, *Legal Science*, pp. 92f.

21  Cf., e.g., Jolowicz and Nicholas, *Historical Introduction*, p. 368.

22  For the development of the Edict, see Watson, *Law Making*, pp. 31ff.

23  See Lenel, *Edictum*, pp. 299f.

24  See, e.g., P. Stein, *Fault in the Formation of Contract* (Edinburgh, 1958), pp. 67ff.

25  *D.*18.1.4, 5, 6pr.

## Chapter 5: Legal Isolationism: I

1 See, e.g., J. Marquardt, *Das Privatleben der Römer*, 2d ed. (Leipzig, 1886), 1:47ff.

2 See, e.g., ibid., pp. 123ff.

3 *De agri cultura*, 146.

4 See also Schulz, *Principles*, pp. 19ff.

5 Of course, a diligent researcher might come up with some hidden clues.

6 Daube, "Fashions and Idiosyncrasies in the Exposition of Roman Law of Property," in *Collected Studies* 2:1327ff.

7 For this approach to *fructus* see, e.g., P. F. Girard, *Manuel élémentaire de droit romain*, 7th ed. (Paris, 1924), p. 262 and n. 3.

8 "An Unacceptable Face of Human Property," in *New Perspectives in the Roman Law of Property*, ed. P. Birks (Oxford, 1989), pp. 61ff.

9 It is enough to think of the famous case of Arescusa, which is discussed later in the chapter.

10 It is noteworthy that in the whole of Roman literature, legal and non-legal, there is no reference to the sexual abuse of slave children by their owners. Are we to assume that such did not occur? Or rather (as I would suppose), that it was a subject unworthy of notice?

11 Watson, "Morality, Slavery and the Jurists in the Later Roman Republic," *Legal Origins*, pp. 266f. The other important texts besides Gaius are Cicero, *de finibus* 1.4.12; *D*.7.1.68pr.

12 Birks has chosen to misrepresent my position, ignoring my observations on the harmful consequences of the decision: "An Unacceptable Face," p. 62.

13 *D*.18.1.1.1; *G*.3.141; cf., above all, Daube, "The Three Quotations from Homer in *D*.18.1.1.1," *Collected Studies* 1:341ff.

14 Cf., e.g., Kaser, *Privatrecht* 1:161.

15 Naturally, we should be looking only at chapter 3, since chapters 1 and 2 are earlier: for the argument see Daube, "On the Third Chapter of the *lex Aquilia*," *Collected Studies* 1:16ff.

16 Attempts have been made, of course, but none has found support. See, e.g., B. Beinart, "Once More on the Origin of the Lex Aquilia," *Butterworths South African Law Journal* (1956), pp. 70ff. A. M. Honoré resorts to redating the statute: "Linguistic and Social Context of the *Lex Aquilia*," *Irish Jurist* (1972), pp. 138ff.

17 See Jerome's continuation of Eusebius's *Chronicles* 11, 139h (in Schöne's edition); Dio Cassius, 48.33.5; Isidorus, *Etymologiae* 5.15.2.

18    See Appian, *Civil War* 5.8.67.

19    Cf. Watson, *Succession*, pp. 170ff.

20    See, e.g., D.24.1.64 (marriage of Maecenas and Terentia); 24.3.66pr (dowry of Licinnia, widow of Gaius Gracchus); 50.7.18(17) (surrender of Hostilius Mancinus to the Numantini, who refused to accept him); 49.15.5.3 (no *postliminium* for Atilius Regulus; citizenship for Menander).

21    Cf. Daube, "Zur Palingenesie einiger Klassikerfragmente," *Collected Studies* 2:793.

22    *Roman Law*, p. 105.

23    *De oratore* 3.33.133; also 1.45.200.

24    See Watson, *State, Law and Religion*, pp. 70f.

25    See, e.g., Livy, 31.9.8. *De oratore* 3.33.133 should not mislead one into thinking that giving advice on marrying a daughter and so on, which would involve knowledge of the questioner's circumstances, meant that the jurist took a personal interest in the outcome of any legal advice he gave. The two activities were dissimilar. A jurist was expected to give his legal opinion to anyone who asked for it. On the other hand, only *clientes*, whether in the technical Roman sense or not, would ask for advice on marrying a daughter, buying a farm, or cultivating a field. When such advice is sought, receiving an answer is but a small part of the purpose.

26    See the sources cited in Watson, *Law Making*, pp. 106ff. They also frequently attended court and advised the judges: Cicero, *Topica*, 17.65f.

## Chapter 6: State Law: Statute and Edict

1    For the argument see Watson, *Law Making*, pp. 6ff.

2    *Res gestae divi Augusti* 6.2; Suetonius, *Augustus*, 34; Seneca, *De beneficiis* 6.32: cf. Rotondi, *Leges publicae*, pp. 443ff; P. A. Brunt and J. M. Moore, *Res gestae divi Augusti* (London, 1967), pp. 46ff.

3    G.1.42, 46, 139; 2.228, 239; *P.S.* 4.14; *Epitome Ulpiani* 1.24; C.7.3.1.

4    G.1.13, 27, 29, 31; *Epitome Ulpiani* 1.11; *Coll.* 16.2.5; D.40.9.5; C.7.2.5.

5    For details see Watson, *Law Making*, pp. 14f.

6    See, e.g., Schulz, *Principles*, p. 6ff.

7    "Texts and Interpretation in Roman and Jewish Law," now in *Collected Works of David Daube*, vol. 1, *Talmudic Law* (Berkeley, 1992), pp. 173ff at p. 174.

8    For my view see Watson, "Personal Injuries in the XII Tables," *Studies*, pp. 253ff.

9   The argument is set out in Watson, *Law Making*, pp. 45ff.

10  For sources and the argument that it was proposed by the *dictator* C. Poetilius Libo Visolus in 313 B.C. see Watson, *Law Making*, pp. 9ff.

11  *Lex Furia testamentaria* (between 204 and 169 B.C.); *lex Voconia* (169 B.C.); *lex Cornelia* (probably 81 B.C.); *lex Falcidia* (40 B.C.).

12  For these see Lenel, *Edictum*, pp. 355ff. There were also edicts on testate succession: Lenel, *Edictum*, pp. 342ff, 361ff.

13  *De legibus* 1.5.17.

14  But my failure to discuss the Edicts of provincial governors has a different reason from the same failure of the jurists. I do not discuss them because their characteristics (if not their substance) are akin to the praetorian Edicts. The jurists did not discuss them because they were not interested in what happened outside Rome.

15  See, e.g., Lenel, *Edictum*, pp. 252ff.

16  See, e.g., ibid., pp. 288ff.

17  See in general, M. Kaser, "Ius honorarium und ius civile," 101 *ZSS* (1984), pp. 1ff.

18  For this evidence, see Watson, *Law Making*, pp. 33f.

19  *C. Tanta* §18; *C.*4.5.10.1; Eutropius, *Breviarium* 8.17; Aurelius Victor, *De Caesaribus* 19.2.

20  *C. Tanta* §18.

21  See, e.g., Schulz, *Legal Science*, pp. 148ff.

22  See above all, Daube, "The Peregrine Praetor," *Collected Studies*, vol. 1, pp. 395ff.

23  For the argument see Watson, *Law Making*, pp. 63ff.

24  For the argument see A. Watson, "Sellers' Liability for Defects: Aedilician Edict and Praetorian Law," 38 *IURA* (1987), pp. 167ff.

25  An example of the mistaken view is in D. Johnston, *The Roman Law of Trusts* (Oxford, 1988), pp. 4f.

26  See, e.g., Watson, *Law Making*, pp. 30ff.

27  See, e.g., W. W. Buckland, *Equity in Roman Law* (London, 1911), pp. 7f.

28  For the argument see Watson, *Law Making*, pp. 21ff.

29  See, e.g., Lenel, *Edictum*, pp. 364f.

30  See, e.g., Lenel, *Edictum*, pp. 364f; E. Volterra, *Senatus Consulta* (Turin, 1969), pp. 67f.

31  See, e.g., Kaser, *Privatrecht* 1:702.

## Chapter 7: Juristic Law: Reasoning and Conceptualization

1    Roman legal reasoning so dominated subsequent thought that the absence of result-oriented argument appears to be natural: see A. Watson, *Joseph Story and the Comity of Errors* (Athens, Ga., 1992), p. 117 n. 29.

2    *G.*3.176ff. See, e.g., Watson, *Obligations,* pp. 214ff; Thomas, *Textbook,* pp. 345ff.

3    See, e.g., Lewis and Short, *A Latin Dictionary* (Oxford, 1879), *s.v. pecus;* the *Oxford Latin Dictionary* (Oxford, 1982) *s.v. pecus.*

4    Varro, *De re rustica* 1.2.18.

5    See, e.g., Varro, *De re rustica* 2.4.

6    Cf. Schulz, *Principles,* pp. 48f.

7    Cf., e.g., Kunkel, *Herkunft,* pp. 114, 258.

8    *G.*3.97ff.

9    Not surprisingly, Ulpian's position has been much misunderstood by modern scholars: cf. Watson, *Obligations,* p. 86.

10    Cf. Watson, *State, Law and Religion,* pp. 8f.

11    See, e.g., Schulz, *Legal Science,* pp. 17f.

12    See Schulz, *Legal Science,* pp. 19, 111, 335.

13    *Ad familiares* 7.10.2.

14    See above all Lenel, *Edictum,* p. 489.

15    See Lenel, *Edictum,* p. 470.

16    *D.*41.2.3.1; *P.S.* 5.2.1; cf. Buckland, *Textbook,* p. 197.

17    For all four jurists the recipient of the *precarium* would not prevail in the *interdictum uti possidetis* against the grantor, precisely because he held *precario* from the grantor.

18    *Das Recht des Besitzes,* 7th ed. (Vienna, 1865).

19    *Der Besitzwille* (Jena, 1889).

20    See, e.g., Thomas, *Textbook,* pp. 138ff.

21    *D.*41.2.12.1; cf. *h.t.* 52pr; 43.17.1.2.

22    *Roman Law,* pp. 11ff.

23    *Roman Law,* p. 17.

## Chapter 8: Jurists and Reality

1    Some instances to protect a dowry will be found in Daube, *Roman Law,* pp. 105ff.

2    *Furtum* may or may not have originally required asportation. I accept the

argument of P. Birks that the derivation of the word from *ferre* is inconclusive; "A Note on the Development of *furtum*," 8 *Irish Jurist* (1973),
pp. 349ff at pp. 350f. For present purposes it is enough that touching was
the requirement by the first century B.C.: see *D*.47.2.21pr; cf. Watson,
*Obligations*, pp. 220f, and the works there cited.

3 See, e.g., *D*.47.2.21pr, 5, 6; *h.t.* 22.1, 2.

4 See, e.g., *D*.47.2.21.8, 9, 10.

5 See, e.g., *D*.47.2.40; *h.t.* 81pr, 1, 2; *G*.3.196; *J*.4.1.6; Aulus Gellius, *Noctes
Atticae* 6.15, 16.

6 See, e.g., *D*.47.2.10; *h.t.* 11; *h.t.* 12; *h.t.* 14.2, 3, 5, 6, 7, 11, 12, 15, 16; *h.t.*
15pr; *h.t.* 46.3, 4, 5, 6; *h.t.* 91pr.

7 For another statement by Paul to the same effect see *P.S.* 2.31.12.

8 *Römische Rechtsgeschichte* 2 (Leipzig, 1901), p. 785.

9 See, e.g., H. F. Jolowicz, *Digest XLVII.2. De Furtis* (Cambridge, 1940),
pp. 48ff.

10 For the proposition see Watson, "*Contrectatio* as an Essential of *Furtum*,"
*Studies*, pp. 283ff; "*Contrectatio* Again," in *Studies*, pp. 291ff.

11 *D*.47.2.36pr; *h.t.* 50.1.

12 See also Watson, "*D*.28.5.45(44): An Unprincipled Decision on a Will,"
*Studies*, pp. 161ff.

13 "*D*.47.2.52.20: The Jackass, the Mares and *Furtum*," now in *Studies*,
pp. 303ff.

14 This is a different understanding of the text from that found in *The
Digest of Justinian*, by T. Mommsen, P. Krueger, and A. Watson (Phila-
delphia, 1985).

15 See chapter 5 for a discussion of dowry or deposit in a slave's "marriage."

16 Nor need it have been. *Mutuum* was necessarily gratuitous only in the
sense that the action on it, the *condictio*, lay only for the principal.

17 Cf., e.g., *D*.16.3.1.11, 12 (Ulpian, *On the Edict*, book 30).

18 See, e.g., Kaser, *Privatrecht* 1:536; Thomas, *Textbook*, p. 278.

19 *Coll.* 10.7.9 = *P.S.* 2.12.9; *D*.12.1.10.

20 For the *actio mandati* against the *procurator omnium bonorum*, the
agent of all one's affairs, see A. Watson, *Contract of Mandate in Roman
Law* (Oxford, 1961), pp. 36ff.

21 See, e.g., Watson, *Mandate*, pp. 102ff; H. T. Klami, "*Mandatum* and
Labour," 106 *ZSS*, pp. 575ff at pp. 580ff.

22 This again is a different understanding of the text from that in *The Digest
of Justinian*.

23   *D*.17.1.7 (Papinian, *Replies*, book 3).

24   Cf. A. Watson, "Roman Law and English Law: Two Patterns of Legal Development," 36 *Loyola Law Review* (1990), pp. 247ff at pp. 253ff.

## Chapter 9: Legal Isolationism: II

1   *The Common Law* (Boston, 1881), p. 1.

2   See Watson, *State, Law and Religion*, p. x and the references therein.

3   Livy, 3.32.7.

4   See, e.g., F. Wieacker, *Römische Rechtsgeschichte* (Munich, 1988), vol. 1, pp. 300ff.

5   The archeological evidence shows that before this time there were contacts between Rome and Greece: see, e.g., Jolowicz and Nicholas, *Historical Introduction*, p. 112.

6   See, e.g., Watson, *Legal Transplants: An Approach to Comparative Law*, 2d ed. (Athens, Ga.; Edinburgh, 1993).

7   See, e.g., Jolowicz and Nicholas, *Historical Introduction*, p. 112.

8   *D*.10.1.13.

9   See, e.g., Jolowicz and Nicholas, *Historical Introduction*, p. 112 n. 4.

10   *D*.47.22.4.

11   *De re publica*, 2.23.59; 2.25.64.

12   For more detail see Watson, *Legal Transplants*, pp. 25ff.

13   For the argument, see, e.g., Watson, *Obligations*, pp. 46ff; Jolowicz and Nicholas, *Historical Introduction*, pp. 290ff.

14   This is also the opinion of Kaser, *Privatrecht* 1:624, n. 11, who cites authors on all sides of the issue.

15   *Historical Introduction*, p. 406.

16   *The Greek Law of Sale* (Weimar, 1950), pp. 478f.

17   *Opere*, vol. 3 (Milan, 1929), pp. 77ff.

18   See, e.g., A. Watson, *Roman Slave Law* (Baltimore, 1987), pp. 49f.

19   By Schulz, *Roman Legal Science*, pp. 38ff.

20   See, e.g., Watson, *Legal Transplants*, p. 33.

21   On reluctance to borrow from Greek law, but with a different emphasis see Schulz, *Principles*, pp. 126ff.

22   *Historical Introduction*, pp. 406, 408, 414ff.

23   *C*.8.37(38).1.

24   *Historical Introduction*, p. 418.

25   *C*.4.30.3.

26    *G.*4.116.

27    *Historical Introduction,* pp. 419f.


## Chapter 10: Conservatism and Absence of System

1    *D.*1.2.2.5.

2    *D.*1.2.2.41.

3    See Watson, *Law Making,* pp. 143ff.

4    For omissions from the *Twelve Tables,* see Watson, *State, Law and Religion,* pp. 14ff.

5    For the argument see Watson, *Law Making,* pp. 143ff; *State, Law and Religion,* pp. 14ff, 26ff.

6    The omission of deposit is surprising since that was the subject of a clause of the *Twelve Tables: Collatio,* 10.7.11.

7    *Legal Science,* p. 150.

8    See, e.g., F. de Zulueta, *The Institutes of Gaius* 2:5; infra, appendix B.

9    E.g., by Schulz, *Legal Science,* p. 180; T. Honoré, *Ulpian* (Oxford, 1982), pp. 106ff.

10    The accepted reconstruction is primarily the work of O. Lenel, *Edictum.*

11    See Lenel, *Edictum,* pp. 490ff.

12    For the order of the clauses see above all, Lenel, *Edictum.*

13    *Juristische Schriften,* vol. 1 (Berlin, 1905), p. 164. For further criticism of the arrangement see, e.g., Schulz, *Legal Science,* pp. 151f.

14    *C. Tanta* §18. For details see, e.g., Jolowicz and Nicholas, *Historical Introduction,* pp. 356f.

15    *C. Tanta* §18.

16    Eutropius, *Breviarium* 8.17; Aurelius Victor, *De Caesaribus* 19.2.

17    See, e.g., Watson, "Know Thyself: Man the Measure—*Implumes Aves Volitant,*" 21 *Georgia Journal of International and Comparative Law* (1991), pp. 591ff, at p. 593 n. 2.

18    For these jurists see above all Kunkel, *Herkunft,* pp. 6ff.

19    *D.*1.2.2.41; for the arrangement see A. Watson, *Law Making,* pp. 143.


## Chapter 11: Conservatism and Tradition

1    For this see Rotondi, *Leges publicae,* pp. 443ff.

2    See Kaser, *Privatrecht* 2:3.

3    See, e.g., Watson, "The Rescripts of the Emperor Probus (276–282 A.D.),"

*Origins*, pp. 61ff; "Private Law in the Rescripts of Carus, Carinus and Numerianus," *Origins*, pp. 45ff; D. Liebs, *Die Jurisprudenz im spätantiken Italiens* (Berlin, 1987); T. Honoré, "Conveyances of Land and Professional Standards in the Later Empire," in *New Perspectives in the Roman Law of Property*, ed. P. Birks (Oxford, 1989), pp. 137ff.

4   The surviving fragments are in O. Lenel, *Palingenesia iuris civilis*, vol. 1 (Leipzig, 1889), pp. 947.

5   *C.Th.* 1.1.5 (429). The first and unsuccessful plan was more ambitious. After all the rescripts were collected and published there was to be a further collection of all currently relevant rescripts together with writings of the jurists.

6   What follows is a shortened and simplified version of chapter 15 of my *Roman Law and Comparative Law*. Omissions here are not indicative of a change of mind. The structure of Roman contracts also obscures social reality: see A. Watson, "Artificiality, Reality and Roman Contract Law," 57 *T.v.R.* (1989), pp. 14ff.

7   See, e.g., Thomas, *Textbook*, p. 226.

8   *Rhetorica ad Herennium* 2.13.19.

9   See M. Kaser, *Das altrömische Ius* (Göttingen, 1949), pp. 256ff; H. van den Brink, *Ius Fasque: Opmerkungen over de Dualiteit van het archaisch-romeins Recht* (Amsterdam, 1968), pp. 172ff; O. Behrends, *Der Zwölftafelprozess* (Göttingen, 1974), pp. 35f; and the authors they cite.

10   Kaser, *Privatrecht* 1:168ff.

11   Kaser, *Privatrecht* 1:170f.

12   See for the argument A. Watson, *Roman Private Law Around 200 B.C.* (Edinburgh, 1971), pp. 126f.

13   The *condictio furtiva*, which is exceptional, need not concern us here.

14   Kaser, *Privatrecht* 1:492f.

15   *Contra* P. Birks, "Fictions Ancient and Modern," in *The Legal Mind: Essays for Tony Honoré*, ed. N. MacCormick and P. Birks (Oxford, 1986), pp. 83ff at p. 86 n. 9. For him: "It is an advanced, not a primitive, jurisprudence that can close the list." He offers no evidence for this sweeping generalization.

16   In French law any noncommercial (in the technical sense) transaction above a very small amount can be proved only by a notarial act or a private signed writing except under article 1348 of the *code civil*, when it is not possible for the creditor to procure writing. "Possible" here refers to moral possibility as well as physical, and in certain close relationships—

such as, at times, those involving one's mother, mistress, or physician—
obtaining a writing is regarded as morally impossible.

17  Some scholars—e.g., Kaser, *Ius*, p. 286—suggest that a real action, the
*legis actio sacramento in rem*, was available for *mutuum* before the
introduction of the *condictio*. There is no evidence for this, and the avail-
ability of such an action would make it more difficult to explain the
introduction of the *condictio*. But the suggestion would not adversely affect the idea expressed here that *mutuum* was given specific protection
because the arrangement was among friends and *stipulatio* was morally
inappropriate. At whatever date, a commercial loan would involve interest, a *stipulatio* would be taken, and there would be no need for the
specific legal protection of *mutuum*.

18  *Collatio* 10.7.11. The action has often been thought to be something
other than an action for deposit or to be an action for what was later
called *depositum miserabile*, but see Watson, *Private Law*, p. 151; and
Kaser, *Privatrecht* 1:160, n. 49.

19  E.g., Watson, *Private Law*, p. 157; Kaser, *Privatrecht* 1:160.

20  E.g., Kaser, *Privatrecht* 1:160.

21  Lenel, *Edictum*, pp. 288f.

22  The literature is enormous, but see, e.g., W. Litewski, "Studien zum soge-
nannten '*depositum necessarium*,'" 43 *Studia et documenta historiae
et iuris* (1977), pp. 188ff, especially 194ff, and the work he cites.

23  Cf., e.g., Plautus, *Bacchides*, 306.

24  Diósdi, *Contract*, pp. 44f.

25  See Watson, *Obligations*, pp. 40ff.

26  See Kaser, *Privatrecht* 1:546; Jolowicz and Nicholas, *Historical Introduction*, pp. 288ff; and the works they cite.

27  T. Mommsen, "Die römischen Anfänge von Kauf and Miethe," 6 *ZSS*
(1885), pp. 260ff.

28  Scholars who take any one of these approaches—especially the first
two—also wish to give a central role in the invention to the peregrine
praetor. This seems to me to be unnecessary, but the point need not
detain us here; see Watson, *Law Making*, pp. 63ff.

29  This appears even in Mommsen, "Anfänge," p. 260; see also E. I.
Bekker, *Die Aktionen des römischen Privatrechts* (Berlin, 1871), 1:156ff;
V. Arangio-Ruiz, *La compravendita in diritto romano*, 2d ed. (Naples,
1956), 1:57ff. Diósdi objects, asking why it would be necessary to cut
up "the uniform contract of spot transactions into two separate con-

tracts, to confirm the two promises with a *stipulatio*, then abandon the *stipulationes* shortly so that at the beginning of the preclassical age the contract appears as already in its classical shape" (*Contract*, p. 45). By "spot transaction," he appears to have *mancipatio* in mind. There are two flaws in this argument. First, the object of the sale-type transaction would not always be a *res mancipi*, in which case *mancipatio* would be inappropriate. Second, even in the earliest times, even when the object was a *res mancipi*, the parties would not always want a spot transaction but perhaps delivery at a later time, and *mancipatio* would not then be used.

30   Watson, "The Origins of Consensual Sale: A Hypothesis," *Origins*, pp. 165ff.

31   In fact, the *stipulatio* could not be taken from a son or a slave with full protection until the introduction of the *actio quod iussu*. That action appears to be based on an edict of the praetor (Lenel, *Edictum*, p. 278), and actions based on an edictal clause giving the plaintiff a new right of action cannot be safely dated earlier than ca. 100 B.C.; see Watson, *Law Making*, pp. 31ff.

32   B. Nicholas does not agree and suggests the stipulations persisted because they imposed strict liability, whereas liability on sale would be based only on good faith; see Jolowicz and Nicholas, *Historical Introduction*, p. 289, n. 8 (at p. 290). This does not address the problem, which is not the continued use of *stipulatio* but the absence of implied warranties in sale. Those who wanted strict liability could still have demanded a *stipulatio* even if *emptio venditio* had implied warranties (which could be excluded). Again, this approach does not lessen the commercial inconvenience of the lack of implied warranties. Moreover, it must be surprising in a contract of sale based on good faith that there is no warranty of title or of quiet possession.

33   Strict textual proof is lacking, but a development from the strict-law *stipulatio* to good-faith *emptio venditio* can have occurred no other way.

34   *De re rustica* 2.2.4; 2.3.4; 2.4.5.

35   The impact of the defects in early consensual sale would be less noticeable, of course, where what was sold was a *res mancipi* and it actually was delivered by *mancipatio*, which did have an inherent warranty against eviction. Even here, however, there was no warranty against latent defects.

36   For views see, e.g., Jolowicz and Nicholas, *Historical Introduction*, pp.

249ff. Significantly, one recent writer on ancient hire, H. Kaufman, offers no view on the origins of the consensual contract; see *Die altrömische Miete* (Cologne, 1964).

37  Actually, *locatio conductio* is so obviously a residual category—every bilateral transaction involving a money prestation that is not sale is hire—that one need not start with the assumption of the priority of sale. From the very fact of the residual nature of hire one can deduce the priority of sale; unless, that is, one were to argue (as I think no one would) that originally sale transactions were within the sphere of *locatio conductio* and that *emptio venditio* was carved out of this all-embracing contract.

38  Cato, *De agri cultura*, 149.

39  *Rhetorica ad Herennium* 2.13.19. See A. Watson, *Contract of Mandate in Roman Law* (Oxford, 1961), p. 22.

40  K. Visky, *Geistige Arbeit und die Artes liberales in den Quellen des römischen Rechts* (Budapest, 1977), pp. 146ff.

41  Watson, *Law Making*, pp. 31ff, especially p. 38.

42  *G*.3.153a.

43  *G*.3.154b.

44  See, above all, Watson, "Consensual *societas* between Romans and the Introduction of *formulae*," *Legal Origins*, pp. 175ff.

45  *G*.3.149.

46  *D*.17.2.29pr, 1; see Watson, "The Notion of Equivalence of Contractual Obligation and Classical Roman Partnership," *Legal Origins*, pp. 239ff.

47  *Laesio enormis* is postclassical, whether it is to be attributed to Diocletian or Justinian: *C*.4.44.2; 4.44.8.

48  *G*.3.159; *D*.17.1.12.16. That damages were doubled for breach in *depositum miserabile* is not a problem. *Depositum miserabile* could still be subjected to special regulation.

49  *D*.45.1.122; 45.1.126.1; 45.1.140pr. There is something illogical in accepting a written document as evidence of a *stipulatio*. It can show the intention of the parties but scarcely that they went through the formalities.

50  D. M. MacDowell, *The Law in Classical Athens* (Ithaca, 1978), p. 233.

51  *G*.3.134.

52  M. Crawford, *Roman Republican Coinage* (Cambridge, 1976), pp. 35ff.

53  The state of development of barter before the time of Justinian is very obscure, much disputed, and need not be gone into here. For literature, see, e.g., Thomas, *Textbook*, pp. 312f; and Kaser, *Privatrecht* 1:381.

54    *G*.3.141; *J*.3.23.1; *D*.19.4.1pr.

55    *D*.19.5.

56    *D*.19.5.5pr.

57    For these see Watson, *Obligations*, p. 257.

58    One might add that it was the power of the *stipulatio* that hindered the classical jurists from giving a remedy for a *nudum pactum;* see K.-P. Nanz, *Die Entstehung des allgemeinen Vertragsbegriff im 16. bis 18. Jahrhundert* (Munich, 1985), pp. 18f.

59    See, e.g., Lenel, *Edictum*, p. 375.

60    On all this see A. Watson, "The Transformation of American Property Law: A Comparative Law Approach," 24 *Georgia Law Review* (1990), pp. 163ff at pp. 164ff.

61    *G*.4.103. See also Schulz, *Principles*, pp. 33f.

62    *G*.4.104.

63    But see, e.g., Buckland, *Textbook*, pp. 687f; M. Kaser, *Das römische Zivilprozessrecht* (Munich, 1966), pp. 116, 228 n. 33.

64    *Vat. Fr.* 47a.

65    *Epitome Ulpiani* 11.27; *Vat. Fr.* 325, 327.

66    *G*.1.184.

67    *G*.3.83.

68    *D*.9.2.2pr.

69    See D. Nörr, "*Mortis causam praebere,*" in *The Legal Mind,* ed. N. MacCormick and P. Birks (Oxford, 1986), pp. 203ff; B. Frier, "Prototypical Causation in Roman Law," 34 *Loyola Law Review* (1988), pp. 485ff.

70    See, e.g., Watson, *Obligations*, pp. 241ff.

71    *D*.9.2.9pr.

72    *D*.9.2.7.3.

73    *G*.3.219.

74    *D*.9.2.7.7.

75    *G*.3.219. An incorrect translation is given by F. H. Lawson, *Negligence in the Civil Law* (Oxford, 1950), p. 143.

76    *G*.3.218.

## Chapter 12: A Central Indefiniteness

1    See, e.g., Schulz, *Principles*, pp. 40ff.

2    *D*.50.17.202 (*Letters*, book 11).

3    See also *J*.1.13.1.

4    For the argument see Watson, *Persons*, pp. 102ff.

5    Another true juristic definition is the much better one for *dolus* by Aquilius Gallus; *D*.4.3.1.2; Cicero, *De officiis* 3.14.60; *De natura deorum* 3.30.74. For others, see Festus, *s.v. noxia;* Cicero, *Topica* 4.24 *(ambitus);* 6.29 *(gentiles).*

6    There is a lacuna in the text.

7    For other nonlegal definitions, see Cicero, *Topica* 7.32 *(litus); D.*50.16.25.1 *(pars).*

8    And other listings were possible: see the discussion in Watson, *Succession,* pp. 134ff.

9    For etymology being used to explain the scope of something see Cicero, *Topica* 8.37 *(postliminium);* 9.38 *(aqua pluvia); D.*33.10.7 *(suppelex);* Macrobius, *Saturnalia* 3.3.8 *(sacellum);* Aulus Gellius, *Noctes Atticae* 7.12.1 *(testamentum).*

10    Cf. G. Wissowa, *Religion und Kultus der Römer,* 2d ed. (Munich, 1912), p. 162.

11    "*Penus legata,*" in *Studi in onore di Emilio Betti* (Milan, 1962), vol. 4, pp. 479ff at pp. 696f.

12    *Res gestae divi Augusti* 6.1.

13    Bruns, *Fontes,* number 56, pp. 202f.

14    *Scriptores historiae Augustae, Opil. Mac.* 13.1.

15    For views held see the writers cited by Thomas, *Textbook,* pp. 43ff; more recently, F. Wieacker, "Respondere ex auctoritate principis," in *Satura Roberto Feenstra Oblata,* ed. J. A. Ankum, J. E. Spruit, and F. Wubbe (Freiburg, 1985), pp. 71ff.

16    See, e.g., Schulz, *Legal Science,* p. 118.

17    We have no texts that clearly indicate the existence of the *ius respondendi* later than Hadrian. If *Const. Deo Auctore* §4 means, as is sometimes held, that Justinian's instructions to Tribonian were to read and to work up the books of those jurists who had the *ius respondendi,* then the instructions were not followed since the republican jurists had no such right. A sentence at the beginning of Eunapius's *Vita Chrysantii* refers to a jurist Innocentius who must have lived in the reign of Diocletian, and it is often said that it shows he had *ius respondendi.* But it need mean only that he held a prominent position in the imperial chancery. See Schulz, *Legal Science,* p. 114, n. 6.

18    Jolowicz and Nicholas, *Historical Introduction,* p. 453; cf. Thomas, *Textbook,* p. 54.

19    For the argument see Watson, "The Law of Citations and Classical Texts in the Post-Classical Period," in *Legal Origins,* pp. 225ff.

20   See, e.g., Jolowicz and Nicholas, *Historical Introduction*, pp. 98ff; Thomas, *Textbook*, p. 35.

21   *G*.2.14a.

22   *G*.2.15.

23   *G*.2.18–25; 1.119–122.

24   *G*.2.79.

25   It is sometimes suggested that the dispute had philosophical roots, but see Thomas, *Textbook*, p. 175.

26   See, e.g., Buckland, *Textbook*, p. 217.

27   *G*.3.103.

28   *G*.3.161; *P.S.* 2.15.3; *J*.3.26.8; *D*.17.1.3.2,4.

29   See, e.g., Jolowicz and Nicholas, *Historical Introduction*, pp. 479f.

## Chapter 13: Legal Isolationism: III

1   This is not to deny that behind much of their reasoning and unexposed may lie traces of education in Greek culture: see, above all, Daube, *Roman Law*, pp. 176ff.

2   *Atti del congresso internazionale, Roma* (1934), 1:117ff.

3   *Rationes decidendi*, vol. 1 (Aalen, 1969), p. 227. This work, from p. 225 onwards, contains the best treatment of the text.

4   See, e.g., Watson, *Law Making*, pp. 188f.

5   *Theseus* 23.1.

6   *Rationes* 1:232.

7   Horak claims that here in Alfenus there is only *Vulgärphilosophie*, in which Stoic and Peripatetic ideas are commingled: *Rationes* 1:232. For the views of other scholars see the references given by Horak, *Rationes* 1:232, n. 24.

8   For a Roman view see Lucretius, *De rerum natura* 2.62ff.

9   Apparently there is no evidence that the theory goes back to Heracleitus, as was once thought.

10   Plutarch, *Moralia* 392D, 559B. The idea seems to go back to Epicharmus: fragment 2 in H. Diels, *Die Fragmente der Vorsokratiker*, 6th ed. W. Kranz (Berlin, 1951), 1.196.

11   What constitutes a genus or species is a relative matter.

12   E.g., *Topica* 3.13, 14; 7.30, 31; 9.39, 40. Cicero prefers to translate εἶδος by *forma* rather than *species*.

13   *D*.33.10.7.1 has Tubero using the word "species" but not referring to the subdivision of a genus.

14    *G.*1.188.

15    *D.*41.2.3.23.

16    *G.*1.188 and 3.183. *D.*33.10.6pr is not relevant.

17    In fact it is not absolutely certain, though it is probable, that they did use the word "genus."

18    *Hecyra,* 198; Cato, *De agri cultura* 46.1; Accius, fr. 15; Lucilius 1100.

19    H. Coing, "Zur Methodik der republicanischen Jurisprudenz," *Studi Arangio-Ruiz* (Naples, n.d.), 1:365ff. at pp. 372ff.

20    Cicero, *Topica* 8.37.

21    Aulus Gellius, *Noctes Atticae* 4.1.17.

22    Cicero, *Topica* 8.37.

23    Aulus Gellius, *Noctes Atticae* 7.12.2.

24    Festus *s.v. vindiciae;* but not, I think, with *noxia:* Festus *s.h.v.*

25    *D.*50.16.239.6.

26    *D.*50.16.180.1.

27    Aulus Gellius, *Noctes Atticae* 7.12.5,6.

28    Cf., e.g., Reitzenstein, *Paulys Real-Encyclopädie der classischen Altertumswissenschaft,* 2d ed. G. Wissowa, 6 (Stuttgart, 1909), 807ff at 807f, *s.v. etymologika;* R. Pfeiffer, *History of Classical Scholarship* (Oxford, 1968), pp. 4, 12.

29    For a brief account of the Stoic doctrine see Reitzenstein, *Encyclopädie,* 6.808ff.

30    Philosophical dependence is too easily claimed by modern scholars; cf. the demonstration by Pfeiffer that Philetas, Callimachus, and their followers were *not* Peripatetics: *Classical Scholarship,* p. 95.

31    Jurists; we are not here concerned with the Roman grammarians. Again nothing relevant should be argued here from the fact that the jurists were aware that a word might have more than one meaning or that Servius observed that a *lex* that uses two negatives permits rather than prohibits. *D.*50.16.237.

32    "Stoische Logik und römische Jurisprudenz," 87 *ZSS* (1970), pp. 85ff; see also C. Krampe, *Proculi Epistulae* (Karlsruhe, 1970), pp. 82ff.

33    For disjunctions in Stoic terminology see, e.g., I. Mueller, "An Introduction to Stoic Logic," in J. M. Rist, ed., *The Stoics* (Berkeley, 1978), pp. 1ff.

34    This is even more true of the other two texts adduced by Miquel: *D.*14.1.29; *C.*6.38.4. In these Stoic terminology does not appear.

35    See also *J.*1.2pr.

36    *Nichomachaean Ethics* 5.7.1.

37  For a few of those who have held this view see A. Watson, "Some Notes on Mackenzie's Institutions and the European Legal Tradition," 16 *Ius Commune* (1989), pp. 303ff.

38  Cf. Schulz, *Legal Science*, pp. 69f. Rather astonishingly T. Honoré claims: "It looks as if the famous passage of Ulpian on the law of nature, in which he asserts that animals are thought to know about marriage, the procreation of children and their education by experience (*peritia*), and hence not merely by instinct is to be taken as Neoplatonic": *Ulpian* (Oxford, 1982), p. 31. Even apart from the fact that this is based on a faulty understanding of the Latin, this claim is impossible. His evidence is that Porphyrius, who was a Neoplatonist, affirmed the rational character of animals. But that is not even what Ulpian is claiming in Honoré's own view. Again, Porphyrius was not born until 234, a decade after Ulpian's murder. The argument must be that, since both Ulpian and Porphyrius were born in Tyre, this was a Neoplatonic idea circulating in Syria. But Honoré believes Ulpian was in Rome by 202: p. 18.

39  *G.*1.1; *J.*1.2.1.

40  *D.*29.5.1.2.

41  *D.*29.5.1.2.

42  *D.*29.5.1.9.

43  *Ad Atticum* 6.1.15.

44  By Schulz, *Legal Science*, pp. 193f.

45  See, e.g., Kunkel, *Herkunft*, p. 235.

46  *G.*1.2. But he does mention that quaestors exercise the jurisdiction of the curule aediles in the provinces of the Roman people, but that there are no quaestors in the provinces of Caesar: *G.*1.4.

47  F. von Velsen, "Das edictum provinciale des Gaius," 21 *ZSS* (1900), pp. 73ff: see the contrary arguments in Lenel, *Edictum*, p. 4.

48  On the boundaries of Rome see Robinson, *Ancient Rome*, pp. 7f.

49  *The Making of the Civil Law*, pp. 14ff.

50  *D.*41.1.7.10.

51  E.g., A. Watson, *The Law of the Ancient Romans* (Dallas, 1970), p. 73.

52  *D.*19.5.5pr.

## Chapter 14: "Law Keeps Out"

1  There was legislation in 1971 derogating from the immunity, but this was repealed in 1974.

2  See A. Watson, *The Nature of Law* (Edinburgh, 1977), pp. 96ff.

3   See, e.g., Schulz, *Principles*, pp. 140ff.

4   See, e.g., Watson, "The Divorce of Carvilius Ruga," *Studies*, pp. 23ff.

5   See, e.g., Buckland, *Textbook*, pp. 117f.

6   For the argument see Treggiari, *Roman Marriage*, pp. 446ff. It seems that a particular form was needed for evidence if a husband wished to avoid penalties when his wife was adulterous: *D.*24.2.9; cf. Treggiari, *Roman Marriage*, pp. 454ff.

7   *G.*2.123ff; *Ulpiani Regulae* 22.16ff; *D.*28.2.1; *h.t.* 2; *h.t.* 3pr, 1; *h.t.* 7; *h.t.* 17; *h.t.* 25pr; *C.*6.28.3.

8   *G.*2.135; *Ulpiani Regulae* 22.23. For minor cases where disinherison was not permitted see, e.g., Buckland, *Textbook*, pp. 326f.

9   For the argument see, e.g., Watson, *Succession*, pp. 62ff. See *J.*2.18; *D.*5.2; *C.*3.28. For more detail see, e.g., Thomas, *Textbook*, pp. 495f.

10  For the history of the exceptional case of partnership see Watson, "The Notion of Equivalence of Contractual Obligation and Classical Roman Partnership," *Legal Origins*, pp. 239ff; see also chapter 11.

11  See, moreover, Cicero, *De officiis*, 3.12.50–17.72.

12  *C.Th.* 3.1.1 (A.D. 319); *h.t.* 4 (A.D. 383); *h.t.* 7 (A.D. 396).

13  For these arguments see Watson, *Roman Law and Comparative Law*, pp. 201ff. See also A. J. B. Sirks, "La *laesio enormis* en droit romain et byzantin," 53 *T.v.R.* (1985), pp. 291ff; H. T. Klami, "*Laesio enormis* in Roman law?" 33 *Labeo* (1987), pp. 48ff; A. J. B. Sirks, "Diocletian's Option for the Buyer in Case of Rescission of a Sale," 60 *T.v.R.* (1992), pp. 39ff.

14  For one attempt among many, see, e.g., H. F. Jolowicz, "The Origin of *Laesio* Enormis," *Juridical Review* 49 (1937), pp. 50ff.

15  Many scholars fail to make or observe the distinction but instinctively choose one hypothesis, and hence can argue to the—for them—obvious conclusion with greater vigor.

16  Hannu Tapani Klami, for instance, takes the latter position: "Let Justinian and his compilers therefore have the merit—or the blame—for the first steps taken toward the adjustment of unequitable contracts." But he also says, "the riddle of *laesio enormis* cannot be solved, I suppose." ("*Laesio*," p. 63.)

17  See Watson, *Slave Law*, pp. 63ff.

## Chapter 15: Simplicity and Economy of Means

1   *State, Law and Religion*, pp. 32ff, 39ff. The simplicity of the *stipulatio* becomes especially clear when we look at other early systems: see, e.g., for

Anglo-Saxon law, T. F. T. Plucknett, *A Concise History of the Common Law*, 5th ed. (Boston, 1956), pp. 628ff; for Bedouin law, Frank Stewart, "Schuld and Haftung in Bedouin Law," 107 *ZSS* (1990), pp. 393ff.

2   See, e.g., Watson, *XII Tables*, pp. 65f.

3   See, e.g., Kaser, *Privatrecht* 1:66f.

4   Cf. Thomas, *Textbook*, p. 480.

5   See Watson, *XII Tables*, pp. 52ff.

6   See, e.g., Watson, *Succession*, pp. 40ff.

7   See, e.g., Watson, *State, Law and Religion*, pp. 30ff.

8   See, e.g., Watson, *Succession*, pp. 122ff.

9   See, e.g., Schulz, *Principles*, pp. 66ff.

10   See, e.g., Watson, *State, Law and Religion*, pp. 74f.

11   See Treggiari, *Roman Marriage*, pp. 61ff.

12   See, e.g., Thomas, *Textbook*, pp. 404f.

13   See, e.g., for the Republic, Watson, *State, Law and Religion*, pp. 4ff; for the Empire, P. Garnsey, *Social Status and Legal Privilege in the Roman Empire* (Oxford, 1970).

14   For the argument see Watson, *State, Law and Religion*.

15   See, e.g., Jolowicz and Nicholas, *Historical Introduction*, p. 138.

16   See, e.g., P. Vigneron, *Le cheval dans l'antiquité gréco-romaine* (Nancy, 1968), pp. 139ff; K. D. White, *Roman Farming* (London, 1970), pp. 288ff. Some use of horses was, however, made by farmers. See Cato, *De agri cultura*, 138.

17   See, e.g., W. J. Ong, *Orality and Literacy* (London, 1982), p. 49.

18   Earlier, I took the view that one could not determine whether the Sabinian or the Proculian view corresponded to the original classification: *XII Tables*, pp. 136f.

19   See, e.g., P. Bonfante, *Corso di diritto romano*, vol. 2, *La proprietà* (Rome, 1927), p. 182; for a different opinion see, e.g., G. Diósdi, *Ownership in Ancient and Preclassical Roman Law* (Budapest, 1970), pp. 22ff.

20   *G.*2.14a, 17.29; *Epitome Ulpiani* 19.1; *Vat. Fr.* 45.

21   *In iure cessio*, which in any event is cumbersome, is unlikely to have existed so early: see, e.g., A. Watson, *The Law of Property in the Later Roman Republic* (Oxford, 1968), p. 93 and especially n. 1.

22   *G.*2.19; cf. Buckland, *Textbook*, pp. 226f.

23   For the extensive literature, see Diósdi, *Ownership*, pp. 109ff.

24   Festus, *s.v. viae*; Tab. 7.7.

25   Diósdi, *Ownership*, p. 114.

26   *D.*8.3.8; Tab. 7.6.

27    Diósdi, *Ownership*, p. 114.

28    For the argument, see Watson, *Obligations*, pp. 72ff; cf Kaser, *Privatrecht* 1:460.

29    For the argument see Watson, *XII Tables*, p. 57.

30    *Epitome Ulpiani* 11.14; cf. *D*.50.16.53pr. Rather different versions appear in Cicero, *De inventione* 2.50, 148 (cf. *Rhetorica ad Herennium* 1.13.23) and *G*.2.224 (cf. *D*.50.16.120). For the argument establishing Ulpian's as the original version, see Watson, *XII Tables*, p. 52.

31    See Watson, *XII Tables*, p. 52 for the full argument.

32    See Watson, *XII Tables*, p. 64 for the argument.

33    *Privatrecht* 1:108 and the authors he cites. Against the notion of divided ownership see above all Diósdi, *Ownership*, pp. 121ff; and Watson, *XII Tables*, pp. 125ff. Most recently, Kaser defended his view of relative ownership and divided ownership in "Relatives Eigentum," *ZSS* 102 (1985), pp. 1ff. P. Birks, "The Roman Law Concept of *Dominium* and the Idea of Absolute Ownership," *Acta Juridica* (1985), pp. 1ff, says nothing apropos.

34    Cf. *G*.1.123; Boethius, *II in Topica Ciceronis* 3.14; Servius, *In Vergilii Georgica* 1.31; Isidorus, *Etymologiae* 5.24; Nonius Marcellus, *s.v. nubentes.*

35    *Nexum* itself may, but need not, be an opportunistic use of *mancipatio* so will not be dealt with here, but see Watson, *XII Tables*, pp. 111ff.

36    For the argument, see Watson, *XII Tables*, pp. 118f. The provision involved *mancipatio* (or no opportunistic use of the provision could have been made for *mancipatio*), but no real sales (or the son would not have returned to the *potestas* of the father).

37    See, e.g., Buckland, *Textbook*, p. 165.

38    See, e.g., *G*.1.115; 2.112; Cicero, *Topica*, 4.18; A. Watson, *The Law of Persons in the Later Roman Republic*, pp. 152f.

39    See, e.g., *G*.1.17.

40    See, e.g., A. Watson, *Roman Slave Law*, pp. 24f.

## Appendix A: Cicero the Outsider

1    N. Wood, *Cicero's Social and Political Thought* (Berkeley, 1988), p. 1.

2    *Brutus* 89.306; *Ad Atticum* 4.16.3; *De legibus* 1.4.13; cf. L. V. Ciferri, "Cicero's Conception of *iurisprudentia*," 38 *R.I.D.A.* (1991), pp. 103ff.

3    *Topica* 12.51.

4    Cf. Schulz, *Legal Science*, pp. 54f, 336 n. J.

5  *De oratore* 1.36.167ff.

6  *De oratore* 1.55.235ff.

7  *De oratore* 1.56.238; cf. 1.57.241f, 1.58.246f.

8  *De oratore* 1.58.248; cf. 1.58.250.

9  *De oratore* 1.37.171.

10  See also, e.g., *De legibus* 2.19.47f.

11  *De oratore* 1.60.254.

12  *De oratore* 1.55.236; cf. *Pro Murena* 13.29.

13  *De oratore* 1.44.197.

14  See, e.g., Schulz, *Principles*, p. 65.

15  Cf. *De oratore* 1.41.185ff.

16  *Noctes Atticae* 1.22.7.

17  *Institutiones oratoriae* 12.3.10.

18  Cf. Wood, *Cicero's Thought*, p. 70.

19  *De legibus* 1.5.17.

20  Cf. *De legibus* 1.11.17–1.12.8, 2.4.9f.

21  *De legibus* 1.7.22ff, 1.11.32–12.34.

22  *De legibus* 2.5.13f; cf. 1.15.42–16.45.

23  *De legibus* 1.15.42.

24  *De re publica* 3.10.17.

25  *De legibus* 1.10.28.

26  *Saturnalia* 6.4.8.

27  *De legibus* 1.4.13.

28  But we should remember that there is a confusion in *De legibus* 3.20.48.

## Appendix B: Gaius and His *Institutes*

1  *Gaius, A Biography* (Oxford, 1962), p. xii; cf. O. Stanojević, *Gaius Noster* (Amsterdam, 1989); J.-H. Michel, "Du neuf sur Gaius?" 38 *R.I.D.A.* (1991), pp. 175ff.

2  Schulz, *Legal Science*, p. 167, regards the *Res Cottidianae* as a work akin in nature to the *Institutes*.

3  G.1.8.

4  But we should not overlook Alfenus's attempt at system: see Watson, *Law Making*, pp. 182f.

5  D.44.7.1, 2, 4, 5.

6  See, e.g., Schulz, *Legal Science*, pp. 180f; F. Wieacker, *Textstufen klassischer Juristen* (Göttingen, 1960), pp. 206ff; T. Honoré, *Ulpian* (Oxford, 1982), pp. 106ff.

7   Wieacker, *Textstufen*, pp. 186ff, 206.

8   *C. Omnem* §2.

9   *C. Omnem* §1.

10   See, e.g., A. Watson, *The Making of the Civil Law* (Cambridge, Mass., 1981), pp. 62ff.

11   For Pomponius see the long text from his *Enchiridion* in one book in *D.1.2.2.*

12   See, e.g., Honoré, *Gaius*, pp. 1ff.

## Appendix C: A Conclusion: The Astonishing Success of Roman Law

1   2d ed. (Oxford, 1929), p. 11.

2   A. Watson, *The Evolution of Law* (Baltimore, 1985), p. 97.

3   The emperors were (necessarily) interested in order, hence there is some material on administration in the *Corpus Juris*. But most of our information comes from nonlegal sources. See, above all, Robinson, *Ancient Rome.*

4   Most recently in *Joseph Story and the Comity of Errors*, pp. 77ff.

# INDEX